Private Choices, Social Costs, and Public Policy

Private Choices, Social Costs, and Public Policy

AN ECONOMIC ANALYSIS OF PUBLIC HEALTH ISSUES

Nancy Hammerle

PRAEGER

Westport, Connecticut
London

*RA
410.53
.H36
1992*

Library of Congress Cataloging-in-Publication Data

Hammerle, Nancy.
    Private choices, social costs, and public policy : an economic
analysis of public health issues / Nancy Hammerle.
        p.   cm.
    Includes bibliographical references and index.
    ISBN 0-275-94172-8 (alk. paper)
    1. Medical economics—United States.   2. Medical policy—United
States.   3. Health behavior—United States.   I. Title.
[DNLM: 1. Attitude to Health.   2. Costs and Cost Analysis.
3. Health Care Costs.   W 76 H224p]
RA410.53.H36   1992
362.1'0422'0973—dc20
DNLM/DLC
for Library of Congress   92-3459

British Library Cataloguing in Publication Data is available.

Library of Congress Catalog Card Number: 92-3459
ISBN: 0-275-94172-8

First published in 1992

Praeger Publishers, 88 Post Road West, Westport, CT 06881
An imprint of Greenwood Publishing Group, Inc.

Printed in the United States of America

@™

The paper used in this book complies with the
Permanent Paper Standard issued by the National
Information Standards Organization (Z39.48–1984).

10 9 8 7 6 5 4 3 2 1

To Oliver and Dora
In memory of my father

Contents

Figures and Tables

FIGURES

TABLES

Acknowledgments

A special thank you is owed Denise Colbert, faculty secretary at Stonehill College. Denise valiantly and uncomplainingly fought her way through the paper clips, scotch tape, post-it notes and white out that clutter the landscape of the computer-averse, never balking at the scores of revisions. Geri Sheehan, reference librarian at Stonehill College, also deserves acknowledgment. Her extra effort saved considerable time and legwork. Appreciation is also due Terri Porter for her work on the graphics.

I would additionally like to thank my husband, Fred, for his assistance, support and culinary efforts as well as my son, Oliver, and the friends who provided much needed encouragement.

The biggest thank you, however, goes to my daughter, Dora, who cheerfully played on her side of the desk while I worked on mine. Her delightful good humor makes every day a pleasure and every task much easier.

Private Choices,
Social Costs,
and
Public Policy

Introduction

Six-year-old Lisa Steinberg was killed in November 1987. She died following a beating at the hands of her adoptive father, a beating that ended with her being picked up and thrown against a wall with such force that it left her brain-dead. The nation was horrified and grief-stricken.

In March 1989, as its hard-drinking skipper rested in his cabin, the *Exxon Valdez* ploughed into Bligh Reef off the coast of Alaska. The crash unleashed 11 million gallons of oil into Prince William Sound and wreaked unparalleled environmental devastation. Hundred of thousands of animals were killed, the Alaskan fishing industry suffered a near-mortal blow, and the overall cost is so huge it has yet to be tallied. The cost to Exxon alone has exceeded $3 billion.

In May 1988 a pickup truck traveling in the wrong direction on an interstate highway in northern Kentucky collided with a church bus bringing teenagers back from an amusement park outing. Almost 30 people were killed and dozens were seriously injured in one of the worst roadway accidents in U.S. history. The truck driver was intoxicated; the victims were young; we were shocked at the loss.

A Florida dentist infected five of his patients with the AIDS-causing human immunodeficiency virus when he performed invasive dental procedures on them without due precautions in the late 1980s. Their visits to his office took place *after* the dentist had been informed he had AIDS. The news sounded an alarm that sent repercussions throughout our entire health care industry and raised our fear of AIDS to new heights.

These episodes sent our collective consciousness reeling and will remain part of our national memory for years to come. But while they are exceptional, these cases are far from unique. In the year Lisa Steinberg died almost 150 children were fatally abused in New York City alone; possibly as many as five thousand were killed nationwide. The Alaskan oil spill was but one of the hundreds of industrial accidents caused each year by substance-abusing employees. Impaired employees cost American business billions of dollars every year. The Kentucky collision was just one of thousands of alcohol-related traffic crashes. Drunken driving is responsible for about 23,000 deaths and 500,000 injuries every year. And while no other cases of AIDS transmission from health care practitioners to patients have yet been revealed, each year thousands of people are unwittingly infected from some source.

What ties these incidents together, and ties them together with millions of other cases, is that they represent the externalities of imprudent individual choices. When people make unhealthful choices they injure not just themselves but others as well. Cigarette smokers foul the air their families breathe with lethal results. They start fires that kill their children. Heavy drinkers abuse their spouses, cause fatal accidents and, if pregnant, give birth to retarded babies. Pregnant crack users bear infants who suffer horribly and whom they abandon at birth. When their children are brought home they are abused or neglected. Intravenous drug users who share injection equipment also share the AIDS virus with their fellow users, their mates and their offspring. Parents who beat their children raise parents who beat their children. They also raise violent criminals.

None of these outcomes are inevitable, of course, but they occur with distressing frequency. Compounding the problem is the fact that harmful behaviors such as these are practiced by significantly large numbers of people.

When an unhealthful behavioral choice is made by enough individuals it creates a public health problem that threatens the well-being of society at large. It also generates substantial external costs, that is, costs that are borne by persons other than the perpetrator. Some of these external costs are financial and may take the form of increased health care expenditures, lost productivity or destruction of property. Their impact is typically broad and thus they are known as social costs. Other costs can be categorized as human costs, such as when the quality of life is diminished by physiological, psychological or environmental deficits. Although these human costs usually affect only individuals initially, they too ultimately exact a social price.

Eventually a critical mass is reached and public pressure is brought to bear for reform and respite. Public opinion demands policy measures that will reduce the incidence of unhealthful behavior and the social costs arising from it.

As its name implies, the purpose of this book is to identify and estimate the social costs of those ill-considered personal choices that have public health ramifications. Whereas everyone knows that private behavior often has a far-reaching impact and that private choices often impose social costs, even the best-informed among us seldom appreciate the complexity or magnitude of those costs. Therefore, every effort has been made to provide comprehensive cost analyses, if not in monetary terms, at least categorically.

The book also evaluates various current and proposed public policy strategies designed to lessen the incidence of harmful choices or reduce or internalize their costs. The objective is to promote those policies that most effectively and cost-effectively reduce the societal burden.

As many readers are aware, some public policy measures are costly to implement but ultimately reduce social costs. Increasing low-income women's access to prenatal care, for example, is expensive. But its costs are recouped very quickly as fewer babies are born preterm or low birth weight and in need of neonatal intensive care. Making health care affordable for the working poor is expensive but it may prevent the onset of costly health problems or allow timely, appropriate treatment to lessen their severity. Better health care will also enhance worker productivity.

Other measures will save society money immediately. Legalizing certain drugs will save billions of dollars in criminal justice costs, both in drug law enforcement and in terms of the crimes addicts commit to finance their drug purchases.

Other measures make money. Increasing taxes on cigarettes and alcoholic beverages will produce greater tax revenues at the same time that it reduces their consumption, reduces their associated externalities and more equitably distributes their remaining costs.

Still other policy suggestions call for a reallocation of social spending away from less-effective strategies to those that produce a greater return. Rather than trying to rehabilitate recalcitrant child abusers, for example, our scarce social resources might be better employed providing quality boarding homes for their children. This could result in reduced social costs for generations to come.

Also as its title indicates, the text makes extensive use of economic concepts and analytical tools. Economic theory provides a valuable framework for understanding human behavior, justifying government intervention to modify that behavior and estimating both the effectiveness and the cost-effectiveness of various public policies. No economic background is necessary to comprehend the meaning of economic terminology as it is applied here. Rather, all readers should find the theoretical constructs employed in such a way as to significantly contribute to their understanding of the subject matter. The dominant methodology, moreover, is far from theoretical. Rather, the approach is primarily empirical and the book provides a great deal of quantitative information.

TECHNICAL NOTES

Numbers are seldom found in their most useful form. They are in absolute values when population rates are needed, show absolute changes when percentage changes are called for, or worse. Consequently, some of the data presented here are the result of extensive working over of original source data. When the functions that have been performed are not obvious from looking at the original data, the term "modified" appears after the source. Also, because the time lag between data collection and publication can be significant, even relatively recent sources often present data that are outdated. When the direction and general magnitude of change can be determined, it has been pointed out.

Many public health problems have escalated in recent years or taken a dramatically different turn. This is especially true of the public health manifestations of crack use (of which there are many) and of AIDS. Most such developments are too recent to yet show up in national data. Therefore, in order to make this book an authoritative reflection of the state of affairs today, there is a good deal of reliance on state and local data. Also, many pertinent issues are so new they have not yet been discussed in the scholarly press. Thus newspaper articles, corporate reports, staff memos, unpublished data and personal interviews are drawn upon more often than usual. The result, hopefully, is information that is not only as up to the minute as possible in a volume like this, but information that also embodies recent shifts in direction. So although the magnitude of the problems may change and the rate of change may change, the direction of change should remain fairly stable for some time and the information provided herein should continue to be useful.

One word of caution is, however, necessary. Demographic data are almost always categorized only by white and black. Occasionally data are also available for the Hispanic population, but when they are, the figures that are provided concurrently for whites and blacks usually include Hispanics as well. Rarely are data provided for Hispanics, non-Hispanic whites and non-Hispanic blacks. Since approximately 95 percent of Hispanics are classified as white, 9 percent of the white population, as of 1988, is Hispanic (USBC). Misinterpretation of the data for whites may result if readers are unaware of that fact. This is especially true of conditions such as teen pregnancy and AIDS, in which the incidence among the Hispanic population greatly exceeds that among the non-Hispanic white population.

Many readers will be surprised by what they find here. Some will be chagrined. The book was not intended to be provocative, only to convey the facts and suggest effective remedies for some of our more intractable public health problems. In consequence, more than a few myths are debunked, though not always explicitly, and a realistic approach is taken to the potential for behavior modification. The approach to policy is pragmatic, rather than idealistic, and treats people as they are, not as they should be. The problems discussed in this volume are too urgent to await any fundamental changes in human nature.

1

Cigarette Smoking

The triad of private choices, social costs and public policy clearly corresponds to the case of cigarette smoking: certain individuals choose to smoke. Their choice imposes costs on society. Policies are needed to stop their smoking or otherwise rectify the inequity of uncompensated externalities.

However, the issues are not as clear-cut as they may appear. Some people might choose to smoke, but their choice is rarely well-informed or freely made. And once made, the decision to smoke is extremely difficult to rescind.

The social costs are great, but are seldom accurately portrayed. Most critics of tobacco use claim smoking increases health care costs, costs that are subsidized by nonsmokers. In actuality, despite their higher prevalence of disease and disability, smokers save society money on health care. Nevertheless, smoking is socially costly.

Yet even though smoking is costly as well as unhealthful, cigarettes should not be banned. To do so would be counterproductive. It would increase costs.

There is one measure we could take that would effectively reduce smoking. We will probably not take it. To do so would be impolitic.

In the meantime, smoking kills over 400,000 Americans each year. Over 7,000 victims are not smokers.

SMOKING-ATTRIBUTABLE MORTALITY AND MORBIDITY

Smoking-Related Deaths

Cigarette smoke contains over four thousand compounds, many of which are toxic, tumerogenic, mutagenic or carcinogenic (USDHHS 1989a).

Cigarette smoking is the single most preventable cause of death in the United States. It is directly responsible for one in six deaths—22 percent of all deaths among men and 11 percent of all deaths among women (USDHHS 1989a). Over 434,000 persons died from smoking-related causes in 1988, including

142,836 from cancer, 200,802 from cardiovascular diseases and 82,857 from respiratory diseases (CDC 1991e). An estimated 30 percent of all cancer deaths, 87 percent of lung cancer deaths, 21 percent of deaths from coronary heart disease, 18 percent of stroke deaths and 82 percent of deaths from chronic obstructive pulmonary disease are attributed to cigarette smoking (USDHHS 1989a).

Reduced Life Expectancy

Cigarettes don't just kill; they kill prematurely. Among males, 10 percent of smokers, but only 4 percent of nonsmokers, die before the age of 55; by age 65, 28 percent of smokers have died compared to 11 percent of nonsmokers; by the age of 75, 57 percent of smokers are dead, whereas 70 percent of nonsmokers are still alive (USDHHS 1989b). Male smokers have approximately 70 percent higher overall death rates than nonsmokers; female excess mortality (i.e., deaths that would not otherwise have occurred) is somewhat less as fewer female smokers smoke heavily (USDHHS 1989a). Each pack of cigarettes smoked reduces life expectancy by 137 minutes (Manning et al.).

Dose Responsiveness

Smoking-attributed mortality is strongly dose-related. Excess mortality rates from smoking-related diseases among men who smoke 25 or more cigarettes a day are roughly twice that of men who smoked less, and men who smoke heavily have almost double the risk of dying from a smoking-related disease before age 65 than do light smokers (Mattson et al.) A 35-year-old smoker who smoked one additional cigarette per day for the rest of his life would live 35 fewer days; conversely, if he smoked one less cigarette per day, he would extend his life by 40 days (Lippiatt).

Other Physiological Effects of Smoking

Smoking also reduces the quality of life and harms the body in numerous ways that are not necessarily fatal. It increases the risk of diabetes and of peptic ulcers. It makes ulcers more difficult to heal and more likely to be fatal. It appears to increase the risk of osteoporosis and bone fractures in older women. It reduces fertility in both men and women and reduces the chances of a successful outcome to pregnancy. Smoking also exacerbates the negative effects of alcohol on the body and may influence the efficacy of prescription drugs, sometimes dangerously. Oral contraceptives, for example, pose little health risk to nonsmoking women but are hazardous to women who do smoke (USDHHS 1989a). Cigarette smoke also saps one's energy, stains the teeth, fouls the breath, dulls the hair and ages the skin.

THE DEMAND FOR CIGARETTES

Despite fairly widespread knowledge of the health risks, over 50,000,000 Americans continue to smoke.

The Joys of Cigarette Smoking

Smokers often report that, once past the coughing, throat-burning, nauseating early stages of smoking, cigarettes perk them up (or calm them down), produce a mild high (or a mellowing out), give them something to do with their hands (always important) and (combining busy hands with cigarette-dulled taste buds) prevent them from overeating. Some smokers even claim to enjoy the taste. Do these benefits (great though they may be) outweigh the costs to health? Of course not. Why, then, do people smoke? They cannot stop once they have started. Why did they start? Usually because they were immature and unable to resist the peer pressure to light up.

Characteristics of Cigarette Smokers

Smokers are found in all sociodemographic groups. However, smoking prevalence is notably greater in some groups than in others.

Gender, Race and Ethnicity

More men smoke than women, and male smokers are twice as likely to smoke heavily as female smokers (NCHS 1989d). As can be seen in Table 1.1, white women and black women smoke at about the same rate, but black men smoke at a rate 30 percent greater than that of white men (NCHS 1991). Non-Hispanics smoke at a slightly higher rate than Hispanics smoke (NIDA 1991).

Surveys of adolescents indicate that the demographic composition of the smoking population will change over time. The National Institute for Drug Abuse (NIDA), surveying 12- to 17-year-olds in 1990, found that slightly less than 11 percent of Hispanic youth smoked, while the rate among young whites, 13.6 percent, was more than triple that of young blacks (NIDA 1991). That particular NIDA survey found smoking rates among young males of 12.3 percent, compared to 11 percent among young females. However, NIDA surveys of high school seniors have consistently found higher smoking rates among girls than among boys since 1977 (in Davis). This and other factors to be discussed shortly led Davis to project that smoking among women will surpass smoking among men by the year 2000.

In total, NIDA surveys have found that smoking prevalence among high school seniors is greater for those who are female, white, not planning to get a bachelor's degree or who live in the Northeast (in USGAO 1989e).

Table 1.1
Current Cigarette Smoking by Persons 18 Years of Age and Over by Sex and Race:
United States, Selected Years

	1965	1974	1979	1983	1985	1987
All persons	42.3	37.2	33.5	32.2	30.0	28.7
All males	51.6	42.9	37.2	34.7	32.1	31.0
- White males	50.8	41.7	36.5	34.1	31.3	30.4
- Black males	59.2	54.0	44.1	41.3	39.9	39.0
All females	34.0	32.5	30.3	29.9	28.2	26.7
- White females	34.3	32.3	30.6	30.1	28.3	27.2
- Black females	32.1	35.9	30.8	31.8	30.7	27.2

Source: National Center for Health Statistics. *Health United States 1990.*

Socioeconomic Status

Smoking is inversely related to education and income. Persons with less than 12 years of schooling are more than twice as likely to smoke as those with 16 or more years; persons whose family incomes are $20,000 or less are 50 percent more likely to smoke than those whose family incomes are $50,000 or more (NCHS 1989d). Holding income and education constant reduces the disparity between black and white smoking rates (Novotny et al.).

Age

Slightly more than half the people who currently smoke are 35 years of age or older; another 27 percent are between the ages of 26 and 34 (NIDA 1991). Smoking rates are highest among 35- to 44-year-olds (NCHS 1991). Smoking prevalence among adolescents, while of great concern, is less than among older cohorts.

The noteworthy fact here is that most of the people who smoke today began when the severity of the health consequences of smoking were less well understood. People made a choice to smoke, but it was not necessarily a well-informed choice. Despite the fact that cigarettes have been called "coffin nails" at least since the turn of the century, the great body of cigarette smoking research has been conducted in the years following the release of the first Surgeon General's Report on Smoking and Health in 1964. And only since then have the deleterious effects of cigarette smoking been widely publicized. By that time, many smokers were unable to quit.

Nicotine Addiction

An important component of the demand for cigarettes is that they contain nicotine, a highly addictive substance. Therefore, according to the Becker-Murphy model of rational addiction, even though the harmful effects of cigarette smoking are so pronounced as to make continued smoking appear irrational, for many smokers continued smoking is a rational choice. Becker and Murphy contend that past consumption of an addictive good stimulates present consumption by increasing the marginal utility of current consumption relative to the present value of the marginal harm resulting from future consumption. Simply put, the discomfort of nicotine withdrawal is so great that the utility derived from relieving it exceeds the smoker's momentary perception of the additional harm continued smoking engenders. This (apparently) rational decision making (apparent because the health benefits of smoking cessation are great), derived from an intense physiological urge to smoke, makes it extremely difficult for cigarette smokers to desist. Yet most smokers realize they should quit. Over 65 percent assert health considerations are their primary reason; most cite concern about their future health as opposed to their present health (NCHS 1989d).

Thus far, more than 38,000,000 Americans have successfully quit smoking, and almost half of all living adults in the United States who ever smoked have quit (CDC 1990l). However, it is difficult. At least two-thirds of smokers have tried to quit at one time or another and at least one-third try in any one year. Most quitters relapse in a short while (USDHHS 1989b). Hunt found that cigarettes are as addictive as heroin and more so than alcohol. Of those who had made serious efforts to quit, 65 percent of alcohol abusers had relapsed by the end of one year, while the relapse rate for cigarette smokers and heroin addicts was 75 percent (in USDHHS 1989b). People who successfully overcome an addiction usually have several periods of relapse before being able to sustain cessation. Recovered alcoholics and heroin addicts who have also been cigarette smokers often report that stopping drinking or drug use was more easily and quickly accomplished than stopping smoking.

Nicotine is so addictive that many people who switch to lower-yield cigarettes, planning to wean themselves gradually, find themselves smoking more intensely in order to maintain nicotine delivery (USDHHS 1989a). Of those who do quit, many manage only by chewing nicotine gum. They remain strongly addicted.

Recruits to the Smoking Population

The addictive power of cigarettes may make continued smoking for those already hooked a "rational" choice. But, given that nicotine's addictive properties are so well known, it is not rational to start smoking in the first place. Who would make such an irrational, health-threatening choice? Teenagers, very young teenagers. Smoking uptake is almost exclusively a phenomena of adolescence.

The concept of rational choice is often thought to be inapplicable to adolescents. They tend to be risk takers by nature, assume a certain invincibility, lack perspective, underestimate their propensity for addiction and confront tremendous peer pressure. They are usually considered too immature to make a rational, informed choice. Yet this supposition underestimates some adolescents and lets others off the hook too easily. Most teens do make the best choice with respect to cigarette smoking—they don't do it.

But far too many teens do smoke, and thousands more take up the habit each day. Although it has long been the case that most smokers began as teens (among smokers born since 1935, 80 percent started smoking by age 20, and almost half started by age 17), studies of smokers today indicate that the age of initiation is falling. Smoking, especially among females and among whites, now begins at an earlier age (USDHHS 1989a). A 1986 University of Michigan survey found that 26 percent of the high school seniors who smoked had their first cigarette by grade six, 73 percent had their first by grade nine (in USDHHS 1989a). NIDA found that 60 percent of new smokers today start by the age of 13 (in Tye et al.).

Changes in the Demand for Cigarettes

Demand has decreased as many Americans have conquered their addiction to cigarettes and more young people have declined to initiate smoking.

Sources of the Decline

Most people credit governmental antismoking activity, largely spearheaded by health advocates, for the decrease in cigarette consumption. Their lobbying activity resulted in more research, widely disseminated information, and restrictions on advertising and smoking behavior.

Tobacco industry spokespeople see it a different way. They claim that "effective anti-smoking guerilla warfare [perpetrated by] self-styled do-gooders [who use] their own First Amendment rights in an arrogant, despotic, inquisitorial way to restrict those same rights and the freedom of choice for others" have encouraged "the ever-growing paternalistic mentality of the federal government" (Burns, pp. 74, 78; Kerrigan, p. 63). The result has been "elite groups of government officials who apparently believe that they have—and should exercise—the power to influence individual adult behavior. They have decided that . . . tobacco is bad for people and are attempting to eliminate it in the guise of the public interest through legislation, regulation and/or by absolute fiat" (Kerrigan, p.63). "When government first decides on a social policy [it] then searches for the facts to support it. . . . Like Hitler in Germany, the spread of the policy itself, becomes its justification. As the masses move to embrace it, all walking to the same drummer, group satisfaction is obtained by castigating a minority" (Delman, p. 51). The "facts" the government finds are largely uncovered by government-supported research. Tobacco is overresearched because "where there is research there are jobs and grants . . . and where there are grants there is a battle for money and results, and where there are results there is need for confirmation, and further research, grants, jobs, etc" (Delman p. 44). (Delman proceeds to suggest that "our Age of Science and Age of the Medical God accept its lack of knowledge and . . . express a greater humility" [p. 44]). Research results are then promulgated by the media as Americans "remain childishly deceived by the fourth estate into believing that what the news presents are 'facts' " (Delman, p. 41). Misinformed citizens are then threatened by a "health scare" (Blaine & Reed, p. 116). And the "fear-production [that is a] result of this information . . . may be [itself] a cause of illness" (Delman, p. 50). In other words, tobacco is not hazardous to our health; fear of tobacco is. That fear is excited by overzealous vigilantes interested only in trampling on the civil rights of others, abetted by medical researchers with strong vested interests and promoted by a fascistic government that has its own agenda to pursue, namely to extend its totalitarian influence.

Whatever the motivation, the program is working. Cigarette consumption is down.

Total and Per Capita Consumption

United States Department of Agriculture economist Verner Grise informs us that total cigarette consumption grew enormously in the first half of the century. New production methods allowed more efficient production and lower product prices, and population and income both increased greatly. Per capita consumption tripled from 1920 to 1950 as smoking spread through most segments of society. It reached its peak in 1963, the year before the Surgeon General's seminal report and the application of warnings to packages and advertisements. In 1964, per capita consumption began to decline gradually. By 1986, it was 25 percent below the 1963 record. But due to population growth, total cigarette consumption increased until 1985. Now both total and per capita consumption fall yearly (Grise 1987). Blaine and Reed (1987) attribute 3.2 percent of the recent yearly 4 percent decline in per capita cigarette consumption to the "health scare." Grise attributes part of the decline to real cigarette price increases and the bevy of federal, state and local restrictions on smoking.

Smoking Prevalence, Quit Rates and Initiation Rates

Over 42 percent of the United States population age 18 or over smoked in 1965. By 1987, the number was down to 28 percent as smokers quit or died and fewer young persons began (NCHS 1991). As was depicted in Table 1.1, smoking rates have decreased for all groups.

Comparing smoking behavior in 1974 to that in 1985, Fiore and associates found that in addition to lesser overall smoking prevalence, quit rates (defined as the proportion of ever smokers who are former smokers) increased among men, women, blacks and whites. The largest increase in quit rates was among black males; although their smoking prevalence is still greater, the gap is closing. If this trend continues, we should eventually see a reduction in smoking-related mortality among black men, which now greatly exceeds that of whites.

The Fiore group also found that initiation rates (measured by the prevalence of current smokers aged 20 to 24) decreased significantly among men, especially black men, but changed very little among women. This, coupled with their observation that the prevalence of smoking among men decreased almost 1 percent a year from 1974 to 1985 but fell at only one-third that rate among women, leads to the conclusion that male and female smoking rates (and smoking-attributable mortality) will eventually converge. It also supports the contention that smoking among women will eventually exceed smoking among men.

Projections of Cigarette Usage

There is cause for optimism. Although relative smoking rates may differ, absolute smoking rates among every group have declined. How much smoking will continue to decline depends upon public policy in the form of excise taxes, antismoking activities, restrictions on smoking and regulation of the tobacco industry. It also depends on real income, new research findings about the health effects of tobacco, and advertising and promotional activities by cigarette manufacturers. Grise estimates that consumption by the year 2000 will have fallen by 20 to 25 percent from its 1987 levels. He feels it may fall as much as 35 percent if excise taxes are greatly increased and restrictions on smoking become more numerous and stringent (Grise 1987).

However, the problem is far from over. More than 50,000,000 Americans still smoke, and each year over 1,000,000 teens begin (USDHHS 1989b). The evidence suggests that those who continue smoking may be more strongly addicted and less responsive to educational efforts. The proportionate decline in smoking was greatest among college graduates and lowest among persons who had not completed high school (USDHHS 1989a). Moreover, it appears that the proportion of smokers who smoke heavily has not declined, and the proportion of those who are very heavy smokers may actually have increased (USDHHS 1989a).

Thus, despite the decline in cigarette consumption, the tobacco industry remains a potent economic force.

THE TOBACCO INDUSTRY

> Ladies and gentlemen, with every tick of the second hand, our industry is enriching the economy of this country by $2600. . . . [T]hat's $156,000 a minute . . . more than $9.4 million every hour . . . 24 hours a day . . . 365 days a year. When we talk about tobacco . . . we're talking about big money.
>
> —Terry J. Burns, tobacco industry spokesman, p. 75

Revenues Generated by Tobacco Production and Sales

Tobacco's Value as a Farm Commodity

Tobacco is a valuable crop. Grown on 137,000 farms in the United States on about 0.2 percent of our cropland, it accounted for 3.5 percent of reported crop cash receipts in 1990. It typically ranks fifth or sixth among legal cash crops and first or second in value per acre (Grise 1991).

Value as a Finished Product

Although domestic consumption has fallen, total cigarette production increased to 700 billion cigarettes in 1990 (USDA). Evidence of the inelasticity of demand for cigarettes is provided by the fact that in spite of increases in real prices markedly greater than that of other consumer items, cigarette manufacturers have enjoyed considerable increases in their revenues and profits. Americans spent a record-breaking $44 billion on tobacco products in 1990, $41.8 billion on cigarettes alone (Grise 1991). Cigarette industry profits have also been setting records. They totalled $7.2 billion in 1989, 10 percent greater than in 1988 (Salomon Brothers). The average compounded annual profit growth rate from 1984 to 1989 was 14 percent. Profits per 1,000 cigarettes totalled $13.84 in 1989, over 18 percent greater than the year before, raising the average annual compounded growth rate to 15.6 percent. Salomon Brothers expects continued double-digit increases over the next several years. They claim to know of no other industry with such a favorable profit-per-unit outlook. Kidder, Peabody asserts that cigarette stocks are a safe investment in times of economic uncertainty. They credit investors looking for a safe haven from the ill economic winds of 1990 for the surge in equity of cigarette stock of over 30 percent relative to the market that year. Many American tobacco companies have restructured their portfolios in order to reduce their risk but find that it is their nontobacco earnings that are at risk. For example, demand for American Brands' lines of office, hardware and home improvement products softened in the recession of 1990, whereas its profits from cigarettes were at an all-time high (Salomon Brothers). Industry leader Phillip Morris, which produces Kraft foods and Miller beer, among other products, receives almost half its operating income from tobacco sales, although only 20 percent of its operating revenue derives from that source. Processed foods and alcoholic beverages are profitable, but not as profitable as cigarettes (Kidder, Peabody)

The Industry's Economic Impact

Tobacco sales benefit more than just farmers and stockholders. The impact is far-reaching.

Income and Employment Induced by the Production of Tobacco Products

Tobacco's core sector, the sector that grows, processes, packages and brings tobacco products to market, employed 422,462 workers in 1986. Total compensation paid was almost $7 billion (Price Waterhouse).

It must be noted, however, that the cigarette industry, because of its homogeneous product line, lends itself to a high degree of automation. RJR Nabisco (formerly R. J. Reynolds) now uses 8,000-per-minute cigarette makers and packers and has greatly reduced its cigarette work force. More cutbacks are expected. New equipment capable of producing 10,000 cigarettes per minute is on the drawing board. It will be available to the industry by the mid-1990s (Salomon Brothers).

The supplier sector, firms supplying everything from pesticides to irrigation equipment, papers, plastics and insurance, employed 278,421 persons in 1986 whose jobs were directly (though perhaps rather generously) attributable to the production of tobacco products. Their compensation was estimated at $7.8 billion (Price Waterhouse).

Later rounds of consumption by core and supplier sector workers were credited with the creation of over 1.6 million jobs with a payroll of over $37.5 billion.

Summing compensation to employees, proprietors' income, corporate profits (estimated at $3.6 billion to core and suppliers' tobacco production share), induced expenditures and the like, Price Waterhouse calculated that the tobacco industry contributed $59.9 billion to the United States gross national product in 1986.

Tobacco-Related Tax Revenues

Price Waterhouse estimates that core and supplier sector employees paid $2.35 billion in personal income taxes and $1.72 billion in FICA taxes in 1986. Corporate income taxes from firms directly involved in tobacco production totalled $2.2 billion.

Tobacco consumers also pay taxes at the point of purchase. Excise taxes paid on tobacco products in 1990 totalled over $10 billion, 42 percent of which accrued to the federal government (Grise 1991).

Balance of Trade Effects

Tobacco exports have provided some relief to our trade deficit problem and have prompted increased cigarette production in spite of reduced domestic demand. The dollar value of tobacco exports increased 25 percent from 1988 to 1989 and 39 percent from 1989 to 1990 (TMA). Even though we are the world's largest importer of tobacco products as well as the world's largest exporter, the value of our net exports in 1990 was $5.8 billion, a record high (USDA).

Export opportunities are expected to increase significantly, as markets in eastern Europe are opening up to American cigarette companies even more rapidly than expected. Phillip Morris and RJR have recently negotiated large sales to what had been the Soviet Union; more are expected (Kidder, Peabody).

Tobacco Subsidies

There are no tobacco subsidies. Contrary to popular mythology, the government does not subsidize tobacco production or pay farmers to grow less tobacco in order to maintain prices. There is a system of price supports, but it runs on the no-net-cost principle. Funds to uphold price supports or provide loans to growers come from a fund to which participants must contribute. No general tax revenues are used; funding is entirely internal.

All this would be wonderful, indeed the tobacco industry would be roundly applauded, if industry data told the whole story. But they certainly do not. Industry data do not reveal the tremendous health risks tobacco and related products pose or the carnage associated with their use. Nor do they reveal the enormous monetary costs such products impose on consumers, on their families, friends, co-workers and employers, and on society at large.

THE COSTS OF CIGARETTE SMOKING

Private Costs

Direct Costs

The most immediate cost of cigarette consumption is the purchase price. At approximately $1.50 per pack, smokers spend an average of nearly $600 on cigarettes each year. The $41.8 billion spent in 1990 represented over 1 percent of total personal disposable income (Grise 1991).

Spending on cigarettes can have a large effect on a household's budget. Families that include at least one smoker spent an average of $850, 2.5 percent of their post-tax income, on cigarettes in 1990 (CBO).

Poor households spent proportionately more. The Congressional Budget Office estimates that families with smokers in the bottom post-tax income quintile spend an average of 8.2 percent of their income on cigarettes, as compared to 3.1 percent for the middle quintile and 1.2 percent for the top quintile. As a group, however, lower-income households spend an even more largely disproportionate amount of their income on cigarettes because of their higher smoking rates.

Health Care Costs

The other costs of smoking that are most obviously internalized are the health consequences—the pain, suffering, disability and death smoking entails. These health consequences also involve monetary expenses, representing about 6 percent of all United States health care expenditures (OTA). According to the

Office of Technology Assessment, total smoking-related health care costs in 1985 were approximately $22 billion, perhaps as much as $35 billion. Over two-thirds of that was incurred on behalf of persons under 65 years of age. Government spending on smoking-related illness approximated $3.5 billion for Medicare, $0.7 billion for Medicaid and $0.4 billion for veterans' health, but may have been as high as $5.4 billion, $1.1 billion and $0.6 billion for those programs respectively (OTA). These figures are far greater today. The Consumer Price Index for medical care rose 56 percent from 1985 to 1991 alone (USDL 1991).

Only a small portion of these costs are borne by the smoker in the form of direct payments, medical deductibles, contributions to health insurance, and tax payments that support government-funded health care. Most of the expense is collectively shared by co-workers, employers and taxpayers.

Lost Wages

Earnings may be reduced by smoking-related absenteeism and premature death. Horowitz found the average smoker to miss 2.2 more days from work per year than the average nonsmoker (in Jackson et al.). Lost wages are commonly considered equivalent to productivity losses, as most analysts, overlooking salaried employees, contend reduced productivity is internalized by the worker in the form of forgone wages. The OTA estimates that smoking-related productivity losses in 1985 were probably about $43 billion, but may have run as high as $61 billion (OTA).

Warner estimated that only 38 percent of the costs of smoking-related health care and lost productivity is borne by smokers (in OTA).

The Social Costs of Cigarette Smoking

Monetary Costs

Warner estimated that nonsmokers pay 62 percent of the economic costs of cigarette smoking (OTA). If that is true, the external costs of smoking in 1985 may have been as much as $22 billion in health care and as great as $38 billion in lost productivity. The estimate of the external costs of lost productivity is especially problematic since, as just mentioned, many analysts consider such losses to be internalized in the form of lost wages. But employers often pay for sick leave, for temporary replacement of ill workers, and for recruitment and training of new permanent workers. Their health insurance premiums may also be increased. In addition, production schedules may be disrupted, nonsmoking employee morale may be dampened, profits may suffer and forgone wages are not subject to taxation. And that which is not produced is missed by all of us, not just by those who would have been paid for producing it.

However, there are monetary benefits accruing to nonsmokers as a result of others' smoking—a monetary windfall, one might say, as these benefits exceed the external costs.

Monetary Savings Accruing to Nonsmokers

Smokers do pay taxes on the cigarettes they buy, but whether those taxes compensate for the external costs cigarette smoking imposes on society is a subject of dispute. Manning and colleagues performed an especially interesting analysis on the external costs of smoking with respect to cigarette tax revenues and concluded that the net external cost was a mere $0.15 per pack. However, they assumed productivity losses were internalized as lost wages. From that perspective, the taxes collected from the sale of cigarettes greatly exceed the external costs—smokers subsidize nonsmokers. Most other analysts include both smoking-related health care costs and productivity losses in their calculations of external costs, usually concluding that cigarette smoking imposes a heavy fiscal burden on society. But the opposite may be true. There appears to be a net economic gain accruing to nonsmokers from others' smoking. This results from the fact that smokers die young. They don't live to suffer other, perhaps more costly and more debilitating diseases, and they die before drawing much of their social security and pension benefits.

Retirement account savings: Smokers who die at precisely the age of retirement have made their full contribution to their pension plan and social security accounts but receive none of the benefits. Since those benefits would have been paid out over time, their worth must be discounted. The resulting sum, the present value of the worth of that future income stream, is essentially "bequeathed" to society. If some portion of those funds can be transferred to the surviving spouse or the deceased's estate, the value is, of course, reduced; but since such monies can rarely be transferred in their entirety, society still reaps a death benefit. That benefit is reduced if the smoker dies before retirement, having not made the maximum contribution, or if he dies some years after retirement, having drawn on his benefits. However, when all possibilities are considered—dying before, at, or after retirement, or transferring benefits—a bequest to society still remains. Due to their earlier-than-average deaths, smokers claim a less than proportionate share of their retirement benefits.

Manning and associates estimate the saving to retirement funds to be only $0.24 per pack of cigarettes (in 1986 dollars, discounted at 5 percent). This is markedly less than the external costs of cigarettes which they estimate to be $0.44 per pack ($0.36 for short-run medical care, $0.05 for group insurance and $0.03 for sick leave). Schelling, however, claims the retirement fund saving more than offsets the costs of short-run medical care. He estimates a discounted bequest to society of twenty billion (1986) dollars in unclaimed retirement benefits. But generally, most observers contend health care costs and retirement savings offset each other.

Yet even if this were true, there would still be a social saving. We have to consider not just what smokers do cost us for health care, but also what they do not cost us.

Health care savings: Nonsmokers are hardly invincible to illness. They may live longer than smokers, but time eventually catches up with them. Nonsmokers may live longer only to suffer longer-lived, more costly diseases.

If far fewer people smoked, we would have a population that was both larger and older, as the average age of death would be greater. We would have fewer doctor's visits and hospital stays, in the population's younger years, but more later. If the real price of health care contacts remained the same and if the average number of contacts per individual remained the same, our spending would be no greater and would serve a larger population, one that enjoyed a longer life. We would get more for our health care dollar. If we took into account that the health care expenditures for an older, nonsmoking population come later than the expenditures for a younger, smoking population, we would find even more favorable results. At equal levels of actual expenditures, the present value of discounted future expenditures for nonsmokers is actually less than current expenditures on behalf of smokers.

But health care costs may not be equal. Examining the effect of a reduction in smoking, Lippiatt found that increased life expectancy is associated with an increase in medical costs even when discounted. The increased medical costs, however, are modest. She estimates the additional medical care costs (undiscounted) to be $280 per extra year of life. While not supporting the oft-made argument that smoking should be reduced in order to reduce health care costs, it is a small price to pay for a longer life of improved quality and greater productivity. It is also a small price to pay to reduce the social costs of smoking for, while we have thus far addressed the external fiscal costs arising from health care and lost productivity, there are other, largely nonfinancial externalities associated with smoking. These can be quite significant, unambiguously demonstrating how one person's choice imposes costs on others.

The Health Effects of Environmental Smoking

Nonsmokers in close proximity to smokers may inhale the smoke exhaled by smokers, known as "second-hand smoke." Or they may inhale the smoke produced by the burning cigarette between puffs, known as "sidestream smoke." Although second-hand smoke is less harmful to the nonsmoker, as the smoker's body filters out some of the toxins, both forms of environmental smoke are injurious. Inhalation of environmental smoke is referred to as passive or involuntary smoking.

Scores of studies have uncovered serious adverse consequences from passive smoking. Nonsmokers who live with smokers generally have a 30 percent increased risk of lung cancer compared to members of nonsmoking households (USDHHS 1989a). They are also at greater risk of other cancers and of heart disease. Studying deaths from all causes in nonsmokers living with smoking spouses, Sandler and associates found an elevated mortality risk that was not only greater than that of persons who were not exposed to tobacco smoke, but slightly exceeded the mortality risk of smokers who consumed up to nine cigarettes a day. The children of smokers, compared to children of non-smoking parents, have an increased number of respiratory disorders, are sick more often and miss more days of school (NCHS 1987). The Centers for Disease Control conservatively attributes 3,825 deaths in 1988 to passive smoking (CDC 1991f). A report sponsored by the Environmental Protection Agency (but not yet approved or released) concluded that environmental smoke kills 53,000 nonsmokers a year, including 37,000 from heart disease ("Secondhand").

But at least adults and children who live with smokers can occasionally escape to a smoke-free environment. The most insidious, indeed treacherous, delivery of cigarettes' toxic agents is that by a pregnant woman to her unborn baby. As will be detailed in Chapter 5, that child is at increased risk of spontaneous abortion, premature birth, low birth weight, and fetal and infant death. Maternal cigarette smoking is responsible for over 4,000 such deaths each year (USDHHS 1989a).

Smoking-Ignited Fires

Improper cigarette usage was responsible for approximately 53,700 structural fires resulting in 1,410 fatalities and 3,210 injuries, not including those among firefighters, in each of the years from 1984 to 1988. Most of the fires occurred in residential structures, and many of the victims were not smokers. They were elderly persons and children trapped in the blaze of another's making. Yearly property damage approximated $333 million (NFPA).

Few private behavioral choices inflict such obvious harm on nonparticipants. Cigarette smoking clearly imposes costs on nonsmokers, costs that go beyond the mere financial, costs that cry out for relief.

CURRENT PUBLIC POLICY

Justification

Government intervention in the market for cigarettes is justified because the market is significantly flawed. It is characterized by grievously imperfect information on the part of consumers, who are unable to freely exit the market upon acquisition of accurate information and who express deep regret at having entered the market initially. It is also characterized by the lethal externalities of environmental smoke and fires and by the imposition of external financial costs. Therefore, since the government is mandated to protect public welfare, it is obligated to intervene in the market for cigarettes. And, in fact, governmental efforts to reduce smoking have been more than moderately successful.

Approach

The government's campaign against cigarette smoking has focused on demand reduction. Its keystone has been education—in schools, through the mass media, during health care contacts and in explicit warnings on cigarette packages and advertisements. The government has also restricted advertising, having banned cigarette commercials on television and radio since 1971. Anti-smoking legislation has been enacted, mostly at the state or local level, restricting smoking in public places such as government buildings, banks, schools, health care facilities, public transportation, retail stores, theaters and sports arenas. Almost half the states (and many cities) have partial restrictions on smoking in restaurants. The federal government restricts smoking at its own work sites and on interstate mass transportation vehicles. It prohibits smoking on all domestic airline flights.

Effectiveness

Testimony to the effectiveness of the government's antismoking campaign is found in the decreased prevalence of smoking among all demographic groups since the first Surgeon General's Report in 1964. It is also found in the decreased total and per capita cigarette consumption, which until that time had been rising. Yet consumption data actually understate the campaign's success, since, as Warner points out, consumption not only would not have declined in its absence, it would have increased. Smoking among women, in particular, was just beginning to follow the earlier pattern of men's smoking and would doubtlessly have increased a great deal. Smoking prevalence has lessened among successively younger cohorts in all subpopulation groups as fewer young people have taken up smoking in each of the years following the initial "health scare" (Warner 1989). Indeed, the antismoking campaign provides us one of the few pieces of solid good news in this entire volume: an estimated 2.9 billion deaths, from 1964 through the year 2000, have been postponed by campaign-related smoking cessation and noninitiation (Warner 1989).

However, even though, by Warner's estimation, over 90,000,000 Americans would be smokers today without the campaign, 50,000,000 still are. And every day 3,000 more teenagers join them. Obviously, much still needs to be done.

RECOMMENDATIONS FOR FUTURE POLICY

Our ultimate objective is a smoke-free society. This necessitates cessation by smokers and noninitiation of potential smokers. It may never be achieved. Therefore, as we pursue our goal, we also must continue to strive to reduce the externalities associated with smoking.

Our policy instruments have thus far proven fairly effective. Even though they may have passed the point of diminishing marginal returns (as those persons most readily influenced have already been influenced), they should be continued, expanded and improved. New measures must be introduced as our knowledge of smokers and smoking increases. Proper application of that knowledge will enhance the efficacy of our policies.

Improved Access to Smoking Cessation Programs

Smoking cessation has major and immediate health benefits, even for persons already stricken with a smoking-related disease. It reduces the risk of various cancers, heart attack, stroke, and chronic lung disease and improves the chances for a successful pregnancy. Former smokers live longer than continuing smokers—for example, persons who quit smoking before age 50 are 50 percent less likely than continuing smokers to die within the next 15 years (CDC 1990l). Townsend estimates that giving up smoking permanently saves, on average, 2.5 years of life per smoker, and that quitting for one year saves, on average, 25 days of life (in Reid & Smith).

Yet very few health insurance carriers cover the costs of smoking cessation programs. Many provide reimbursement for nicotine gum but usually only after the patient has been diagnosed with a smoking-related disease (Moore in USDHHS 1989a).

When legislation providing universal access to health care is enacted, which will surely be before the end of this decade, it should include coverage of those programs that have been found to be cost-effective. Until that time, private insurers should be encouraged to cover smoking cessation and Medicaid should be mandated to cover it. Local governments must also provide cessation programs in schools and in neighborhood clinics. To do otherwise is to jeopardize public health and safety. To strictly enforce antismoking regulations yet fail to assist in breaking nicotine addiction is unjust.

Educational Efforts

Publicity

New research findings on the adverse effects of smoking and the benefits of cessation should continue to be well publicized, as publicity has been found to be the most effective tool in reducing smoking (Reid and Smith). Antismoking public service messages on television and radio should be increased. Required to counterbalance cigarette commercials when they were still permitted, their near disappearance represents the downside of the advertising ban. And, just as cigarette companies flagrantly target specific groups, notably women, teens and minorities, so should we. American advertising genius could be used in a socially productive way.

School-Based Prevention Programs

In-school antismoking education does not get the high grades publicity gets from Reid and Smith, but it surely deserves some credit for the decline in smoking and must be continued. Hinging on the principle that preventing the onset of addiction is easier than conquering it once it has been established, antismoking education today must commence in the earliest grades.

To reach their full potential, prevention programs must also take creative cognizance of the psychosocial predictors of smoking uptake. Studies have shown that children most at risk of smoking are those whose parents, friends or siblings smoke, who are of lower socioeconomic status, who are left unattended for long periods of time, who have low self-esteem, who perform poorly in school, who are less able to withstand peer pressure, or who perceive smoking as a risk-taking, sensation-seeking adventure or rite of passage. Although lectures on why smoking is bad for one do have some value, they appear to be most influential among low-risk children, those who share few or none of the above-mentioned characteristics, and who, in today's climate, would probably not have smoked anyway. Proof of the failure to educate students who are most at risk of smoking is found not only in the fact that more of them smoke, but also, as Leventhal and associates discovered, in that smoking teens know comparatively little about the health hazards and addictive nature of smoking. They also greatly overestimate smoking prevalence, even within their own social circles, and underestimate social disapproval of smoking. Traditional educational approaches are less successful with them, as they tend to be low academic achievers.

A greater variety of school-based smoking prevention programs addressing specific risk factors is evidently needed. Best and company, evaluating the impact of several program types, concluded that those that treat social modeling are most effective. Friedman and colleagues claim the best prevention programs help children develop assertiveness and other social skills that enable them to better resist (or avoid) peer pressure situations, obviously useful in other contexts as well. Programs that alert children to the insidious nature of advertising promote a healthy skepticism and are also obviously of transferrable value.

We must provide adequate basic care for our children, a recurring theme in this volume, as no society can flourish in good health unless children are properly cared for. Later we will discuss the need for infant stimulation programs, preschool education and day care. When the threat to children's well-being is cigarette smoking, after-school programs for the estimated two to six million latchkey children are the deterrent. While many latchkey children thrive, developing personal resources they may not otherwise have, others are endangered. There is a direct relationship between hours of self-care and consumption of cigarettes, alcohol and marijuana by eighth graders (Richardson et al.). Of these, despite the relief parents might feel to find their children "only" smoking cigarettes, cigarette consumption is probably the most harmful for the most young people. Moderate use of alcohol and (some) drugs, while undesirable, can be less harmful. Immoderate use is frequently a passing phase. But cigarette smoking is harmful in any degree, highly likely to increase in frequency once begun, and not unlikely to last a lifetime. Users are more likely to become addicted to nicotine than to heroin, cocaine or morphine and, once established, nicotine addiction is the most difficult to overcome (Glazer).

But education, even creatively packaged innovative programs, will not deter all potential smokers. Publicity will not prompt all smokers to quit. Some people are resistant to education; some are ineducable; some simply deny the evidence. Such denial is apparent in the National Center for Health Statistics' survey, which found smokers to be much less well informed about the hazards of smoking than nonsmokers or former smokers (NCHS 1989d). Smokers must have heard the warnings, but somehow they just did not register. Therefore the force of the law is required to further propel the antismoking campaign.

Legal Approaches to Smoking Deterrence

Restricting Smoking Activity

Smoking prohibitions, few in number prior to 1964, were originally designed to avert fire hazards. Now in the thousands, the impetus comes from antismoking activists endeavoring to protect the right of nonsmokers to breathe unpolluted air. But, while intended to reduce externalities, prohibitions on smoking in large numbers of public places have also effectively raised the internal cost of smoking. The inconvenience, coupled with the greater social awareness prohibition promotes, has contributed to the decline in smoking. Comparing smoking behavior in communities with highly restrictive antismoking ordinances to that in nonrestrictive communities, Lewit found smoking cessation rates up to 10 percent greater in the stricter localities than could be accounted for by personal characteristics alone (in USDHHS 1989a). Restrictions also reduce the time available for smoking, thereby reducing total consumption.

Amid growing evidence of the health hazards of environmental tobacco smoke, public support of a total ban on all smoking in public places has increased in recent years. The latest Gallup poll on the issue found that 60 percent of the population, including 75 percent of nonsmokers and 26 percent of smokers, support such a ban ("Majorities").

Support has also been growing for more smoking restrictions in the private workplace, although it is far from unanimous. The AFL-CIO has declared its opposition to legislated smoking policies. Hazel Duke, president of the New York state NAACP, also objects. She claims such legislation discriminates against minorities, who are typically at the bottom of the totem pole in most workplaces and seldom possessed of access to private offices where smoking would still be permitted (in Glazer).

Legislators and the courts have been reluctant to intervene. The Occupational Safety and Health Act has not been found to protect nonsmokers' rights; the Employee Retirement Income Security Act may, under some circumstances, preclude the discharge of smokers who violate their company's smoking policies; and the National Labor Relations Act forbids an employer operating under a collective bargaining agreement from unilaterally establishing a smoking policy (Vaughn).

Yet private employers generally have a great deal of discretion regarding smoking policies. Consequently, current corporate policies differ widely. Few firms, primarily health care facilities and insurance companies, ban it entirely. Very few firms refuse outright to hire smokers. To do so could conceivably leave them open to charges of racial discrimination against black men because of their higher smoking rates. Most firms that do restrict smoking in some way merely designate certain areas as smoking or nonsmoking. Some have restructured work spaces; others have simply installed ventilation systems. All can expect growing pressure to protect nonsmokers both internally and legislatively, especially at the municipal level. When the rights of smokers and nonsmokers have come into conflict, resolution increasingly tends to favor nonsmokers. Public policy is working to reduce social costs.

If we want to reduce smoking and the externalities associated with it, smoking restrictions must clearly be extended and made more stringent. This would provoke hardship in cigarette-addicted persons, but we can righteously claim it is for their own good and that, in any case, our imposition on them is of a higher moral order than their imposition on us. But just as clearly, there are limits as to how much further antismoking laws can be extended, especially since smoking remains a legal activity. Increased restrictions on smoking will have only a marginal effect.

Restricting Cigarette Sales

Sales restrictions are designed to deter smoking by children, necessitated by the fact that, of the 3,000 children who each day smoke their first cigarette, roughly 750 will die from smoking-related diseases. Referring to nicotine addiction as a childhood disease, DiFranza and Tye inform us that 90 percent of first-time smokers today are under the age of 18 and that almost 3,000,000 children 17 or younger smoke on a daily basis. Over 100,000 daily smokers are 11 years old or less.

The sale of tobacco products to minors is illegal in 45 states and the District of Columbia. The possession of tobacco products by minors is also illegal in many states. Yet enforcement is rare and penalties are light. An informal nationwide study found that 70 percent of the stores approached by minors sold them cigarettes; in Massachusetts, 75 out of 100 stores that were approached by an 11-year-old girl sold cigarettes to her (Kirn).

Mid-1991 saw a legal breakthrough that is expected to have national repercussions, prompting stricter observance of the laws by retail stores. The outcome of a suit filed by two nicotine-addicted teenagers against a convenience store chain that illegally sold them cigarettes firmly established the store's liability for the youths' addiction and any future health problems that may result from their smoking (Jones). Although it may go too far in relieving the adolescents of any responsibility, such a liability does provide for a more equitable reassignment of smoking's costs. But the real benefit, one hopes, will be lessened opportunities for children to obtain cigarettes.

Enactment of a proposed ban on cigarette vending machines (except in bars and other places not frequented by children) would also reduce the availability of cigarettes to minors. It should be particularly effective in reducing sales to young children who often lack the confidence to approach a clerk. A study commissioned by the National Automatic Merchandising Association found that 13-year-olds are 11 times more likely than 17-year-olds to purchase cigarettes from a vending machine (in Slade). Children can and do acquire cigarettes by other than direct purchase, but machines facilitate acquisition and thus encourage smoking. They make cigarettes far too accessible and should be retired.

Restricting Cigarette Advertising and Promotion

Cigarette advertising should be strictly prohibited; promotional activity must be severely curtailed. Cigarette merchandisers have been too successful in marketing their product—a product that promises the high life but delivers a premature death.

A ban on cigarette advertising would, however, result in a genuine loss of income to the advertising industry and the media for, despite having been banned from the airwaves, cigarettes are the most heavily advertised product after passenger cars. They rank number one in outdoor media, number two in magazines and number six in newspapers (CDC 1990b). More money is spent on the advertising and promotion of tobacco products than on that of any other consumer good (Mahar). Expenditures in 1988 totalled $3.28 billion—$1.05 billion for advertising, $2.23 billion for promotion (CDC 1990d). This represents a 300 percent increase in real expenditures since 1975 and continues the shift away from direct advertising to promotions in the form of coupons, giveaways, and sponsorship of cultural and athletic events (CDC 1990d).

According to the tobacco industry, the rationale behind its merchandising activity is not to expand the market for cigarettes but to enhance market share, that is, to prompt current smokers to switch brands. That explanation rings hollow. Less than 10 percent of smokers switch brands in any given year; when they do, they usually switch between brands produced by the same company (Tye et al.). The cigarette industry is highly oligopolistic. Six companies produce almost all the 250 brands on the market. Two-thirds of the brands are produced by just two companies—Phillip Morris and RJR. As Tye and associates point out, if the only purpose of cigarette advertising is to induce brand switching, expenditures of the magnitude the tobacco industry incurs are irrational given that interindustry switching is so negligible. Such expenditures are rational only if they encourage smoking uptake or discourage smokers from quitting. And cigarette advertising does just that. It also provokes recidivism among former smokers, increases smokers' daily consumption by cueing smoking behavior and contributes to the perception that smoking is less hazardous, more prevalent and more socially acceptable than it is (CDC 1990d).

Moreover, a form of censorship appears to be at work. Warner and associates have found strong statistical evidence that cigarette advertising in magazines, especially in women's magazines, is associated with lesser coverage of the health hazards of smoking. Fear of economic reprisal by cigarette manufacturers is apparently the primary motivation since the degree of restriction appears to be a function of the publication's proportion of revenues received from cigarette advertising.

Merchandising efforts, including advertising, promotions, packaging and the ubiquitity of the product, have been especially creative (and successful) when aimed at specific groups. Although public outcry forced the demise of the notorious Uptown, the cigarette designed expressly to appeal to blacks, cigarette companies still target minorities. Black neighborhoods are inundated with billboards depicting upscale blacks enjoying the good life of which cigarettes are presumably a part. And cigarettes are heavily advertised in minority-oriented publications.

Cigarettes are also heavily promoted in women's magazines. Indeed, the entire industry pitch to potential female customers is a textbook case of successful campaigning. With slogans like Marlboro's "Mild as May" and "Ivory tips protect the lips," buzzwords like "slim" and "thin," phrases like "You've come a long way, baby," portrayals of women smokers as glamorous movie stars, loving mothers or wholesome nymphs, and sponsorship of women's athletic events, the pitch to women is credited with, in Davis's words, "making lung cancer an equal opportunity disease" (p. 101). The campaign also imperiled many more children, both in utero and in the home.

Most of the industry's heavy ammunition, however, has recently been directed at teenagers, a perfectly rational move from the industry's point of view. Male, female, white, black and brown, they comprise the largest pool of potential smokers. Considering the addictive power of nicotine, inducing youngsters to smoke represents an investment that will generate returns for decades to come. It is an investment tobacco companies must undertake to sustain their shrinking domestic market. They need to replace smokers that die or quit. So they feature cartoon characters in their advertisements, promote heavily in teen magazines, distribute beach towels, baseball caps and tee shirts with company logos and, most blatantly, give out free samples of cigarettes at rock concerts and other places frequented by teenagers. But most reprehensible of all, fiendish in fact, is the placing of notices in teen and mass-market publications stating that children should not smoke, that they should wait until they are 18, that smoking is an adult activity. There is no more effective way to induce teenagers to do something than to tell them they are too young to do it.

All this must stop. Cigarette advertising and promotion have been empirically demonstrated to increase cigarette consumption (Tye et al.). If we genuinely want to reduce cigarette smoking, if a smoke-free society is a serious public policy goal, we cannot permit what so flagrantly works contrary to our purpose. These practices simply must be stopped. Most of the public supports such a ban ("Majorities"). However, we should not expect the elimination of cigarette advertising to result in greater media coverage of the health hazards of smoking. As the Warner group reminds us, cigarette manufacturers have become huge conglomerates in recent years. Thus, even if a ban on cigarette advertising were enacted, the media may still be reluctant to cover the risks of smoking for fear of losing the cigarette-producing conglomerates' nontobacco advertising.

Banning Cigarettes

It seems rather halfhearted to ban cigarette advertising but not cigarettes themselves. We forbid the manufacture, distribution and consumption of numerous other products, many of which are less hazardous to our health and less addictive. Yet we tolerate cigarettes and allow them to be openly pitched to our young, many of whom are successfully seduced. Nevertheless, it would be a mistake to ban cigarettes entirely. Not because of empathy for the poor addicted smokers, unable or unwilling to quit. They would still get their cigarettes, though perhaps in lesser quantity. The underground market would provide tobacco much the same way it provides illicit drugs. It is more out of empathy for the poor convenience store clerks and gas station attendants, already jeopardized by drug addicts seeking funds to procure their supply. Only organized crime would benefit, and the government would have fewer tax revenues to combat it.

Modifying the Product

This can take several forms, depending on whether the intent is to protect the smoker or to reduce externalities.

Establishing content maximums: The European Economic Community, as of 1992, has disallowed the sale of cigarettes with a greater than specified tar and nicotine content. Only those cigarettes commonly known as low-yield are permitted. This, however, was not a wise move. As have filter-tip cigarettes before them, low-yield cigarettes have been promoted as a safer choice. Since they were perceived as less hazardous, persons who might not have begun smoking otherwise may have been less reluctant to start. This is especially true of younger persons and women. The availability of "safer" cigarettes, furthermore, may have encouraged many smokers to continue rather than quit. It was easier to switch than to fight.

However, filter tip and low-yield cigarettes are not safer; they are even more deadly. Nicotine's grip is so very tenacious that smokers who switch maintain nicotine delivery by smoking more cigarettes, inhaling more deeply and inhaling more frequently. Consequently, smokers of "light" or filter-tip cigarettes have significantly shorter life expectancies than smokers of regular cigarettes (Schmidt 1990).

Mandating fire safety: Although several pieces of legislation calling for self-extinguishing cigarettes have been introduced in Congress, no such cigarette is yet on the market. Intended to reduce deaths and damage arising from cigarette-ignited fires, the tobacco industry maintains they are not technically or commercially feasible. While it may be true that the necessary additives may increase health risks and worsen taste, it is also true that the industry has a vested interest in producing cigarettes that continue to burn when at rest. We must resolve the health and consumer-acceptance issues and, if feasible, insist on cigarettes that impose fewer dangerous externalities.

Regulating the Cigarette Industry

Rather than legislate specific restrictions, Congress could expand the authority of particular regulatory agencies to better control the tobacco industry. The Federal Trade Commission could be empowered to forbid vending machine sales, ban advertising completely or restrict it to black and white "tombstone ads" displaying only text rather than sexy models, fast cars or other mood settings. It could prohibit sponsorship of musical, artistic or sporting events which, since they sometimes air on television, not only impact on attendees, but are also a means of circumventing the advertising ban. It could also bar distribution of free samples or discount coupons. Tobacco could be defined as a drug, which would not be unreasonable given its addictive properties, and brought under the aegis of the Food and Drug Administration. Tobacco could be categorized as a controlled substance and overseen by the Drug Enforcement Administration. In either case, content, distribution and sales could be more strictly regulated. Tobacco could also be classified as a chemical substance. That would allow the Environmental Protection Agency to require full disclosure of the type and levels of chemical constituents in tobacco smoke, which alone might dissuade some current and potential smokers.

Whichever route is chosen, one thing is certain: the tobacco industry must not be allowed to freely develop, modify, merchandise and sell its products. Strict oversight and effective intervention are required to protect the public interest.

Increasing the Excise Tax: A Weapon that Will Work

Successful as the antismoking campaign has been, smoking has decreased an average of only 1.5 percent per year. At that paltry rate, with over 50,000,000 continuing and beginning smokers, it will take decades to seriously reduce smoking. A more drastic measure is necessary to accelerate the rate of decline.

Taxation is just such a measure. The demand for cigarettes may be inelastic but it is far from perfectly so. A large enough increase in price will lower consumption dramatically.

Tax Levies to Date

Cigarettes are subject to taxation at the federal and state levels. Some cities tax them as well. But it is the federal excise tax that must be increased. A steep but uniform tax is required; otherwise smuggling and bootlegging will undermine our effort.

Congress raised the federal excise tax on cigarettes from $0.07 to $0.08 per pack in 1951, the first increase in over 30 years. The one cent increase did not begin to compensate for inflation during that time. In real terms, the eight cent tax on cigarettes was one-third what it had been in 1950. Congress doubled the nominal tax to $0.16 per pack in 1983, raising the real tax rate to what it had been in 1977 (CBO). Although the real prices of cigarettes increased in the 1980s, this was largely because of price increases on the part of cigarette companies. That did abet the decline in consumption somewhat, but it primarily increased industry revenues and profits. In 1950, the federal excise tax made up over half the wholesale price of cigarettes; by 1986, despite doubling the tax, the proportion had fallen to 23 percent (Grise 1991). It was raised to $0.20 per pack in 1991, hardly enough to make a difference in consumption.

Estimated Effects of a Tax Increase

On consumption: Cigarette smoking is price responsive. Following the tax increase in 1983, total cigarette consumption fell by 5 percent. Yet it had decreased by only 1 percent the year before and not at all the following year (Grise 1991). Canadian data is even more convincing. Since 1980, the real prices of cigarettes have increased much more than in the United States, while consumption has fallen much more. Imposition of a $.40 per pack tax increase in 1989 led to a 7.8 percent drop in per capita consumption that year and an additional fall of 10 percent in the first ten months of 1990 (CCS). Provincial taxes have also increased greatly, making the total average tax per pack of cigarettes $3.69 and raising the average price per pack in Canada to $5.50. These fiscal measures, combined with severely restrictive smoking laws and the banning of virtually all cigarette advertising, including the printing of cigarette brand names on sportswear, is having a tremendous effect. Final figures for 1991 are expected to reveal a 43 percent decline in the per capita adult consumption of cigarettes just from 1980 (Koretz). Future consumption should decline even more as far fewer Canadian teenagers take up the habit.

Estimates of the impact of a tax increase on smoking in the United States are derived from estimates of cigarette price elasticities, the most widely accepted being that of Lewit and Coate. They found an overall adult price elasticity coefficient of −0.42, meaning that a 10 percent increase in prices could be expected to induce a 4.2 percent decline in cigarette consumption. Over two-thirds of the decline stems from nonparticipation in the market as potential smokers are dissuaded from starting and current smokers are persuaded to quit. The remainder of the decline results from the reduced daily consumption of continuing smokers.

Their estimates have proven very accurate. In 1981 they had written that if the excise tax was doubled to $0.16, the resultant impact on the price of cigarettes would lead to a 4.8 percent drop in quantity demanded. As noted, when the increase was passed in 1983, consumption fell by 5 percent.

Lewit and Coate also computed elasticities by sex and age. They found men to be much more price responsive than women. Among 20 to 25 year olds, the price elasticity coefficient for males was -1.40; for females it was an almost insignificant -0.30. Younger adults, less habituated than their elders, were also more price responsive. The overall coefficient for persons 20 to 25 was -0.89; for persons 26 to 35 it was -0.47. Working with Grossman, they calculated the elasticity of demand for 12 to 17 year olds to be -1.40. For all groups, potential increases in the price of cigarettes had a greater impact on the decision to not smoke than on a simple decline in daily consumption. Not surprisingly, the nonparticipation effect was much greater for teens. They are less affluent and either have not yet started or find it relatively easy to quit.

Applying Lewit and Coates elasticity coefficients, Warner (in 1986) estimated that an eight cent tax increase would encourage 1.8 million persons (including over 400,000 teenagers) to quit or not begin smoking. A 16 cent tax increase would increase cigarette prices by 15 percent and encourage 3.5 million persons (including 800,000 teens) who would have otherwise smoked to forgo consumption.

The General Accounting Office (GAO), however, believes that the elasticity of demand among teens is not as great as when Lewit and Coate made their determination. The GAO contends that the antismoking campaign and the increasing social disapproval of smoking resulted in an increased proportion of hard-core cigarette smokers among the current pool of adolescent smokers. They are more addicted and less price responsive. (Also, although the GAO report does not mention it, today's teens have higher labor force participation rates. Real teenage incomes, even among working class youth, have increased. In addition, smoking has become more concentrated among school dropouts, many of whom may have become full-time workers.) So, whereas Warner wrote that a 15 percent increase in the price of cigarettes would deter 800,000 adolescents from smoking, the GAO estimates that a 15 percent price increase would (as of 1989) reduce the number of teenage smokers by about 500,000 (USGAO 1989e).

On health: Assuming that Warner's estimates are reasonably accurate, that there are no radical changes in medical technology, and that one of every four tax-induced quitters or nonstarters would have died from smoking, the eight cent tax increase would have averted 450,000 smoking-related premature deaths. The sixteen cent increase would have, over time, averted 860,000 such deaths (Warner 1986). Savings in morbidity- and mortality-related expenses would not be immediate, but would accrue over decades. However, any potential gains would be diminished if inflation is allowed to erode the value of the tax.

On tax revenues: Congress finally did raise the cigarette tax again, but only by four cents. It became $0.20 in 1991, barely enough to maintain the real value of the $0.16 tax. It is due to increase again in 1993 to $0.24 per pack. Neither of these increases is large enough to substantially curtail smoking. The increases are so small that they may have no impact at all. But then, they were not enacted to curb smoking; they were designed to reduce the budget deficit. However, a significantly larger increase in the tax can do both.

Employing the model of smoking elasticities he developed with Becker and Murphy, Grossman (in 1989) calculated the revenue maximizing tax on cigarettes to be $0.75, an increase of $0.59 over the then current $0.16 tax. Using elasticities formulated by Chaloupka, Grossman determined the revenue maximizing tax to be $1.29 per pack. The effect of either tax would be tremendous. In the long run, the $0.75 tax would generate revenues of $13.3 billion and reduce smoking by 40 percent. The $1.29 tax would generate revenues of $18.6 billion and lead to a reduction in smoking of about 50 percent ("Smoking"). In the short run the revenue effect would be greater and the consumption effect would be less. But over time, more smokers would succumb to the economic pressure to quit and fewer young persons would be inclined to start.

It sounds like the ideal fix. Impose a whopping tax, index it to inflation and watch the budget deficit decline, smoking decrease and social costs and externalities fall as Americans lead longer, healthier lives. And it virtually is ideal. However, nothing is without trade-off.

On the economy: Such a major increase in taxes, with its subsequent change in behavior, would engender a redistribution of income and resources which, while benefitting some interest groups, would provoke vehement opposition from others. The opposition would come from very powerful parties and is the reason we will probably never enact a tax that would so effectively reduce smoking.

The most noticeable shift in income would be from the tobacco industry to the federal treasury. And as the tobacco lobby would surely stress, those individuals who continue to smoke would be paying a very high price, transferring money to the federal government that they could have enjoyably spent elsewhere. They might also be paying an amount in excess of the social costs of their smoking, raising legitimate questions about the fairness of the tax.

The relative burden of the tax also provokes the fairness issue. Excise taxes are regressive. If, however, lower-income persons have a higher price elasticity with respect to smoking, which they probably do, their smoking will decrease that much more. Therefore, while the tax may be regressive and place an unequal burden on low-income persons who continue to smoke, those who desist will enjoy a proportionately greater income effect, that is, a greater proportion of their income will be freed to purchase other goods and services. Furthermore, since the tax would reduce smoking to a greater extent among poorer people, they, as a group, would experience a progressive health benefit. (However, considering the addictive strength of nicotine and the fact that the economically disadvantaged have higher rates of smoking, such a large tax may indeed be unfair. The Congressional Budget Office suggests possibly increasing food stamp allotments or the earned income tax credit to compensate. But not all low-income families receive either benefit, and those that do are not necessarily smokers. A better solution might be to channel some of the additional tax revenues into enhanced social services in low-income neighborhoods.)

There would also be a regional redistribution of income and employment away from the tobacco-producing states. Many would undoubtedly suffer, just as happened during the switch from coal to oil. Hopefully, unemployment would be minimized through attrition, farmers would be assisted in substituting new crops, and factor mobility would reduce the macro impact. If the money not spent on cigarettes were used to buy other domestically produced items, there would be no net loss. Some regions and industries would benefit. The economic impact calculated by Price Waterhouse for the tobacco industry would still be felt. It would just originate elsewhere.

Should we do it? Yes—if only to reduce teenage smoking. The increased incidence of teenage pregnancy and parenting underscores the urgency.

Will we do it? Probably not. The tobacco lobby is rich, powerful and influential. Together with the slick and capable advertising and merchandising industries, motivated by the 63,000 jobs and almost $4 billion in revenues that would be lost if promotional activity is banned, they constitute a formidable opposition to any measure that would substantially reduce smoking or corporate profitability. The stakes are also high for institutional investors. Pension funds, insurance companies, mutual funds, college endowments, banks and investment firms own stock in tobacco companies. Such weighty interest groups held 60 percent of Phillip Morris's equity in 1987 (Pytte). And the major brokerage firms, who know at least as much as the best of us, continue to recommend tobacco as a solid, safe investment.

2

Substance Abuse

Unlike cigarette smoking, which is always harmful, consumption of alcohol and certain drugs is not necessarily injurious. Adverse consequences arise from their misuse, consequences that can generate very high personal and social costs. Therefore a large body of public policy measures has evolved to restrict or prohibit alcohol and drug use. Some measures have been helpful, some useless. Others have only exacerbated the health and social problems they were intended to relieve.

Nothing, however, could eradicate all the problems as we will never totally eliminate the use of psychoactive substances. Humankind has practiced some form of chemical consciousness altering since the dawn of history. It is no wonder. Psychoactive agents can relieve pain, induce relaxation, reduce stress, enhance spirituality, heighten sensuality, incite passion, release creative muses and produce euphoria. They can enhance the pleasure of food, music, art, sex and the company of friends.

But misuse (and for some substances, any use is misuse) can provoke serious health problems, functional impairment and foolish, impulsive, high-risk, erratic, aggressive or violent behavior. Some individuals may experience addiction, which, differing markedly from that to cigarettes, evokes pathological patterns of consumption. The drug addict or alcoholic is overwhelmingly involved with procuring and using his preferred substance, is often intoxicated throughout the day, and needs increasing quantities of the drug to achieve inebriation. He has great difficulty discontinuing use, relapsing after repeated attempts to stop and suffering extreme physical distress upon cessation. Withdrawal may be accompanied by vomiting, delirium, tremors, seizures, hallucinations or paranoia. Misuse, which may involve addiction or merely inappropriate use, is characterized by myriad externalities and terrible social costs.

The external costs of cigarette smoking are great but less immediate and, in many ways, less severe than those associated with psychoactive substances.

Smoking does not interfere with one's ability to drive, operate machinery, reason, remember, make decisions, or fulfill obligations. Smokers seldom smoke the rent or grocery money. Smoking does not incite men to murder their wives; nor is it associated with the sexual abuse of children. And, since smoking is legal, neither does it lead to muggings or turf wars. Cigarette smoking is more deadly and affects more people. But drug and alcohol abuse do more than kill. They seriously impair personal, social and occupational functioning, at times destroying lives, families and entire communities in the process. Many more nonusers are put at risk. Controlling their use, therefore, is in the public interest.

ALCOHOL

Alcohol is a toxic chemical, primarily affecting the brain and the digestive system, but associated with deleterious effects on virtually every part of the body. Its effect on the central nervous system classifies it as a depressant. Consumed in moderate amounts, in low-risk situations, it may provide utility well in excess of any possible danger. Moderate consumption even provides health benefits, for as alcohol is metabolized by the liver, it apparently produces a form of cholesterol that helps clear fat out of the circulatory system. Thus men who average one-half to two drinks per day are 41 percent less likely to suffer fatal heart disease (Rimm et al.).

Patterns and Prevalence of Alcohol Use

Drinking Patterns

Most drinkers imbibe moderately, generally defined as taking 60 or fewer drinks in one month. Known as social drinkers, they experience no serious long-term alcohol-related health or social problems. Cessation of use presents no difficulties. However, these drinkers may occasionally engage in high-risk alcohol use, such as driving while intoxicated.

Alcohol abusers drink more heavily and more often engage in binge drinking, that is, ingesting more than five drinks in one drinking episode. Referred to as problem drinkers, their acute and chronic high-risk alcohol use often results in serious adverse consequences to themselves and to others.

Alcohol abusers who are physically dependent on alcohol are known as alcoholics or alcohol-dependent persons. They crave alcohol, have an impaired ability to control their drinking and suffer withdrawal when consumption is discontinued.

Prevalence of Alcohol Use and Abuse

A National Institute on Drug Abuse survey found that 66 percent of Americans age 12 or older had at least one drink in 1990. Almost 40 percent drank 12 or more times, and 20.7 percent drank at least once a week (NIDA 1991).

Estimates of alcohol abuse vary. A household survey of persons aged 18 and older found that 34 percent of the respondents were nondrinkers, 56 percent were social drinkers, 4 percent were nondependent alcohol abusers, and 6 percent were alcoholic (Harwood and Parker in USDHHS 1990c). The Public Health Service estimates that about 10 percent of Americans are problem drinkers, with 10.5 million exhibiting some symptoms of alcohol dependence. They estimate that an additional 7.2 million adults abuse alcohol but do not yet exhibit symptoms of dependence (USDHHS 1990c). The American Psychiatric Association estimates that 13 million persons in this country are alcoholics.

By gender: Men are 16 percent more likely than women to drink at all and 2.4 times more likely to drink at least once a week (NIDA 1991). Over 8 percent of men, compared to 2 percent of women, admit to heavy drinking, that is, drinking five or more drinks on five or more days during the month prior to NIDA's National Household Survey (NIDA 1990). The result is an age-adjusted alcohol-induced death rate for males 3.4 times that for females (NCHS 1990a).

By race: Blacks are 23 percent more likely than whites to abstain from drinking, the prevalence of alcohol consumption among black youth is far less than that among white youth, and only 4 percent of blacks admit heavy drinking compared to 5 percent of whites (NIDA 1990). Yet blacks experience far more social and medical problems associated with heavy drinking than do whites (USDHHS 1990c). The unexpected disparity in adverse consequences may perhaps be explained by greater underreporting of drinking among blacks, variations in drinking patterns, or racial differences in biological vulnerability to alcohol. As discussed in Chapter 3, the age-adjusted death rate for alcohol-induced causes among the black population is 2.7 times that among the white population (NCHS 1990a).

Among adolescents and young adults: Excluding caffeine, alcohol is the drug of choice among youth just as in society at large. More than 6 percent of 12 and 13 year olds, 23 percent of 14 and 15 year olds, 42 percent of 16 and 17 year olds and 61 percent of persons aged 18 to 21 reported using alcohol in the month prior to NIDA's household survey. This was roughly double those who smoked cigarettes and over five times those who used marijuana, the second- and third-ranked favorites. Heavy drinking was reported among 2.3 percent of those aged 12 to 17 and 10.3 percent of those aged 18 to 25, the largest proportion of any age group (NIDA 1990). Over 4 percent of high school seniors drink on a daily or near daily basis; one-third engage in fairly frequent binge drinking (NIDA 1989). Overall, heavy drinking among persons under 21 exceeds that among older individuals, with heavy drinking among young males about four times that among females for all but the youngest teenagers (NIDA 1990). An estimated 3,000,000 children and adolescents are alcoholics (APA).

Unfortunately, even moderate drinking can pose problems for young people. Since they typically weigh less than adults, they have less body water to dissolve alcohol. They thus have a lower tolerance for alcohol and are more susceptible to its effects (Gordis).

Trends in Alcohol Consumption

Average per capita alcohol consumption for persons aged 14 or older, expressed in gallons of pure alcohol, peaked in 1980 and has declined each year since. By 1987 it averaged 2.54 gallons, down from 2.76 gallons in 1980 (USDHHS 1990c). The decrease was almost totally due to the decline in the consumption of spirits, which have high alcohol content. Beer consumption has decreased slightly since its peak in 1981; wine consumption, which had been increasing prior to 1984, has since stabilized. Principal reasons for the decrease in consumption include changing tastes, lesser social acceptability of heavy drinking and increased emphasis on health and fitness.

Population surveys reveal that more people abstain from drinking alcohol and that abstention rates have increased most among men (USDHHS 1990c). Some surveys indicate decreased alcohol use among adolescents. But a survey of Massachusetts youth found that, while drinking among high school juniors and seniors had remained fairly stable (at frightfully high rates), drinking among younger students had increased substantially. Nearly 70 percent of seventh graders experimented with alcohol in 1987, compared to 50 percent in 1984; 24 percent were continuing drinkers, up from 17.6 percent earlier (Williams et al.). Other population surveys reveal evidence of an increasing proportion of heavy drinkers among persons in their twenties and a small increase in the prevalence of dependence problems (USDHHS 1990c).

The Etiology of Alcoholism

Alcoholism is a disease as it has an identifiable cluster of symptoms predictive of a course and outcome. It is not an infectious disease or one in which cells multiply wildly. Rather it is the result of a biopsychosocial process. Environmental factors, such as availability of alcohol, social acceptance of drinking and drunkenness and peer pressure to drink play a decided role. But its primary root appears to be biological. It is estimated that one-third of alcoholics have at least one parent who is also an alcoholic (USDHHS 1990c). Family studies reveal a three- to fourfold increased risk of alcoholism in the children of alcoholics; adoption studies have found the same risk in the children of alcoholics whether they were raised by an alcoholic parent or not (Schuckit 1987). Using family, twin and adoption studies, Cloninger and colleagues have estimated the overall rate of inheritability for alcoholism to be about 64 percent (in Schuckit 1987). That is, about 64 percent of alcoholism is explained by genetic predisposition. But it is important to note that biological vulnerability does not imply biological inevitability. Less than one-half of children of alcoholics develop drinking problems, and only a portion of these become alcohol-dependent (Zucker in USDHHS 1990c).

The Health Consequences of Alcohol Misuse

It has been estimated that each ounce of alcohol consumed in excess of two drinks per day reduces life expectancy by twenty minutes (Manning et al.). As alcohol is the most widely used drug after caffeine, consumed by more than twice as many Americans as the next most popular drug, nicotine, it is not surprising that drinking is second only to smoking as the most preventable cause of death in the United States.

Alcohol-Related Mortality

Over 105,000 deaths, 4.9 percent of total national mortality, were classified as alcohol-related in 1987 (CDC 1990c). Almost 54 percent were from diseases attributed to chronic alcohol abuse; the rest were intentional or unintentional injury deaths. Two-thirds of the alcohol-related deaths were of males. Alcoholic men have a mortality rate that is two to six times higher than that of the average male (Bullock et al.).

Disease: Alcohol abuse increases the risk of cancer at several sites. Most notably, abuse is responsible for 75 percent of the deaths from cancer of the esophagus and 50 percent of those from cancer of the larynx and the lip/oral cavity/pharynx. It also contributes to cardiovascular, respiratory and digestive system diseases and to fatal mental disorders. Alcohol abuse was held responsible for 10,747 deaths from cardiovascular diseases and 15,860 deaths from liver diseases in 1987 (CDC 1990c).

Injury: Alcohol impairs physical and psychological functioning. It lessens visual acuity, diminishes motor control, slows reflexes and increases risk taking. Hence alcohol is associated with a great many injury deaths, 31,106 in 1987 alone (CDC 1990c). Such deaths are usually unintentional and exhibit a dose-response relationship. Persons who typically drink five or more drinks per occasion are nearly twice as likely to die from injuries as are those who drink less. Those who usually drink nine or more drinks per occasion have a risk of fatal injury that is 3.3 times greater (Anda et al.).

Not all alcohol-related injury deaths involve alcohol abusers; simple misuse is sometimes the culprit. Reviewing accidental deaths in New Jersey, Haberman found that although 53 percent of traffic fatalities and 47 percent of non-traffic fatalities showed evidence of alcohol use, that is the decedent had a Blood Alcohol Count (BAC) of 0.01 percent or greater, autopsies revealed that only 34 percent of the accident victims with positive BACs were alcoholics. Another interesting finding was that 29 percent of the accidentally killed alcoholics had BACs of 0.00 percent—that is, they had not been drinking prior to their death. Yet their accidental death rate far exceeded that of nonalcoholics. Their physical and psychological characteristics, such as hangovers, seizures, visual disturbances, impulsiveness, distractability and aggressiveness, possibly make alcoholics more accident-prone even when sober (Haberman).

Roughly 20 percent of all alcohol-related deaths result from motor vehicle accidents. A traffic accident is classified as alcohol-related if either a driver or other active participant had a BAC of 0.01 percent or greater; intoxication is cited if an active participant has a BAC of 0.10 percent or more. Applying that criteria, the National Highway Traffic Safety Administration (NHTSA) found that 49 percent of traffic fatalities (22,415 deaths) were alcohol related in 1989. Accidents in which the driver was alcohol involved claimed 46 percent of the fatalities; driver intoxication was responsible for 37 percent. Other participants were alcohol involved in the remaining cases. Nearly half the 2,611 pedestrians and bicyclists aged 20 to 39 killed in accidents involving motor vehicles were intoxicated (NHTSA 1991). All told, there is, on average, one alcohol-related traffic fatality every 22 minutes in this country (NHTSA 1989).

The association between alcohol and other unintentional injury deaths is even greater. In the New Jersey study, alcoholics, who comprise approximately 10 percent of the population, experienced 37 percent of the traffic fatalities and 63 percent of the nontraffic fatalities (Haberman).

The Centers for Disease Control attributes 38 percent of the accidental drownings (1,657 deaths) in 1987 to alcohol use. Earlier CDC estimates and state studies put the proportion at 65 to 69 percent (CDC 1990c; Wright). As many as 70 percent of recreational boating fatalities involve alcohol; about 38 percent involve intoxication (Wright).

Alcohol increases the risk of fatal falls; 35 percent (4,050 fatalities) were alcohol related in 1987 (CDC 1990c).

Alcohol is a factor in fire fatalities. It may contribute to the start of a fire or inhibit appropriate response. The Centers for Disease Control estimates that 2,119 deaths, 45 percent of total fire fatalities, were attributable to alcohol use in 1987 (CDC 1990c). Studies of fire fatalities in the mid-1980s found that 50 percent of the deceased were intoxicated at time of death (Howland & Hingson).

Alcohol is also implicated in intentional injury deaths. That it has been demonstrated to increase aggression and induce depression partly explains its involvement in 46 percent of the homicides and 28 percent of the suicides in 1987, totalling 9,107 and 8,552 respective deaths (CDC 1990c). A Pennsylvania study found alcohol involvement in 46 percent of teen suicides in 1983 (Brent et al.). In addition, Beasley estimates that 60 percent of suicide attempts might be directly or indirectly related to alcoholism (in Doweiko).

In many cases of alcohol-related injury deaths, especially those resulting from roadway accidents, fires and homicides, the decedents were not necessarily alcohol involved. Nor were they alcohol-impaired but sober alcoholics. Rather, they were victims of the externalities of alcohol use.

Many victims are young. The great majority of the years of productive life lost to alcohol-related causes are lost to injury deaths, the leading cause of death among young persons (CDC 1990c; NCHS 1990a). Almost 65 percent of the roadway fatalities among persons aged 20 to 24 are alcohol related, as are 45 percent of those among 15 to 19 year olds (NHTSA 1991).

Alcohol-Related Morbidity

The 1985 National Hospital Discharge Survey found that 4 percent of the discharges involved an alcohol-related diagnosis. An alcohol-related disorder was the principal diagnosis in over 2 percent. Although underreporting no doubt understates the incidence, the discharge data revealed important associations between alcohol and disorders of the liver, pancreas, digestive tract, respiratory system, nervous system and cardiovascular system, as well as drug abuse, nonfatal injuries, accidental poisoning, infection, anemias and malnutrition. Males were three times more likely than females to have an alcohol-related diagnosis (in USDHHS 1990c).

Alcohol consumption is implicated in up to 72 percent of head injury cases. Alcohol not only increases the risk of injury but its presence in the system exacerbates the neurobehavioral effects of head injury, delays cognitive recovery and significantly increases the length and cost of resultant hospitalization (Sparadeo & Gill).

Alcohol-related traffic accidents injure about 500,000 persons each year. Approximately 40,000 are injured seriously (NHTSA 1989).

Fetal Alcohol Syndrome

Resulting from the perinatal transmission of alcohol to a child whose mother drank heavily during pregnancy, Fetal Alcohol Syndrome (FAS) is perhaps the most heartbreaking consequence of alcohol abuse. As discussed in Chapter 5, victims of FAS not only suffer severe physiological abnormalities but often are so profoundly retarded as to require a lifetime of institutional care. Over 7,000 FAS babies are born in the United States each year, making FAS the leading cause of mental retardation today (Abel & Sokol). Another 21,000 babies can anticipate a lifetime of impairment to a less serious degree (Abel). Their mothers did not necessarily drink heavily. Even moderate maternal drinking can endanger a fetus.

Psychiatric Disorders

Alcohol abuse or dependence is strongly associated with psychiatric disorders. Studying psychiatric comorbidity in patients in treatment for alcohol and for drug abuse, Ross and colleagues found that two-thirds had a current psychiatric disorder in addition to substance abuse. Of those in treatment for alcoholism, 78 percent had had a psychiatric diagnosis at some point in their lifetime, including 42 percent for antisocial personality disorder, 31 percent for phobias, 30 percent for psychosexual dysfunctions and 23 percent for major depression. Although comorbidity does not signify causality, alcohol abuse can produce symptoms compatible with any of the above diagnoses. In his study of men in treatment for alcoholism, Schuckit observed that 43 percent of the patients exhibited psychotic symptomatology. Although some psychoses, particularly that of sociopathic behavior, were apparently unrelated to alcohol use, in general, psychosis was related to number of drinks per day and duration of problem drinking. The most frequent diagnosis was alcohol psychosis, characterized by visual or auditory hallucinations, paranoia and the feeling that one's mind is being manipulated (Schuckit 1982). Beasley additionally notes that alcohol-induced brain damage is second only to Alzheimer's disease as a known cause of mental deterioration in adults (in Doweiko). One-third of nursing home patients are estimated to be permanently brain damaged as a result of alcohol abuse (Schuckit 1984). And more than 5,300 deaths in 1987 were attributed to alcohol-induced mental disorders. (CDC 1990c).

The Social and Economic Costs of Alcohol Misuse

Alcohol misuse imposes such great and varied costs on society that it would be a disservice to simply quantify them and express them in monetary terms, if that were even possible. Alcohol misuse takes a dreadful human toll as well as a heavy fiscal toll. This must not go unrecorded.

The American Psychiatric Association claims that as many as 40,000,000 people in this country are indirectly affected by alcoholism through family ties to either an alcoholic or to a person killed or injured by an alcoholic. Advocates of improved clinical services to "alcoholic families" contend that for every alcohol misuser, five other persons suffer directly (Steinglass). And alcohol-abusing employees cause employers, and the economy in general, to suffer enormous losses. Thus the psychological, physiological and occupational impairments of alcohol abusers impact on virtually everyone.

Antisocial Behavior

Intrafamilial stress and violence: Families harboring an alcohol abuser often exhibit severe pathologies. Although underreporting of physical aggression in the home can be assumed to understate its prevalence, Leonard and colleagues found that 25 percent of white male alcohol abusers engage in physical marital conflict. Beasley reports that 50 percent of spousal abuse cases and 38 percent of child abuse cases involve alcohol (in Doweiko). Sever claims that 71 percent of the cases of child sex abuse are alcohol related (in Daro). And Black's clinical experience suggests that 66 percent of the children raised in "alcoholic families" were either abused themselves or witnessed the abuse of others. (in Doweiko).

The extraordinary psychological stress experienced by the children of alcoholics often leads to psychological, social, behavioral or academic difficulties, difficulties that may persist (Woititz).

The families of alcholics not only endure physical abuse and emotional trauma, but frequently experience financial deprivation as well. The consumption of large quantities of alcoholic beverages is expensive, and alcoholics often have alcohol-related employment problems. Over 70 percent of Schuckit's patient population admitted problems with missing work; 49 percent had been fired at least once (Schuckit 1982). Spouses may also lose income and employment because of the demands on them as caretakers. The family's standard of living may be seriously compromised and undesirable changes of residences may be necessary.

The cumulation of stresses causes extraordinarily high rates of marital disruption and divorce among alcoholic families. Over 45 percent of Schuckit's patients were divorced at the time they entered treatment.

Crime and violence: Underreporting also misrepresents the relationship between alcohol and criminal aggression, especially when the aggression involves acquaintances or is relatively minor. Also, since numerous psychological and sociodemographic factors contribute to violent behavior, it is not possible to definitively determine alcohol's role. Yet alcohol's involvement in antisocial aggression is obvious and extends beyond mere barroom brawling. Wolfgang and Strohm found that 54.4 percent of the persons arrested for homicide in Philadelphia had consumed alcohol prior to committing the crime (in Leonard et al.). Although their study encompassed the years 1948 to 1952, when overall alcohol consumption was greater, as noted earlier, 46 percent of the homicides in 1987 were classified alcohol related (CDC 1990c). Nicol and company found that alcoholics are disproportionately represented among persons arrested for attempted homicide, rape and assault (in Leonard et al.). A survey of state prison inmates found that 20 percent of those incarcerated for violent crimes were under the influence of alcohol at the time they committed the crime; another 20 percent were under the influence of both alcohol and drugs (USDJ 1988d). Furthermore, Schuckit found that 11.3 percent of his patients in treatment for alcoholism had been arrested before the age of 16, 41 percent had been arrested after that age, 23 percent had injured someone, and 10 percent had used a weapon (Schuckit 1982).

Much of the alcohol abuser's violence is directed at other drinkers. Wives of alcoholics are sometimes problem drinkers also and instigate violent episodes. Among the violent offenders in state prisons, 57 percent of those who had been drinking victimized someone who had also been drinking (USDJ 1991a). Victims of homicide and rape in particular have high frequencies of alcohol consumption (Goldstein). Their impairment increased their exposure to risk.

But a victim's possible alcohol involvement does not diminish the external costs of alcohol-related aggressive behavior. In addition to the pain and suffering of the injured party and his or her family and friends, the criminal justice and health care costs associated with alcohol-related violent behavior are shared by all.

Nonintentional Injury and Death

Victims of alcohol-attributed fires and accidents frequently include more than the drinker. Children and the aged are overrepresented among fire fatalities, and accidents often involve innocent parties as well. Among Schuckit's patients, 44 percent had been in at least one automobile accident. They survived, but the cost to others may have been great. In 1989, over 14 percent of the drivers who survived fatal crashes were legally intoxicated. Another 7 percent had BACs of 0.01 to 0.09 percent (NHTSA 1991).

We are all in jeopardy. Each year about 600,000 auto accidents, 10 percent of all police-reported motor vehicle crashes, are alcohol related (NHTSA 1989). Forty percent of the people in this country, far more than are problem drinkers, will be involved in at least one alcohol-related traffic accident at some time in their lives.

The risk is great because drinking and driving is a fairly common activity in the United States. A 1986 survey of nearly 35,000 drivers in 26 states revealed that 4 percent of the survey population, over 7 percent of the responding drinkers, and one in eight men aged 18 to 24 years drove after drinking at least once in the month prior to the survey (Smith et al.). Extrapolation of the survey results led Smith and colleagues to conclude that there were more than 150 million instances of drinking and driving in the United States that year. While not every person who drinks before driving is significantly impaired, survey respondents who admitted drinking and driving were more likely to report binge drinking and heavier drinking than those who denied drinking and driving. The aforementioned Massachusetts student survey found that 44 percent of hign school seniors drove after one drink in the month prior to the survey; 25 percent drove after five drinks (Williams et al.). One drink might not appear to pose a great risk, but perusal of NHTSA data supports the theory that young inexperienced drivers, with their lesser alcohol tolerance, sustain greater impairment at low BAC levels than do older drivers. Alcohol figures prominently in their car crashes. Moreover, although adolescents drive far less than older drivers, teen drivers are responsible for about five times as many crash deaths, deaths that occur disproportionately to persons other than the teen driver (Williams & Karpf).

Substance-abusing transportation workers imperil literally thousands of individuals traveling by air, bus, subway and railroad. From January 1987 to April 1988 Amtrak averaged one major alcohol- or drug-related rail accident every ten days. More than 375 people were killed or injured in those accidents, and over 65 percent of the rail fatalities in that time were linked to substance abuse by key personnel (Feron).

Economic Costs

The total economic costs to the nation were estimated by Rice and colleagues to have been $70.3 billion in 1985, a year in which 94,765 deaths were attributed to alcohol (USDHHS 1990a). Individual components of their cost estimate are presented in Table 2.1. Their treatment is comprehensive and excellent in many respects, yet it appears to greatly underestimate the cost of alcohol-related motor vehicle accidents. The cost of alcohol-related crashes is disproportionately large. Although they comprise only 10 percent of police-reported crashes, they account for a third of all crash costs (Miller 1991). Their cost is almost five times that of other collisions as they result in more severe injuries and victims have a lesser

Table 2.1
The Economic Costs of Alcohol Abuse: United States, 1985

Type of costs	millions of dollars	percent of total
Core costs		
treatment and support*	$ 6,810	9.7%
morbidity**	27,388	38.9%
mortality**	23,983	34.1%
(discounted at 6%)		
Related costs		
criminal justice system	3,734	5.3%
private legal defense	342	0.5%
property destruction	175	0.3%
victims of crime**	465	0.7%
incarceration**	2,701	3.9%
motor vehicle crashes	2,584	3.7%
fires	457	0.7%
social welfare administration	88	0.1%
Fetal Alcohol Syndrome	1,611	2.3%
Total Costs	$70,338	+

* research, administration and training of professional staff.
** productivity lost due to incapacitation, incarceration or premature death.
\+ percentages do not total 100.0 due to rounding.

Source: United States Department of Health and Human Services. *The Economic Costs of Alcohol and Drug Abuse and Drug Abuse and Mental Illness: 1985*, modified.

chance of survival. Thus Miller estimates the alcohol-related crash cost to be about $100 billion a year, far more than the $2.9 billion estimated by Rice and colleaques.

The Rice group may also have underestimated the cost of alcohol abuse to industry. While American productivity is greatly reduced by alcohol-related morbidity and mortality, the problem is not merely that alcohol abusers are out sick more often or die prematurely. They are expensive to employ, dangerous to themselves and others, disruptive, and morale dampening. The Bureau of National Affairs (in Kaighan) reported the following:

- Alcohol is involved in 40 percent of industrial fatalities and 50 percent of industrial accidents
- The accident rate among employees with a substance abuse problem is four to six times higher than that of nonabusing employees
- Absenteeism among employees with a drinking or drug problem is five to eight times higher
- Absenteeism among employees with an alcoholic family member is ten times higher
- Medical claims are three times higher in substance-abusing families
- The productivity of employees with a drug or alcohol problem is 25 to 40 percent less; yet they bring four times as many grievances

Lodge informs us in addition that:

- alcohol-abusing employees are late to work three times more often than other employee,
- alcohol-abusing employees request early dismissal or days off 2.2 times more often,
- employees with alcohol problems are involved in on-the-job accidents 3.6 times more often, and
- substance-abusing employees are five times more likely to file workmen's compensation claims.

The National Council of Compensation Insurance estimates that substance abuse cost American business $16 billion for workmen's compensation alone in 1987 (in Kaighan). Two-thirds of substance-abuse workplace costs are generally attributed to alcohol use. Firms whose work force tends to be older incur a greater proportion of alcohol-related costs.

The costs can be extremely burdensome. A NIDA study found that American firms spend at least 25 percent of substance-abusing employees' wages responding to their performance deficiencies (in Lodge). Eleven percent of the human resource executives responding to Mercer-Meidinger-Hansen's survey reported that substance abuse cost their companies 6 to 10 percent of their total payroll; 3 percent reported the costs as greater than 10 percent. The sources of greatest costs were increased medical benefit claims, increased absenteeism and decreased productivity. They also reported that although substance abusers had much higher rates of absenteeism and work-site accidents than other employees, the greatest difference was in the number of disciplinary actions.

The costs of alcohol misuse are clearly great but difficult to accurately estimate. We cannot, for example, adequately price the pain, anxiety, dashed expectations and diminished lifestyle of alcoholics and their families. Nor can we adequately value a life lost. We generally quantify loss of life in terms of forgone earnings, but even from a strictly economic standpoint, that approach may greatly underestimate the value of some people's contribution to society, particularly women's.

External Costs

The external costs of alcohol misuse are yet more difficult to estimate. Probably the best effort is that by Manning and associates, who calculated the external costs of excess drinking (i.e., consumption of alcohol in excess of two drinks per day) as $1.56 per excess ounce undiscounted, in 1986 dollars, and $1.19 when discounted at 5 percent. Unlike their findings regarding cigarette smoking, they found that heavy drinking increases costs in every category (at a 5 percent discount rate) because problem drinkers are more likely to retire early, triggering pension and disability benefits. The large effects of early retirement outweigh the lesser longevity of heavy drinkers.

High as the external costs may appear, the Manning group's estimates are low as they assume a very conservative value of life lost, do not account for the deaths of nondrinking persons resulting from alcohol-related motor vehicle accidents, and overlook deaths resulting from alcohol-related fires. Neither do they include costs to the drinker's family or the medical and disability costs of surviving nondrinking victims of alcohol-related accidents.

Some of the external costs are offset by tax revenues. Collected on all alcohol sold, not just excess alcohol, federal and state tax revenues, averaged across the variety of alcoholic beverages, approximated $0.37 per ounce in 1986 dollars (Manning et al.). As the Manning group determined the external costs of each ounce of alcohol sold to be $0.48 (when discounted at 5 percent), the net external costs are obviously great even when conservatively estimated. They would undoubtedly be great even if the coronary health benefits uncovered by Rimm and associates were factored in.

Public Policy Instruments

Protecting Adolescents

It is imperative that we discourage teen drinking, as both the short- and long-term effects can be tragic. Since their tolerance for alcohol is lower, their judgment, perception and coordination, perhaps not fully developed to begin with, are more severely impaired. Their inhibitions against risk taking, already lower than the typical adult's, is reduced yet more (Gordis). The result can be a variety of problems ranging from poor scholastic performance, delinquency and unintended pregnancy to disability or death. Also, alcohol abuse in adolescence is associated with alcohol abuse in later life.

Environmental approaches: A significant reduction in teenage drinking will not be possible as long as our culture is awash in inducements to drink, many of which are deliberately aimed at young people. Commercials for beer, the drink of choice among teenagers, are the most blatant. When not featuring former athletes, they invariably feature exceptionally attractive young people either surrounded by beer and having a terrific time or not enjoying themselves until the beer arrives. The message is obvious and effective.

Beer commercials must be banned or, at the least, severely restricted. It is inconsistent to forbid the advertisement of spirits and wine on television and radio yet allow beer to be glamorized and made to appear a necessary requisite for a good time and a successful social life. It is especially bad policy since those commercials are likely to exert their strongest appeal to those who are socially insecure, more vulnerable to alcohol and underage.

With respect to the print media, the entire alcoholic beverage industry should be allowed to picture only their products and describe only attributes of the products themselves, refraining from any high-time lifestyle characterizations.

Promotional activity should also be restricted, though it is not clear exactly how. Alcohol is, and should remain, a legal product. Moderate use in low-risk situations can enhance life's pleasure. And the musical events beer companies sponsor, from rock to country, are greatly appreciated. But it is no coincidence that they appeal primarily to young people and that they are as much commercials as concerts, with company logos on every possible surface and on tee shirts and baseball caps, which are distributed at little or no cost. College campuses, too, are often inundated with beer advertisements despite the fact that most students are under 21. College administrators purport concern about underage drinking yet allow Welcome Back to School—Miller Lite banners to be draped across dormitory fronts and Budweiser to sponsor campus rock concerts and give away sportswear decorated with its logo. They hang Just Say No to Drugs posters and distribute This Is a Drug-Free Campus notices to faculty informing them they will be fired if found to be using drugs, yet campus stores sell tee shirts picturing Spuds MacKenzie hoisting a glass of beer with one paw and a college banner with the other.

We must create an environment that puts alcohol consumption in proper perspective and does not disparage sobriety. Responsibility rests not only with the industry, the media and college administrators, but within communities as well. Many communities today are doing their part utilizing strategies such as sponsorship of alcohol-free events and incorporation of antidrinking messages into their antidrug campaigns. The most forceful strategies, however, require federal or state intervention.

Legal approaches: The foremost legal deterrent to teen drinking has been the increase in the minimum alcohol purchase age. Since the decrease in the voting age made it seem appropriate, many states had reduced their legal drinking age in the 1970s, usually from 21 to 18. Increases in alcohol consumption and in alcohol-related car crashes among young persons followed (USDHHS 1990c). States that did not lower their drinking age but that neighbored states that did also experienced increases in youth auto fatalities as the "border effect" lured teenagers across state lines, increasing the number of miles they drove while alcohol impaired. As numerous studies documented the inverse relationship between the legal drinking age and youthful fatalities, many states eventually increased their drinking age, though sometimes just from 18 to 19, and youthful fatalities did decline somewhat (USGAO 1987). But it soon became apparent that a national, uniform minimum purchase age was necessary. Congress thus passed the Federal Uniform Drinking Age Act in 1984, which enabled the withholding of a portion of federal highway funds from states failing to increase their drinking age to 21. As states complied, alcohol-related fatalities among teens fell yet more. Fatal crashes involving intoxicated drivers under age 18 decreased by 47 percent from 1982 to 1989; they decreased by 33 percent among 18- to 20-year-old drivers (NHTSA 1991).

Although underage individuals often can procure alcoholic beverages, raising the drinking age increases the difficulty of "passing" and of finding a legal-age accomplice to do the buying. Coate and Grossman estimated that if a uniform drinking age of 21 had been in effect from February 1976 through February 1980, the number of adolescents who abstained from drinking beer would have been 19 percent greater. The number of teens who drink frequently (defined as drinking four to seven times a week) would have been 29 percent less, and the number who drink fairly frequently (one to three times a week) would have been reduced by 15 percent.

In 1991 Rhode Island reduced the maximum legal BAC for teen drivers to 0.04. This lower maximum is easily justified and has great potential for reducing the incidence of teenage drinking and driving. It should be considered by every state.

Other legal instruments designed to protect teens include raising the minimum driving age, imposing a curfew on younger drivers, and limiting the general availability of alcohol by restricting the number of outlets and hours of business. Some states could benefit from further restrictions. For example, gas station minimarts should not be allowed to sell alcohol. They are often staffed by young employees, who may more willingly sell to underage customers, and beer purchased there is much more likely to be consumed while driving (USDHHS 1990c).

Also important is the strict enforcement of alcohol purchase and drunk driving laws. Swift, certain and severe punishment is necessary to keep the cost of teen drinking high.

Reality-based aprroaches: Realizing that teenagers will drink and that alcohol consumption figures prominently in adolescent social activities, many communities support programs designed to reduce the adverse possibilities. Organizations such as Students Against Drunk Driving encourage safer drinking through strategies such as safe rides, designated drivers, alternative transportation, direct intervention (e.g., taking car keys), and parent-teen contracts allowing teenagers to call home to be picked up, no questions asked. Some schools also teach techniques in assertiveness and peer pressure resistance.

Promoting Highway Safety

Most of the above strategies are useful in reducing the incidence of drinking and driving by persons of all ages and should be encouraged. But such measures must be backed up by strict legal sanctions. Prodded by groups such as Mothers

Against Drunk Driving, many states have given their drunk driving laws more clout. They have enhanced enforcement and impose more severe penalties on violators. Persons convicted of driving under the influence (DUI) now lose their licenses and are often required to participate in driver training and alcohol rehabilitation programs. As a result, the DUI arrest rate increased 127 percent from 1970 to 1986, peaking in 1983 (USDJ 1988c). It has decreased every year since as the heightened deterrent effect combined with increased public approbation and lesser per capita alcohol consumption to reduce the incidence of drinking and driving. There has consequently been a welcome decrease in alcohol-related traffic fatalities from 25,165 in 1982 to 22,415 in 1989. The proportion of drivers involved in fatal crashes who were intoxicated fell 19 percent during that time, while the proportion of traffic fatalities that were alcohol related fell from 57 percent to 49 percent (NHTSA 1991).

Technologies designed to promote highway safety also help avert the adverse outcomes of alcohol-impaired driving. These include improved highway design, such as median barriers, breakaway signposts, banked curves and prominent stripes delineating lanes and roadway edges, and vehicle technologies such as elevated rear brake lights, air bags, penetration-resistant windshields and padded dashboards. Strictly enforced seat belt legislation also averts serious injury.

Taxation of Alcoholic Beverages

Legal sanctions, whether designed to curtail teen drinking or alcohol-impaired driving, have the advantage of targeting a specific undesirable activity. While they have been fairly successful, their disadvantage is that they are susceptible to evasion and entail enforcement costs. Increased taxation, on the other hand, although seldom mentioned in deterrence literature, may be far more effective in reducing alcohol use and the external costs associated with it as it has the advantage of being difficult to evade. (Only minimal moonshining or bootlegging should ensue if the tax is reasonable.) A tax increase also has the advantage of providing revenues to finance remaining external costs, thereby reallocating those costs more fairly. The disadvantage is that a tax penalizes those who drink legally and safely. However, the net economic benefit is likely to be high.

The tax that must be increased is the federal excise tax. Variable state taxes only encourage smuggling and may prompt driving while alcohol impaired over greater distances.

Federal excise tax rates: In 1951, the federal excise tax was $0.16 per six-pack of 12-ounce containers of beer, $0.03 per 750-milliliter bottle of table wine, and $10.50 per 100-proof gallon of distilled spirits. The tax on spirits was raised to $12.50 in 1985. No other increase in the federal excise tax on alcoholic beverages was enacted until 1991, when the tax was raised to $0.32 for beer, $0.21 for wine and $13.50 for spirits. Only the increase in the tax on wine was enough to compensate for inflation, but it is still such a small amount as to be virtually inconsequential. Federal and state excise taxes constitute a much smaller proportion of the purchase price of alcoholic beverages today than they did 30 years ago, so there exists considerable room for increases.

Equity issues: Excise taxes are generally considered unfair because they impact more heavily on lower-income persons and because they discriminate among persons of similar incomes on the basis of tastes and preferences.

The first argument is theoretically sound; however it must be qualified by the fact that alcohol is a superior good. Only 49 percent of families in the bottom post-tax income quintile purchase alcoholic beverages, compared to 89 percent of those in the top quintile. Of those families who do purchase alcohol, those in the lowest quintile spent an average of $631 in 1990; the most affluent spent $1,356 (CBO). In addition, lower-income persons are likely to have a more elastic demand for alcohol, that is, an increase in its price will induce a greater decline in consumption (Cook). Thus, an increase in price will lead to a decrease in their total spending on alcoholic beverages and possibly an increase in their earnings as well. Poorer persons who are not alcohol dependent will receive a disproportionate health and income benefit.

It is also theoretically correct that excise taxes penalize certain consumer choices. However, while persons who choose to purchase alcohol would face an overall greater tax rate than persons of similar incomes who do not purchase alcohol, persons who drink expose themselves and others to greater risks. A higher tax would provide an incentive to curtail excess drinking, hence reducing risk. It would both reduce costs and internalize them to a greater extent, thereby reducing social costs. And, since government expenditures for medical care, rehabilitation, income support and social services related to alcohol use increase with chronic excess consumption, it is fair that heavy drinkers incur a greater tax liability.

Effect of a tax increase on average total consumption: Even though alcoholic beverages vary greatly by price and drinkers could thus adjust to a price increase by substituting "down," existing studies suggest that there is little substitution, at least between types of beverage. A price increase does result in reduced consumption. Estimates of the price elasticity of demand for beer range between −0.3 and −0.7, that is, a 10 percent increase in the price of beer reduces consumption by 3 to 7 percent. Elasticity estimates range between −0.6 and −1.0 for spirits, −1.0 and more for wine (CBO).

The effect on heavy drinkers: If a tax increase affected only moderate drinkers, it would have little effect on alcohol-related morbidity and mortality. Intuition argues that it would. Heavy drinkers are likely to be addicted and therefore possessed of a highly inelastic demand for alcohol. They would maintain consumption levels, substituting lower-priced alternatives if necessary. For many alcoholics this is doubtlessly true; but many heavy drinkers do consume less alcohol when its price increases.

Data linking decreases in cirrhosis deaths to increases in the price of alcoholic beverages confirms the price responsiveness of heavy drinkers. Since cirrhosis is usually caused by years of chronic excess drinking, cirrhosis mortality rates are a reliable proxy for the prevalence of excess alcohol consumption (Cook 1980). With cirrhosis, scarring of the liver tissue impedes the liver's ability to perform vital functions. A reduction in alcohol consumption slows or stops the scarring process, prolonging the life of the cirrhosis victim. Thus, since cirrhosis is an "interruptible" disease, a decrease in cirrhosis mortality rates is convincing evidence of a decrease in heavy drinking.

Evaluating other analysts' studies, Cook (1980) determined the median price elasticity of alcohol with respect to cirrhosis deaths to be − 0.9; that is, a 10 percent increase in the price of alcohol brings about a 9 percent decrease in cirrhosis deaths. From data covering 16 years and 30 states, Cook and Tauchen estimated that an increase in the liquor excise tax by $1.00 (in 1967 dollars) would reduce the cirrhosis mortality rate by 5.4 percent in the short run and by perhaps twice as much in the long run, as the pool of potential cirrhosis victims shrinks.

The effect on adolescent drinking: Focusing on beer, Coate and Grossman computed several sets of elasticities demonstrating substantial price responsiveness among teens, especially those who drink more heavily. Price elasticities for frequent and fairly frequent teen drinkers were found to be − 1.18 and − 0.59 respectively. The price elasticity of the probability of abstention was a significant 0.65.

They also found that a tax increase that raises the real tax on beer to what it had been in 1951 causes the number of teens who drink frequently to fall by 8 percent and the number who drink fairly frequently to fall by 6 percent. A tax increase that equalizes the tax on the alcohol in beer to that of the alcohol in spirits, now taxed at half the rate, produces corresponding reductions of 11 and 8 percent. Most effective is a tax that both equalizes the tax rates and compensates for inflation. It reduces the number of frequent drinkers by 32 percent, of fairly frequent drinkers by 24 percent and of infrequent drinkers by 8 percent (Coate and Grossman).

A uniformly high tax is a particularly effective tool for curtailing adolescent alcohol use since, unlike drinking age laws, it is difficult to circumvent. Moreover, since it disproportionately reduces heavier drinking, it would substantially reduce the adverse outcomes of teen drinking. An excise tax is, however, nonselective; all beer drinkers, not just teens, would pay it. This could be considered unfair were it not that auto fatalities among adult beer drinkers would also decline and that alcohol-impaired teen drivers kill people of all ages. Also, it is in the public interest to minimize high-risk adolescent behavior.

The effect on automobile fatalities: Since increased taxes would reduce alcohol consumption, they would also reduce alcohol-related crash deaths. The elasticity of the death rate with respect to a tax that equates the real tax on beer to its 1951 level is estimated to be − 0.7 for 15- through 17-year-olds and − 1.3 for 18-through 24-year olds (Saffer and Grossman). The price elasticity of alcohol-related auto fatalities generalized for all ages and all alcoholic beverages is − 0.7 (Cook 1980).

Raising taxes on alcoholic beverages can thus be an effective instrument of public health policy. Increasing taxes on alcohol sold by the drink, coupled with stricter server laws, would also be helpful in reducing crash deaths, as it may well be that persons leaving bars and clubs intoxicated are responsible for a disproportionate share of fatalities. However, although an increased tax on alcohol will ameliorate some of the worst outcomes of alcohol consumption, promote a healthier lifestyle and even assist in deficit reduction, it is not without cost. Much of that cost would be borne by the alcoholic beverage industry, which, like the cigarette industry, is wealthy and influential and could be expected to strongly resist.

In any event, the issue is practically moot for, whereas cigarettes and alcohol are the most widely used health-threatening substances and issue terrible externalities, our national attention has been riveted elsewhere. It has been focused on substances that, while used to a much lesser extent, have generated disproportionate social costs and wreaked more than their share of social havoc. Some of the resulting costs and problems have, however, been a direct result of our policy toward the substances. Those substances are, of course, drugs.

DRUGS

In the context of this volume, the term "drugs" refers to any illicit drug, including prescription psychotherapeutic drugs when used for nonmedical purposes. "Drug use" refers to any use of drugs as defined here, while "drug abuse" refers to drug use that results in personal, social or medical problems. For some drugs the terms are virtually synonymous.

The term "current drug use" indicates use of a drug within the month prior to a NIDA survey. It is an imprecise estimate of ongoing use as survey data will also capture infrequent partakers, one-time samplers and since-quitters who happened to have used drugs during that month.

"Drug addiction," aka "drug dependence" or "chemical dependence," involves lack of control over drug use, an intense physical and/or psychological craving for the drug and withdrawal when use is discontinued.

Classifications and Properties of Common Drugs

Since an abundance of information is available elsewhere, only a brief sketch of the drugs that most concern us today will be provided here. Except where otherwise noted, the source of information is the Drug Enforcement Agency's *Drugs of Abuse* (1989).

Narcotics

Persons who abuse narcotics are sometimes introduced to them through medical channels, as many narcotics serve legitimate medicinal purposes. Primarily analgesics, cough suppressants and antidiarrheals, they include morphine, codeine and analgesics selling under the trade names Dilaudid, Percodan, Percoset and Darvon, among others, and are usually administered orally. Opium is one that can be smoked. As most narcotic medications were once made from opium, and many still are, narcotics are frequently referred to as opiates or opoids.

The most societally troublesome narcotic is heroin, largely because of its association with crime. While a powerful painkiller, it is not prescribed for medical purposes. Methadone is. It is used to treat heroin addicts, as it eases detoxification and allows supervised maintenance of addicts who are unable to totally abstain from narcotic use. But ironically, methadone itself, with effects lasting 12 to 24 hours compared to heroin's 3 to 6, is emerging as a drug of abuse and a major cause of overdose deaths in some metropolitan areas.

Narcotics can produce a highly pleasurable rush, followed by an extended period of euphoria and drowsiness. They may also produce respiratory depression and nausea. An overdose can lead to convulsions, coma or death. Additional dangers to the heroin user include uncertain potency, impure diluents and, since heroin is usually injected, the risk of exposure to AIDS or hepatitis from shared needles (see Chapter 3).

Heroin use during pregnancy greatly endangers the fetus. As described more fully in Chapter 5, heroin-exposed babies have a greatly reduced chance of survival, undergo the pain of withdrawal and often experience persistent physical, intellectual and developmental deficits (Kumpfer).

Narcotics are highly addictive, both physically and psychologically. Withdrawal may be accompanied by panic, muscle tremors, cramps, vomiting, chills and sweating.

Depressants

These also serve a legitimate and highly useful medical purpose when used under proper supervision. Primarily sedatives, hypnotics, anticonvulsants and antianxiety agents, they are taken orally. More often obtained by prescription rather than through the black market, the major groups are barbituates, including Nembutal, Seconal, Tuinal and Phenobarbital, and the benodiazepines, which include Dalmane, Diazepan, Librium, Xanax and Valium.

In contrast to narcotics, depressants may impair coordination and produce slurred speech and disorientation. A high is generally achieved only in combination with another drug, such as alcohol. An overdose can result in coma or death and may be deliberate. Depressants are sometimes used as suicidal agents, especially by women.

The depressants tend to be only moderately addictive, but withdrawal is of longer duration and more medically dangerous than that from other drugs. Possible reactions include tremors, delirium, convulsions or death from respiratory arrest.

Stimulants

The primary medical uses of stimulants are weight control and treatment of attention deficit disorders in children. Amphetamines, such as Dexedrine, constitute the most well-known group. Administered orally when used under medical supervision, stimulants used for illegitimate purposes are sometimes injected.

The stimulants most often abused and responsible for the greatest social problems are cocaine and its high-potency derivative, crack. Although once used in patent medicines, cocaine today serves no legitimate medical purpose. As a drug of abuse, cocaine (and other stimulants in large doses) produces a euphoria that makes users feel stronger and more self-possessed. Snorted or injected for a more intense and prolonged high, it produces a temporary sense of exhilaration, superabundant energy, hyperactivity, extended wakefulness and loss of appetite. It may also produce irritability, anxiety and apprehension. A sudden pleasurable rush is quickly followed by a harrowing crash that is easily counteracted by further consumption of the stimulant. This abusive pattern becomes increasingly difficult to break, especially as tolerance to the drug's euphoric properties develops rapidly. Doses large enough to overcome the insensitivity may cause mental aberrations such as suspiciousness and the feeling that one is being watched. Continued high doses produce a toxic syndrome characterized by paranoia with auditory and visual hallucinations. Sublethal overdoses often produce tremors, agitation, hostility, panic, headache, excessive sweating, vomiting, abdominal cramps, high fever and convulsions. Lethal overdoses provoke cardiovascular collapse. The use of crack has especially virulent consequences of all types—personal, familial, societal and medical. It is one of the most rapidly addictive and dangerous of drugs and plays a leading role in many of the social problems currently plaguing our urban areas. In addition, cocaine users who choose to inject incur an even greater risk of exposure to AIDS or hepatitis than do heroin users. Heroin is usually injected but once a day, whereas cocaine is injected as often as ten times a day.

Maternal use of cocaine is extremely hazardous to a fetus. As this is extensively discussed in Chapter 5, it will suffice to note here that the risk of perinatal mortality and morbidity are greatly increased and that cocaine-exposed babies suffer terribly. They may be physically deformed and, like heroin-affected babies, may experience a lifetime of intellectual, developmental and neurobehavioral disability (Chasnoff et al. 1986).

Stimulants have not been determined to be physically addictive, but they are considered to be highly addictive psychologically. Withdrawal is marked by impairment of perception and thought processes, profound depression, anxiety and, sometimes, persistent suicidal tendencies as well. Since the effects are so intensely pleasurable and so short-lived, and the crash that follows is so awful, stimulants are among the most potent agents of reward and reinforcement that underlie the problems of dependence. And to complicate matters, tolerance, at least to cocaine, may develop within days or hours (Schuckit 1984). Users need ever larger doses to achieve intoxication, and their lives quickly become totally absorbed in drug use.

Hallucinogens

Hallucinogens such as LSD, mescaline and peyote are relatively benign. Sometimes referred to as psychedelic drugs, they may occasionally induce depression, but more often produce excitation and euphoria lasting six to 12 hours. They distort the perception of objective reality and may disorient the perception of direction, distance and time. They enhance the appreciation of color, light and sound and may also produce pleasurable delusions or hallucinations. Inexperienced users may experience the panic of a "bad trip" but can usually be "talked down" by a reassuring voice. However, LSD is thought to be capable of activating latent psychosis requiring long-term psychiatric care (Mirin and Weiss in Doweiko).

Usually ingested orally, LSD, peyote and mescaline are safe drugs in terms of direct physical mortality, although LSD may at times be adulterated with a toxic substance (Doweiko). The greatest danger comes from the accidents and rash decisions that may result from the user's impaired perception.

PCP, on the other hand, is a hallucinogen that oftentimes has effects that are much more negative, undesirable to the user and more extreme. Usually smoked, but sometimes administered orally, intranasally or intravenously, it can produce frightening or dangerously compelling auditory hallucinations as well as image distortions and mood disorders. With effects persisting at times for days, PCP can arouse anxiety, paranoia and violent hostility. High doses are associated with paranoid delusions, unpredictable assaultiveness and unusual physical strength, making PCP a very dangerous drug in a social context (Jaffe in Doweiko). Danger exists for the user as well. In fact, with the possible exception of crack-cocaine, PCP poses greater risk to the user than any other drug of abuse. In addition to extreme psychotic reactions, high doses may cause death by respiratory arrest.

With the exception of PCP, which may evoke psychological dependence, hallucinogens are not addictive. No withdrawal syndrome is associated with their use.

Cannabis

The cannaboids include marijuana, hash and the more potent hash oil. All are typically smoked but may be ingested orally. Marijuana effectively relieves the violent nausea caused by chemotherapy as its anti-nausea properties are great and, because it is smoked rather than swallowed, the nauseous patient is able to retain it. Marijuana also reduces the intraocular pressure of glaucoma victims and controls the spasms accompanying multiple sclerosis (Randall in Kleiman), but cannot be legally used for these purposes in most states. Otherwise, like the hallucinogens, the cannaboids appear to have no medical value.

Their effects peak at about 20 minutes after use but may linger for two or three hours. Low doses produce a state of intoxication characterized by an increasing sense of euphoric well-being, a dreamy state of relaxation, lessened inhibitions, increased appetite and a more vivid sense of sight, smell, touch, taste and hearing. Sexual pleasure is heightened (Masters and Johnson in Doweiko). Aggression is suppressed rather than released (Kleiman). Stronger doses intensify responses but may be accompanied by fragmentary thought and temporarily impaired memory. Too large a dose produces fatigue.

Heavy smoking of marijuana over many years may injure the respiratory system. Since marijuana contains more toxins than tobacco smoke and marijuana smokers typically inhale more deeply and hold the smoke in the lungs longer than do cigarette smokers, one joint of marijuana is generally considered to be as potentially damaging to the lungs as four cigarettes (Kleiman). However, no case of lung cancer has yet been attributed to marijuana smoking, largely because of greatly disparate rates of consumption. Marijuana smoking tends to be a phase, rather than a lifelong addiction, and most continuing marijuana smokers consume moderate amounts. Fewer than 1 percent of the persons who smoked marijuana in 1988 smoked as often as two out of every three days (NIDA 1990). Although the quantity they smoke has not been measured, it is surely less than that of the typical cigarette smoker. Cigarette smokers indulge on a daily basis; most smoke twenty or more cigarettes per day (NIDA 1990).

The safest of illicit drugs (and safer than alcohol), cannabis is not physically addictive. However, psychological dependence has occasionally been reported. The withdrawal symptoms are insomnia and decreased appetite, but these are only rarely experienced.

Inhalants

Included in this category are the anesthetic gases used in dental surgery and inexpensive chemical agents such as nail polish remover, cleaning solvents, gasoline and glue. Inhaling them produces a hazy euphoria or an intoxication similar to that from alcohol, lasting about thirty minutes (Doweiko).

In most cases, the mental changes following use disappear quickly. But, although rare, permanent damage to the liver, kidneys, sinus membranes and nasal tissue may result (Schuckit 1984). Usually engaged in by adolescents, inhalant use is generally discontinued after one or two years with no apparent withdrawal process (Doweiko).

Drug Use in the United States

Reliability of Estimates

Because of the illegal nature of drug use, it is impossible to obtain a precise census of users. Two ongoing studies, the NIDA High School Senior Drug

Use Survey and the NIDA Household Survey on Drug Abuse, provide the best estimates, although their numbers are decidedly conservative. This is especially true of the Household Survey which, as its name implies, interviews only members of households. It excludes persons living in group quarters or institutions such as military installations, college dormitories, boarding homes, prisons and rehabilitation centers as well as the homeless. Many excluded groups have disproportionately high rates of drug use.

The number of heroin, cocaine and crack users, particularly addicts, is believed to be significantly understated (USDHHS 1991a; Murray). NIDA estimates that there are 500,000 heroin addicts in this country, but Joseph Biden, Senate Judiciary Committee chairman, claims that NIDA "misses more addicts than it counts" (USGAO 1990h; Murray). Even Health and Human Services Secretary Louis Sullivan concedes that "little confidence" can be put in the numbers on hard-core drug users (in Murray). This is partly because heroin and cocaine are strongly associated with the populations the survey does not reach, such as prison inmates and the homeless, and because the sample size is small and underrepresents minorities who disproportionately use hard-core drugs (NIDA 1990). Another major limitation of the survey is that only about 80 percent of those selected for the study agree to be interviewed. There is good reason to believe that a disproportionate share of those who refuse to participate use drugs, perhaps heavily (ONDCP 1990). Also, while under-reporting of illegitimate activity is always a possibility, it is more so in the case of the Household Survey. Only about half the interviews are conducted in complete privacy (NIDA 1990). Nevertheless, NIDA's findings are quite informative and are cited frequently throughout this volume.

Prevalence and Trends

There is a great deal of drug use in this country. According to NIDA's household survey, 37 percent of household members aged 12 or older (74.4 million persons), conservatively estimated, had used drugs at some time in their lives; 13.3 percent (26.8 million people) used drugs in 1990. The drug most frequently used was marijuana, consumed at some time by an estimated 66.5 million Americans and used in 1990 by 20.5 million. Cocaine was a distant second, used at least once by an estimated 22.7 million persons and used by 6.3 million people in 1990 (NIDA 1991).

As can be inferred from these numbers and from several of the tables in this chapter, many Americans sample drugs, but far fewer continue using them. Those who do continue using drugs do not necessarily indulge with great frequency. Of those who reported smoking any marijuana in 1990, fewer than half smoked as often as once a month and only one-third smoked once a week or more. Of those who admitted to cocaine use, only one-third reported using it as much as once a month; only one-tenth used it once a week or more (NIDA 1991).

The demographic data presented in Tables 2.2 and 2.3 reveal that drug use is very widespread in American society. Although prevalence rates are somewhat

Table 2.2
Percentage of Persons 12 Years of Age or Over Reporting Ever, Past-Month, or
Past-Year Illicit Drug Use by Demographic Characteristic: United States, 1988

Demographic Characteristic	Ever Used	Used Past Year	Used Past Month
Total	36.6	14.1	7.3
Sex			
Male	40.0	16.4	9.0
Female	33.4	12.0	5.8
Race/ethnicity			
White	37.0	13.9	7.0
Black	35.9	13.3	7.8
Hispanic	32.3	14.7	8.2
Population density			
Large metro	40.8	16.1	8.5
Small metro	35.1	13.4	7.0
Non metro	31.3	11.6	5.6
Region			
Northeast	36.6	12.7	6.3
North Central	36.9	15.4	7.9
South	32.9	10.7	5.9
West	43.2	20.5	10.1
Education*			
Less than high school	27.7	10.6	5.8
High school graduate	37.5	15.2	8.5
Some college	44.0	15.9	7.0
College graduate	46.9	13.2	6.4
Current employment*			
Full-time	47.0	16.6	8.2
Part-time	43.7	16.1	8.9
Unemployed	49.6	26.2	17.4
Other**	18.5	6.4	3.1

* Refers only to respondents eighteen years of age or older.
** Refers to non-labor market participants such as homemakers, students and retirees.

Source: National Institute on Drug Abuse. *National Household Survey on Drug Abuse: Main Findings 1988.*

Table 2.3

Percentage of Persons 12 Years of Age or Over Reporting Illicit Drug Use in Past Year by Sex, Race and Ethnicity: United States, 1990

Drug	Male	Female	White	Black	Hispanic	Total
Any illicit drug use	15.5	11.4	13.1	14.9	14.8	13.5
Marijuana and hashish	12.1	8.4	10.1	11.2	10.9	10.2
Inhalants	1.7	0.7	1.3	0.9	1.1	1.2
Hallucinogens	1.7	0.6	1.3	0.3	1.1	1.1
Cocaine (including crack)	4.3	2.0	2.8	4.0	5.2	3.1
Crack-cocaine	0.8	0.3	0.4	1.7	**	0.5
Heroin*	1.1	0.5	0.7	1.7	1.2	0.8
Any needle use	0.5	0.2	0.3	0.6	0.3	0.4
Non-medical use of psychotherapeutics	4.5	4.1	4.2	4.6	4.2	4.3

* estimates of heroin use are for ever having used heroin.
** low precision, no estimate reported.

Source: National Institute on Drug Abuse. *National Household Survey on Drug Abuse: Population Estimates 1990.*

greater in the West and in large cities and among males and the unemployed, use is pervasive. Patterns of use, however, vary. Whites, for example, are three times more likely than blacks to use hallucinogens. Blacks are three times more likely to use crack and twice as likely to use heroin.

Tables 2.4 and 2.5 reveal the trends in drug use and the welcome news that almost all forms of drug use are declining. Not provided by the tables is the additional welcome news that overall drug use declined in almost every sociodemographic group. The sole exception was 18 to 25-year-old college graduates; their drug use increased almost 15 percent from 1985 to 1988 (NIDA 1991).

There is also unwelcome news. While fewer people overall were using cocaine, the proportion of frequent users essentially doubled from 5.3 percent of the cocaine-using population in 1985 to 10.5 percent in 1988 (ONDCP 1990). Not coincidentally, 1985 was the first year in which the highly addictive crack-cocaine became widely available. There was also a significant increase in the lifetime prevalence of cocaine use among Hispanics—from 7.3 percent in 1985 to 11.5 percent in 1990 (USDHHS 1991a; NIDA 1991).

NIDA surveys may underestimate the increase in crack-cocaine and heroin use, but there are other telling indicators. The Drug Use Forecasting Program (DUF), which samples arrestees for drug use, reports a greatly increased prevalence of cocaine use in its subjects. For example, in 1984 16 percent of the males and 27 percent of the females arrested in Washington, D.C., tested

Table 2.4

Percentage Reporting Ever Having Used Illicit Drugs by Age and Type of Drug: United States, Selected Years

Drug/Age	1972	1974	1976	1979	1982	1985	1988	1990
Any illicit drug use								
12-17 years	–	–	–	34.3	27.6+	29.5	24.7	27.7
18-25 years	–	–	–	69.9	63.3	64.3	58.9	55.8
26-34 years	–	–	–	23.0*	24.7*	62.2	64.2	62.6
> 35 years	–	–	–			20.4	23.0	25.9
Marijuana and hashish								
12-17 years	14.0	23.0	22.4	30.9	26.7	23.6	17.4	14.8
18-25 years	47.9	52.7	52.9	59.9	68.2	64.1	60.3	52.5
26-34 years	7.4*	9.9*	12.9*	19.6*	23.0*	58.5	62.1	60.8
> 35 years						15.9	19.6	21.9
Inhalants								
12-17 years	6.4	8.5	8.1	9.8	–	9.2	8.8	7.8
18-25 years	–	9.2	9.0	16.5	–	12.4	12.5	10.4
26-34 years	–	1.2*	1.9*	3.9*	–	5.0*	3.9*	7.2
> 35 years	–							2.6
Hallucinogens								
12-17 years	4.8	6.0	5.1	7.1	5.2	3.3	3.5	3.3
18-25 years	–	16.6	17.3	25.1	21.1	11.3	13.8	12.0
26-34 years	–	1.3*	1.6*	4.5*	6.4*	16.9	17.7	15.7
> 35 years	–					2.4	2.7	4.5
Cocaine								
12-17 years	1.5	3.6	3.4	5.4	6.5	4.9	3.4	2.6
18-25 years	9.1	12.7	13.4	27.5	28.3	25.2	19.7	19.4
26-34 years	1.6*	0.9*	1.6*	4.3*	8.5*	24.1	26.5	25.6
> 35 years						4.2	4.0	5.9
Heroin								
12-17 years	0.6	1.0	0.5	0.5	**	**	0.6	0.7
18-25 years	4.6	4.5	3.9	3.5	1.2	1.2	0.3	0.6
26-34 years	**	0.5*	0.5*	1.0*	1.1*	2.6	2.1	1.4
> 35 years	**					0.5	0.8	0.7
Nonmedical use of psychotherapeutics								
12-17 years	–	–	–	7.3	10.3	12.1	7.7	10.2
18-25 years	–	–	–	29.5	28.4	26.0	17.6	15.8
26-34 years	–	–	–	9.2*	8.8*	27.2	22.1	19.6
> 35 years						9.0	7.5	8.7

– estimate not available.
* estimate available only for persons aged 26 or more.
** low precision, no estimate reported.
+ the exclusion of inhalants in 1982 is believed to have resulted in underestimates of any drug use for that year, especially for 12 to 17 years old.

Source: Data for 1972 to 1988: National Institute on Drug Abuse. *National Household Survey on Drug Abuse: Main Findings 1988.*

Data for 1990: National Institute on Drug Abuse. *National Household Survey on Drug Abuse: Population Estimates 1990.*

Table 2.5

Percentage Reporting Illicit Drug Use in Past Month by Age and Type of Drug: United States, Selected Years

Drug/Age	1972	1974	1976	1979	1982	1985	1988	1990
Any illicit drug use								
12-17 years	--	--	--	17.6	12.7+	14.9	9.2	8.1
18-25 years	--	--	--	37.1	30.4	25.7	17.8	14.9
26-34 years	--	--	--	6.5*	7.5*	21.1	13.0	9.8
> 35 years	--	--	--			3.9	2.1	2.8
Marijuana and hashish								
12-17 years	7.0	12.0	12.3	16.7	11.5	12.0	6.4	5.2
18-25 years	27.8	25.2	25.0	35.4	27.4	21.8	15.5	12.7
26-34 years	2.5*	2.0*	3.5*	6.0*	6.6*	16.9	10.8	8.6
> 35 years						2.3	1.4	1.9
Inhalants								
12-17 years	1.0	0.7	0.9	2.0	--	3.4	2.0	2.2
18-25 years	--	**	0.5	1.2	--	0.8	1.7	1.2
26-34 years	--	**	**	0.5*	--	0.5*	0.9*	**
> 35 years	--	**	**		--			
Hallucinogens								
12-17 years	1.4	1.3	0.9	2.2	1.4	1.2	0.8	0.9
18-25 years	--	2.5	1.1	4.4	1.7	1.9	1.9	0.8
26-34 years	--	**	**	**	**	1.5	**	**
> 35 years	--	**	**	**	**	**	**	**
Cocaine								
12-17 years	0.6	1.0	1.0	1.4	1.6	1.5	1.1	0.6
18-25 years	--	3.1	2.0	9.3	6.8	7.6	4.5	2.2
26-34 years	--	**	**	0.9*	1.2*	6.1	2.6	1.7
> 35 years	--	**	**		1.2*	0.5	0.3	0.2
Heroin	reliable estimates of current heroin use are not available for any year for any age group.							
Nonmedical use of psychotherapeutics								
12-17 years	--	--	--	2.3	3.8	3.0	2.4	2.7
18-25 years	--	--	--	6.2	7.0	6.3	3.8	2.6
26-34 years	--	--	--	1.1*	1.2*	5.3	2.7	1.6
> 35 years	--	--	--			1.5	0.7	0.8

-- estimate not available.
* estimate available only for persons aged 26 or more.
** low precision, no estimate reported.
+ the exclusion of inhalants in 1982 is believed to have resulted in underestimates of any drug use for that year, especially for 12 to 17 years old.

Source: Data for 1972 to 1988: National Institute on Drug Abuse. *National Household Survey on Drug Abuse: Main Findings 1988.*
Data for 1990: National Institute on Drug Abuse. *National Household Survey on Drug Abuse: Population Estimates 1990.*

positive for cocaine; in 1988, 60 percent of the males and 80 percent of the females tested positive (USDJ 1991a). Other indicators, not just of the increase in abusive cocaine use but also of its serious health consequences, are reported by the Drug Abuse Warning Network (DAWN) which monitors drug-related health emergencies and deaths across the country. DAWN found that cocaine-related emergency room cases increased over 400 percent from 1985 to 1989, while cocaine-related deaths more than tripled (ONDCP 1990). Heroin emergency room mentions increased by 47 percent from 1984 to 1988; heroin-related deaths increased by 59 percent (USDHHS 1991a). Yet DAWN's mortality data also understates the problem, as it excludes New York City, home to a disproportionate share of crack and heroin users.

The most recent trends in hard-core drug use are particularly difficult to measure and are subject to dispute. While most sources agree that occasional use of cocaine has fallen considerably, authoritative estimates of the number of cocaine addicts varies. NIDA estimates there were 662,000 cocaine addicts in 1990, 23 percent fewer than its 1988 estimate (ONDCP 1991a). The Senate Judiciary Committee claims there were 2.4 million cocaine addicts, an increase of 10 percent from its 1989 estimate (in Murray).

NIDA's estimates of the number of cocaine addicts may be low, but there are indications that its direction of change is accurate. DAWN recorded a 23 percent decline in cocaine emergency room admissions from mid-1988 to mid-1990 (ONDCP 1991a).

DAWN also recorded a decrease in heroin cases in early 1990, but according to the Office of National Drug Control Policy (ONDCP), that may have been due to transient factors such as a temporary disruption in supply (ONDCP 1990). Other sources suggest that heroin use has been rising. Furthermore, Drug Enforcement Administration (DEA) and Customs Service reports indicate that we are on the brink of a new heroin epidemic (Isikoff). Improved growing and processing methods will combine with an increased number of crack addicts seeking a drug providing a longer-lived high. The result will be large numbers of new users involved with a far more potent product. Such a development would indeed be unfortunate, not merely because of the social stresses arising from heroin use per se, but also because heroin use is strongly associated with the spread of AIDS. Drug abuse gives rise to a multiplicity of costly personal and social problems.

The Social Cost of Illicit Drug Use

The Psychosocial Costs

The frequent use of drugs, particularly hard drugs like heroin, cocaine, crack, and PCP, can be emotionally and psychologically devastating to users and to everyone around them. It destroys potential, self-esteem and relationships as heavy users become absorbed in a drug lifestyle. Much of their time is spent under the influence of drugs or trying to procure them.

The mind- and behavior-altering properties of drugs can induce lethargic, erratic, volatile or violent behavior. Thus drug abuse is associated with, among other things, both the neglect and the physical abuse of children.

Addicts rob their parents, mates and offspring of hopes, dreams and an orderly, stable existence. They rob their neighbors of security and peace of mind. They evoke suffering and despair, fear and trepidation. They diminish the viability of the social fabric.

The Economic Costs

Rice and colleagues (USDHHS 1990a) calculated the economic costs of drug abuse in 1985 in a fashion similar to their analysis of the costs of alcohol abuse. Their findings are depicted in Table 2.6, together with a reiteration of their estimates for alcohol abuse. The comparison is an interesting one. The total cost of drug abuse was $44.1 billion, whereas for alcohol it was $70.3 billion. Core costs (medical and morbidity- and mortality-related costs) for drug abuse were $10.6 billion for a year in which 6,118 deaths were attributed to drugs, including possible suicides and accidental poisoning unrelated to illicit drug use. Core costs for alcohol were $58.2 billion, yet alcohol-attributed deaths numbered 94,765 (USDHHS 1990a).

The relative distribution of costs is even more interesting. Core costs comprise a much smaller proportion of the total costs of drug abuse—24 percent in contrast to 83 percent. The great bulk of the costs of drug abuse are essentially of our own making. They derive primarily from our efforts to control drug use—both the expense of drug law enforcement and the expense induced by the very success of our efforts. Thus they could be reduced by a reordering of our public policy agenda.

More recent estimates are not yet available in such detail; however, the Justice Department, in 1989, estimated the social costs generated by each addict to have been about $200,000 per year (in Cook 1989). The costs associated with drug use are much greater today than at the time of the Rice group's analysis for several reasons: Federal spending for drug control was $1.6 billion in 1985; it was $10.5 billion in 1991, and $11.7 billion has been requested for 1992 (USDHHS 1990a; ONDCP 1991b). Drug-related criminal justice costs have since skyrocketed. Only 1,501 cases of the costly disease AIDS were attributed to drug use in 1985; by 1990 the number was 8,248 and growing rapidly (NCHS 1991). But an even greater source of increasing costs is due to the rise in the use of crack-cocaine.

Barely known at the time the Rice group performed their computations, crack has since spread like wildfire through many inner city communities. It has fueled great increases in both property and violent crimes, thereby increasing criminal justice costs and generating terrible negative neighborhood externalities. It has greatly increased the demand for health care for users, their prenatally affected offspring, and innocent bystanders caught in the crossfire of dealers' turf wars. It has also greatly increased the demand for social services of all types,

Table 2.6

The Economic Costs of Alcohol and Drug Abuse: United States, 1985

Type of costs	Alcohol Abuse		Drug Abuse	
	millions of dollars	percent of total	millions of dollars	percent of total
Core costs				
treatment and support*	$ 6,810	9.7%	$ 2,082	4.7%
morbidity**	27,388	38.9%	5,979	13.6%
mortality**	23,983	34.1%	2,563	5.8%
(discounted at 6%)				
Related costs				
criminal justice system	3,734	5.3%	11,063	25.1%
private legal defense	342	0.5%	1,381	3.1%
property destruction	175	0.3%	759	1.7%
victims of crime**	465	0.7%	842	1.9%
incarceration**	2,701	3.8%	4,434	10.1%
crime careers**	-	-	13,976	31.7%
motor vehicle crashes	2,584	3.7%	-	-
fire destruction	457	0.7%	-	-
social welfare administration	88	0.1%	6	-
Fetal Alcohol Syndrome	1,611	2.3%	-	-
AIDS	-	-	967	2.2%
Total Costs	**$70,338**	+	**$44,052**	+

* research, administration and training of professional staff.

** productivity lost due to incapacitation, incarceration, choice of a career of crime rather than legal employment, or premature death.

\+ percentages do not total 100.0 due to rounding.

Source: United States Department of Health and Human Services.
The Economic Costs of Alcohol and Drug Abuse and Mental Illness: 1985, modified.

especially for the children of users, who often need everything from foster care to special education.

National estimates of the cost of crack are not yet available. However, the *San Francisco Chronicle* compiled a comprehensive accounting of the cost to the city, that is, costs over and above those covered by the state and federal governments, insurance companies and private individuals. Comparing drug-related municipal costs in 1986, when crack's presence was just beginning to be felt, to 1988, when the crack epidemic had not yet begun to peak, the *Chronicle* found the following:

- Police incidents involving cocaine increased 278 percent (cost: $9.80m).
- Felony court cases specifically tied to cocaine possession or sales (61 percent of total cases) increased 218 percent (cost: $5.80m).
- Juvenile cocaine-related arrests increased 440 percent (cost: $4.58m).
- Jailings (mostly of people arrested for crack) increased 21 percent (cost: $15.50m).
- Adults released on probation into the drug diversion program increased 21 percent (cost: $1.01m).
- Felony lawyers in the public defender's office spent almost 50 percent of their time representing people with cocaine-related offenses (cost: $1.60m).
- Foster care cases involving children of addicted parents increased 148 percent (cost: $22.18m).
- Addicts in treatment for crack increased 144 percent (cost: $3.00m).
- The number of infants born who tested positive for drugs increased 73 percent (cost: $3.50m).
- The demand for adult health services increased substantially (cost: $4.72m).

The total cost to San Francisco was $71.69 million, not including a $9 million addition to the jail required to house arrestees who, because of overcrowding, were being released by the score. Nor does it include the cost of the inability to provide critical services to noncrack clients. City agencies from child welfare services to the emergency response system to health care services are over-burdened by crack cases. Money the city spends dealing with crack is money not spent on education, housing or parks. City services are drained, making San Francisco a "dirtier, poorer, riskier place to live" (Gordon p. 12).

Money industry spends dealing with drug-abusing employees is also money not spent on other endeavors. As discussed earlier in this chapter, substance abuse is very costly to American business, perhaps more costly than the Rice group's study indicates. While, overall, alcohol abuse creates more expense for employers, firms with a younger work force may find drug abuse a serious problem. In addition to increased levels of absenteeism, on-the-job accidents and medical claims, drug abuse is also associated with greater employee embezzlement, theft and pilferage (Lodge). The impaired performance, health problems and criminal activity associated with drug use is very costly to business and to us all.

Drugs and Crime

Drug law violations: The production, distribution and use of illicit drugs are crimes by definition. Enhanced drug law enforcement and the increase in viola-tions engendered by the crack epidemic have resulted in a great increase in arrests for drug law violations, from 395,000 in 1979 to 640,000 in 1985 and 994,000 in 1990 (USDJ 1990b; ONDCP 1990). The costs today are great, far greater than the Rice group had estimated for 1985. By 1989 taxpayers spent

$30 billion just for drug trafficking court costs (Coletti). Not only had arrests for drug violations increased, but a larger proportion of arrests resulted in convictions and a larger proportion of convictions resulted in incarceration (USDHHS 1990c). The average length of sentence had also increased, so that by 1991, 70 percent of the inmates in federal prisons were incarcerated for drug offenses. Federal prisons were operating at 69 percent above capacity, necessitating new and costly construction (ONDCP 1991b). A similar situation existed at the state and local level. Drug law violators had comprised 13 percent of state and local inmate populations in 1986 (USDJ 1990b). Since then they have increased both absolutely and relatively, as evidenced by the case of San Francisco. A 1990 survey of inmates in Atlanta jails found that 45 percent had been charged with drug violations (USGAO 1991b).

Stepped-up enforcement together with increased drug law violations have given rise to gross distortions in the criminal justice system. Courts are overwhelmed with drug cases, which comprise up to 85 percent of their dockets, and correctional institutions are severely overcrowded (USGAO 1991b). To relieve pressure on the courts and to comply with court orders to reduce prison overcrowding (since new construction cannot keep pace with demand) measures are being taken that reduce offender accountability, threaten public safety and turn the entire process into an expensive farce. Plea bargains abound, felonies are reduced to misdemeanors, convicted felons are put on probation rather than jailed and inmates are paroled earlier than is prudent. Paradoxically, since drug offenders are generally considered nonviolent, they are among the first to be released. Thus defendants increasingly opt for jail time rather than paying fines because they know they will spend little or no time in jail. In Los Angeles in 1989, inmates served only 1 day for each 37 days of their sentences. In Atlanta, a typical sentence for trafficking 60 bags of crack is 15 to 20 years, but actual time served is only 6 to 12 months. In Detroit, persons arrested for selling relatively small amounts of drugs are only held overnight and are likely to be seen selling on a street corner two days later (USGAO 1991b). This is no way to win a war. Rather it is a burlesque that diminishes respect for the system, demoralizes and endangers police officers for naught and jeopardizes public safety. And it is very expensive.

To consider only the costs associated with drug law violations per se, as the *Chronicle* study did, greatly underrepresents the total criminal justice costs associated with drugs. It overlooks the strong relationship between drugs and other crimes. According to Rice and colleagues, 26 percent of our total police protection expenditures can be attributed to drug-related crime (USDHHS 1990a, modified). As this was in 1985, before crack turned our streets into war zones, we can safely assume that both the proportionate and the absolute costs are greater today.

Drug use and the corrections population: Drug use is highly pervasive within the criminal population. Surveys of persons arrested by local police, state prison inmates and juvenile offenders all reveal substantially higher rates of drug use than non-justice-involved persons of the same age, race and ethnicity. Among arrestees surveyed in 1988 by DUF (which excludes individuals arrested for drug violations and so is thought to represent minimum levels of drug use among arrestees), roughly 16 percent of the males used heroin, 52 percent used cocaine and 17 percent used crack. The corresponding proportions among female arrestees were 23 percent, 54 percent and 21 percent (USDJ 1990a, modified). Major drugs (defined by the Justice Department as cocaine, heroin, methadone, PCP and LSD) were used by 52 percent of the inmates in state prisons in 1986; 35 percent used them regularly (USDJ 1988b). Frequent major drug use was most strongly related to robbery, burglary and murder, in that order. Over 33 percent of the inmates were under the influence of drugs or drugs and alcohol combined at the time they committed the offense for which they were then incarcerated (USDJ 1988d). Drugs were more strongly associated with crimes for economic gain than was alcohol; alcohol was more strongly associated with crimes against the person such as murder, assault and rape. However, this was before the widespread use of crack, which is frequently associated with crimes of violence in addition to property crimes (Williams). By 1990, as many as 75 percent of the inmates in state prisons were drug abusers, as were up to 90 percent of probationers. (USGAO 1991b).

The drug-crime connection: As much as 75 percent of all crime is drug related (USGAO 1991b). Some analysts see this relationship as largely coincidental. Since the subpopulations that exhibit high crime rates also exhibit high rates of drug use, considerable overlap is inevitable. Probing more deeply, other analysts conclude a common causality—that is, the same circumstances that contribute to crime also contribute to drug use. The social conditions of poverty and discrimination may limit opportunity, promote risk taking and reduce an individual's investment in society, leading to both drug abuse and criminal behavior. Additionally, some people may be both risk takers and thrill seekers, desirous of possessions or experiences not available by legitimate means and willing to violate the law in their pursuit.

But most experts view the relationship between drugs and crime as more direct. They see drug abuse as encouraging criminal behavior in several ways: (1) drug use may stimulate aggression or reduce inhibitions, (2) the illegal nature of drug trafficking with its high profit potential sets the stage for crimes such as homicide and assault, and (3) the illegality of the business results in high prices for drugs, which can often only be met by criminal activity.

In the first case, an individual may take drugs to muster the courage to commit a crime. But a more direct connection occurs when the psychopharmacological properties of a drug incite violent behavior. The drugs most commonly linked to assaultive behavior are, in order, barbituates, alcohol, amphetamines and PCP (Goldstein). Today we would include crack near the top of the list. Conversely, some drugs, notably heroin, tranquilizers and marijuana, have a reverse psychopharmacological effect and ameliorate violent tendencies (Goldstein).

In the second scenario, the highly profitable yet illegal nature of the drug trade makes violence more probable at every stage of operation. Managed by criminals, the drug trafficking industry employs violent personnel. Major distributors and small-scale dealers engage in literally murderous battles over markets and profits. They strong-arm competitors and retaliate against informers and persons who may have cheated or stolen from them. Users, too, may engage in violent disputes over money, drugs and drug paraphernalia.

Drug trafficking violence has escalated in recent years with the emergence of crack-cocaine. Since it is a high profit-margin drug, its distribution rights are worth fighting over. In addition, crack profits have financed the purchase of the high-powered weaponry now proliferating throughout our urban neighborhoods and giving rise to a horrorific increase in violence in virtually all our large cities (B. Miller 1990).

Former Philadelphia Police Commissioner Willie Williams has testified that the "paramount causes" of the increase in homicides, robbery, burglary, theft and assault in American cities are the increase in drug abuse and the increasing use of semiautomatic weapons as tools of the drug trade. Not only are drug dealers "more heavily armed than the law enforcement agencies charged with their apprehension," but their use of weaponry is highly indiscriminate, often killing innocent bystanders, including children. In Philadelphia, 35 percent of the homicides in 1989 were directly related to drugs. As elsewhere, drug users under the influence of cocaine more often end up killing an intended robbery or burglary victim and domestic violence more often results in murder by spouses, parents and children on drugs, who today are more likely to have a gun in hand (Williams).

Ironically, the increase in homicides among drug dealers in 1991 may be due more to the decline in crack use. The shrinking market has aggravated the fight for market share (ONDCP 1990).

The third component of the drug-crime connection, the need for money to finance drugs, is also causally related to the fact that drugs are illegal. The supplier's risk of apprehension and conviction and cost of avoiding detection are reflected in high product prices.

Frequent use of drugs is thus very expensive. The median expenditure for drugs by arrestees in the DUF reporting cities in early 1990 was $100 per week. Arrestees in three-quarters of the cities reported weekly expenditures of $4,000 or more; one individual admitted spending $9,000 per week (USDJ 1991b). Not surprisingly, the correlation between arrestees' drug use and acquisition of income from illegal sources was very high. The frequent use of expensive drugs is strongly associated with high levels of illegal income (Collins et al. 1985).

Also unsurprisingly, government agencies such as the FBI, the DEA and the ONDCP all downplay the relationship between addiction to high-priced drugs and income-generating crime. While conceding that daily drug users are disproportionately represented among inmates sentenced for crimes of gain and that convicts admitting to major drug use were almost five times more

likely to have received income from illegal sources and much less likely to have
been employed, government sources stress the fact that only 13 percent of inmates (in 1986) seemed to fit the pattern of drug addicts who committed crimes
for gain (USDJ 1988b; ONDCP 1990). They also point out that most inmates
who use major drugs began using them after their first arrest and that major
drug users are also disproportionately involved in noneconomic crimes. They
claim that abolishing drug use would not abolish crime. All this is true, but
the government's position denies the obvious: *our drug control policies encourage
criminal activity.*

Although only 13 percent of inmates appeared to have committed crimes
for funds to purchase drugs, even the Justice Department acknowledges that
they may have been responsible for a disproportionate share of crimes (USDJ
1988b). Field research with heroin addicts have shown that they commit crimes
with far greater frequency than do nonaddicts. It has been estimated that over
50 million crimes per year are committed by narcotic addicts, yet fewer than
1 percent result in arrest (in Nurco et al. 1985). The criminogenic properties
of heroin addiction under a system that encourages high heroin prices have
been verified by studies following heroin users over the course of their addiction
careers. Their criminal activity soars as they move into periods of addiction
and falls dramatically when they enter phases of rehabilitation and nonuse.
It soars again when use is resumed (Nurco et al. 1985). The sharpest surges
in criminal behavior occur among addicts who had a lesser propensity for crime
prior to the onset of their addiction (Nurco et al. 1988). A cross-sectional analysis
of methadone clients and narcotic users not in treatment found greatly disparate
rates of criminal activity, especially robbery and burglary (Hunt et al.). And
a report issued in 1972 by the American Bar Association estimated that between one-third and one-half of the robberies committed in urban areas are
committed by heroin addicts (in Goldstein).

Crimes for gain are also associated with cocaine use (Collins et al. 1985),
and, although not yet well documented, with crack use as well. Although inexpensive at first, since crack is so rapidly addictive and so many doses are
required throughout the day, it quickly becomes a very expensive habit. Thus
in some cities today over 70 percent of burglaries and robberies are estimate
to be drug related (USGAO 1991b).

There is, of course, considerable overlap among the three drug-crime
scenarios. Thus the tendency to violent behavior on the part of males who are
heavy crack users found by Goldstein and colleagues, and the increasing incidence of crimes against property and persons associated with greater involvement in the crack-cocaine trade on the part of youth found by Inciardi and
Pottieger, may be a function of all three—the psychopharmacological effect
of the drugs, the requisites of drug trafficking, and the need to finance drug
purchases. In addition, some coincidental manifestion of lifestyle is also likely.
But there can be no doubt that the illegality of drugs contributes to the drug-
crime relationship.

The social costs of drug-related crime: The social costs are great. The criminal activities of each heroin addict was estimated (in 1985) to cost society approximately $55,000 per year (Johnson et al.). The crack tally may be far greater. In addition to the criminal justice costs and to the direct costs incurred by victims, we must include the tremendous emotional and psychological costs to victims and potential victims alike.

Compounding the costs are the far-reaching externalities arising from the crime associated with drug trafficking and addiction. Incalculable economic damage is done to neighborhoods and to entire cities as businesses, homeowners, shoppers and tourists perceive the danger of drug-related crime too great a risk to undertake. Something must be done. It is time to reevaluate our drug policies.

Current Public Policy: The War on Drugs

Our national drug control strategy, commonly known as the War on Drugs, is overseen by the ONDCP, headed by current drug czar Robert Martinez, successor to William Bennett. Its lead agency is the DEA. It is primarily funded by the federal government; however, billions of dollars are also expended by state and local governments and the private sector.

The nomenclature "war" is appropriate. Our effort is massive and multipronged, simultaneously attacking domestic production, foreign production destined for the U.S. market, and distribution at every stage, with the heaviest artillery targeted at wholesalers and large suppliers. The offensive has been launched in the fields and in the air, on the high seas and on the streets, and against clandestine labs. Captured enemy agents can expect fines of up to $10 million, seizure of assets, and up to life imprisonment (DEA 1989). The death penalty has been proposed for drug kingpins. Ancillary theaters of operation include schools, workplaces, government research laboratories and rehabilitation centers, wherein we have deployed a fifth column determined to discourage domestic demand.

Resource Allocation

The war effort has been increasingly well funded, as can be seen in Figure 2.1 and Table 2.7, which depict federal budgetary allocations. Approximately 70 percent of the war chest is targeted to supply-side activity. This allocation is lopsided. Since supply is largely created by demand, demand reduction is a more effective tactic. However, it is true that relative financing is an imperfect measure of relative effort. Supply reduction measures often entail international initiatives, necessitating federal involvement. They employ considerable manpower and require extensive capital outlays for patrol cars, aircraft, ships and prisons. Demand reduction activities are less costly and can more readily be carried out at the local level with local funding. Also, the supply measure of arrest and imprisonment may act as a deterrent, reducing demand. In addition,

Figure 2.1
Federal Drug Control Budget Authority in Billions of Dollars by Allocation: Fiscal Years 1981 to 1992

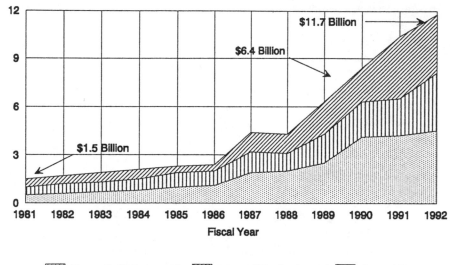

Fiscal Year

Domestic Enforcement   Internat'l/Border Control   Demand

Source: Office of National Drug Control. *National Drug Control Strategy: Budget Summary.*

insofar as accessibility encourages use, supply also generates demand. Reducing supply therefore could reduce demand, if only marginally.

Even so, our antidrug resources are misallocated—overemployed in supply-side efforts, underemployed in the demand side. This arises from a basic conceptual fallacy: that prohibition and interdiction can work despite an indomitable demand and the profits to be made by meeting that demand. Our War on Drugs has thus been a campaign of logistical error, waged against an indefatigable enemy. It has been outrageously cost-ineffective and has done more harm than good.

Effectiveness

Not every battle has been lost. Some campaign objectives have been met; some have been exceeded. For example, drug policy goals in 1988 included reducing both overall drug use and adolescent drug use by 10 percent by 1990. Overall use fell 11 percent, and adolescent use fell 13 percent. Another objective was to reduce occasional cocaine use by 10 percent; it declined 29 percent (ONDCP 1991a).

However, social and public health problems arise not so much from drug use as from drug abuse. While discouraging drug use may help reduce abuse, since occasional users may use drugs irresponsibly, endanger their health or

Table 2.7
Federal Drug Control Budget Authority in Millions of Dollars: Fiscal Years 1990
to 1992

Program	1990	1991	1992	1991-1992 Increase $1	1%
Criminal justice system	$4,238	$ 4,368	$ 4,995	$ 627	14%
Drug treatment	1,279	1,499	1,655	156	10%
Education, community action and the workplace	1,217	1,442	1,515	73	5%
International initiatives	500	647	779	132	20%
Border interdiction and security	1,752	2,023	2,109	86	4%
Research	328	435	488	53	12%
Intelligence	65	108	114	7	6%
Total*	$9,378	$10,521	$11,655	+$1,134	+11%

* Detail may not add to totals due to rounding.

Source: Office of National Drug Control Policy. *National Drug Control Strategy: Budget Summary.*

become addicted, it does not appear to be the case that we have lessened the social problems associated with drug use or reduced the number of hard-core addicts.

Nor have we reduced the supply of drugs. Eradification efforts have been intensified, international initiatives have been enhanced, and border interdictions, domestic seizures, arrests, and convictions have all reached record levels (DEA 1990a; NNICC). Yet the supply of marijuana quadrupled just from 1988 to 1989, and the availability of cocaine, heroin, amphetamines and hallucinogens is as high or higher than ever (NNICC). In fact, the supply of cocaine has grown so enormously it has outstripped demand, aggravating the violence among cocaine traffickers. We have spent billions of dollars to stop the flow of drugs but have merely shifted the routes by which they travel to market. We have also forced prices up, increased profits to remaining suppliers, and increased the mayhem associated with the drug trade.

When we have (temporarily) succeeded in reducing supply, the costs exceed the benefits. In the case of the softer drugs, spending billions of dollars to suppress the use of relatively harmless agents is irrational. In the case of the harder drugs, our approach has only exacerbated the associated problems and greatly increased social costs.

The Supply-Side Approach and Addictive Drugs

Attempts to reduce the supply of heroin and cocaine have succeeded only in raising their price. Since the demand for addictive drugs is highly inelastic, quantity demanded falls little. Rather, addicts resort to more crime to pay the higher price. Streets become more violent and community life is further destabilized.

Our antidrug policy has not only not reduced the number of addicts, it may have inadvertently created more. It may have been responsible for the emergence of crack-cocaine.

Despite the expenditure of vast sums of money and enormous international effort, great quantities of cocaine still found its way to the United States market in the 1980s. But the price, which had been high, was now much higher, a reflection of greater risk (ONDCP 1991a). Because of its high price, cocaine had largely been a drug of the affluent, although lower-income persons sometimes used it, frequently turning to crime if they became addicted (NIDA 1990; Collins et al. 1985). Eventually a California entrepreneur discovered that cocaine hydrochloride salt could easily be processed into potent crystals using baking soda and water. Compared to freebased cocaine, it was easy and safe to process and administer. Better yet, in perhaps the most evil manifestation of American marketing genius, it enabled a dealer to break $1,000 worth of cocaine into 2,500-milligram units worth about $2500 when sold by the dose for as little as $2.50. A gram of cocaine was unaffordable to many but a hit of crack was within everyone's grasp. Thus a great business opportunity opened up as the demand associated with a price reduction was found to be very elastic—price fell and quantity demanded increased immensely. So did profits. Consumers bought a drug that provided an intensely pleasurable rush and immediately craved more, much more. As a result they spent an enormous amount on drugs, suffered serious personal and medical consequences, imposed dreadful costs on society and increased drug profits by buying a drug that may not have existed were it not for our drug control policies. The same could be said of certain other drugs, primarily the amphetamine analog "designer drugs." They may have emerged primarily in response to our restrictive drug policies.

This conclusion is, of course, highly speculative. But other conclusions are inescapable: The War on Drugs has been both costly and cost-ineffective. It has resulted in increased crime and produced tremendous collateral damage. And it has generated terrible social costs. We had underestimated the enemy.

Alternative Approaches

A more effective and rational drug policy would place greater emphasis on demand reduction through education, research and rehabilitation. It would also, paradoxically, embody legalization and regulation.

Legalization

A growing number of economists, foremost among them Milton Friedman, favor restricted legalization of illicit drugs (Coletti). Their justification is partly rooted in civil libertarianism—that people should be free to make choices—informed choices, that is—even if those choices are harmful, as long as they do not impose costs on others. The weakness of this argument with respect to drugs is that consumers' knowledge of drugs and their addictive potential is often highly imperfect and that, for a great variety of reasons, people sometimes make choices that appear rational at the moment but are decidedly not. Thus teenagers take up smoking, men drive intoxicated and women take their first hit of crack. Another weakness is that drug use does impose costs on others.

Yet therein lies the strength of the legalization argument: drug use does generate social costs but the criminalization of drug use has only increased those costs. Legalization will substantially reduce social costs. It may also enhance the effectiveness of our educational and rehabilitative efforts.

Most drugs should be legalized and their use restricted. However, not all drugs should be given the same legal status. Some should not be legalized at all.

Marijuana: Marijuana should be legalized. It is absurd that the government continually identifies the dangerous drugs as cocaine, heroin, marijuana, and PCP. Marijuana simply does not fit into that category. It is far less dangerous than many other drugs, both licit and illicit. Approximately 2,500,000 people died from cigarette smoking during the years 1984 to 1988. Another 500,000 died from alcohol-related causes. About 7,500 deaths were related to heroin during that time, and 6,500 to cocaine. Yet none were attributed to marijuana (USDHHS 1991a).

Marijuana appears to have neither the acute nor the chronic deleterious effects on the body that other substances have. Smoking great quantities over a very long period of time would do severe damage to the lungs but, as noted earlier, such use is rare and, despite the fact that marijuana use has been pervasive for over 25 years, no lung cancer deaths have yet been attributed to it. (Ironically, as Kleiman pointed out, the toxins in marijuana smoke are greatly reduced when inhaled through a water pipe. Yet most states have antiparaphernalia laws that forbid their sale and thus force users to smoke marijuana cigarettes, a more injurious delivery system.)

Marijuana does impair perception and judgment and could therefore contribute to accidents. Yet few marijuana-related motor vehicle crashes have been uncovered, and the great majority of those involved drivers who had also consumed large quantities of alcohol (Dufour & Moskowitz).

Maternal marijuana use has not been associated with birth defects, developmental delays or preterm births as have cigarettes, alcohol, heroin and cocaine (Silverman; Zuckerman et al.). Heavy marijuana smoking during pregnancy conceivably could, like cigarette smoking, impede fetal oxygenation and impair the baby's growth (Zuckerman et al.). However, studies of maternal marijuana smoking have not yet found this outcome (Silverman).

Indeed, there is much that has not been found about marijuana but not for lack of looking. Millions of Americans have smoked it over the last three decades and hundreds of studies have been conducted on its effects, yet no short-, medium- or long-term marijuana-related diseases or disorders have been uncovered. If any existed they should have been apparent by now. As Kleiman remarked, the silence of the literature on these issues is striking.

Cigarettes and alcohol have killed millions and are legal. Marijuana has killed no one, yet over 400,000 people were arrested on marijuana charges in 1988 alone (USDJ 1990b, modified).

The reason most frequently given for marijuana's prohibition is that it is considered a "gateway" drug, that is, marijuana use is assumed to lead to the use of other drugs. As evidence, government sources point out that 75 percent of those who have used marijuana 200 or more times have also tried cocaine, whereas fewer than 1 percent of those who never tried marijuana have used cocaine (USDHHS 1991a). On the surface, this argument appears convincing, but a closer examination reveals it to be spurious. People who more frequently use marijuana may be more willing to try other drugs and, since drugs are traded only on the black market, are more likely to have access to other drugs. But such drug use appears to be far from compulsive. Indeed, marijuana use does not appear to be a gateway even to further marijuana use. Over 55 percent of all persons who ever smoked marijuana smoked it at most 10 times; only 23 percent smoked it 100 times or more. More marijuana smokers may have gone on to use cocaine but, of everyone who ever tried cocaine, over one-third used it 10 times or less. Only 9 percent used it more than 100 times (NIDA 1990). If marijuana truly was a gateway drug, millions more people would be using dangerous drugs and would be using them more frequently. Yet the number of persons who ever used marijuana is more than 3 times the number of those who used cocaine and 35 times the number of those who used heroin (NIDA 1990). To assume that persons who use hard drugs use them because they first used marijuana is to commit a post hoc fallacy.

There are several good reasons to legalize marijuana other than that consumers should be free to purchase a product providing utility in excess of internal and external costs. Legalization would greatly reduce the social costs of marijuana, as those costs stem not so much from consumers' choice to use marijuana, but from the government's choice to forbid its use. Legalization would save billions of dollars in drug law enforcement and its associated criminal justice costs. A significant portion of our war chest could thus be put to more productive use. Furthermore, marijuana is a multibillion-dollar industry that could, and should, be taxed—both to discourage excessive use and to raise revenue. Legalizing marijuana would additionally relieve drug merchants of billions of dollars of illegal and untaxed income, thereby reducing the incentive for crime and the funds that may finance more unsavory ventures. Also, marijuana that is legally packaged and sold could be uniformly graded for potency, providing useful consumer information and reducing consumer fraud.

This is not to say that marijuana use should be encouraged or endorsed. The use of any psychoactive substance entails certain risks. The downside of legalization is that it would increase demand, especially at first when legal accessibility is a novelty. The increase would subside as some new users found they had little taste for the product, but, unfortunately, some new users might experience psychological dependency.

Marijuana should not be left to an unregulated market partly for this reason. It should be restricted. No advertising must be permitted. Advertising would only encourage use as it does for cigarettes and alcohol. As with cigarettes, marijuana smoking must be restricted. It should not be allowed in public places, as the environmental smoke it produces is potentially hazardous to the nonuser and may elicit unwanted consciousness altering as well. As with alcohol, sales should be limited to state-licensed outlets, both for revenue enhancement purposes and to limit use by minors. This restriction would not be difficult to circumvent, however, as marijuana, unlike alcohol, can be easily and cheaply produced. The market can be very easily entered. Yet it would not be wise to devote many resources to tracking such evasions. They are needed elsewhere and, unlike illegally produced alcohol, which may be hazardous to consume, moonshine marijuana is not a dangerous product.

We should also forbid distribution to and use by minors. Research suggests that use by adolescents is amotivational and interferes with schoolwork. This is doubtless true, especially of frequent smokers, as concentration and memory are impaired when one is inebriated and marijuana use is frequently followed by sleepiness. However, adolescents being what they are, they will and do smoke marijuana. Making it legal will no doubt increase its availability, reduce the risks associated with it and lead to more adolescent marijuana use. Therefore our antidrug educational programs must stress responsible use.

The point must be made that any psychoactive substance should be used only in strictest moderation and in low-risk situations. Misuse can be dangerous. Marijuana, like alcohol, should not be used when responsibility or sharp faculties are demanded, such as at work or during the school week. Use on the job can impair productivity, cause accidents and be costly to employers. It could endanger the public safety. Use during the school week is bound to be detrimental to scholastic performance. And never should anyone drive when under the influence. Although marijuana may not impair driving to the extent alcohol does, it does affect judgment, perception and reflexes. Worse still is the use of marijuana and alcohol together, a combination favored by teenagers and young adults. It results in exponentially greater performance deficits, as marijuana exacerbates the impairment properties of alcohol (USDHHS 1991a). Drunk driving laws should be expanded to cover driving when inebriated by any substance. Even though there is no easy way to definitively gauge intoxication from drugs like marijuana (a blood or urine test is required), high-profile publicity could be a deterrent.

Another reason, perhaps the best reason, marijuana should be legalized and honestly discussed is that it would give our antidrug campaign greater credibility. When marijuana is put in the same category as heroin, cocaine, PCP and psychotherapeutic pharmaceuticals, suspicion is cast on the entire program. The evidence of tens of millions of Americans having smoked marijuana with little ill effect casts doubt on the truth of our claims about the harmfulness of other drugs, drugs that truly are hazardous.

Hallucinogens: LSD, peyote and mescaline should also be legalized. They are relatively harmless and the cost of prohibition, both in terms of law enforcement and civil liberties, is great. However, since they cause greater distress to a larger proportion of users, since they are more impairing, since their effects are longer lasting and since frequent heavy use can be damaging, their use should be strongly discouraged. Legalizing use must not be construed as condoning use. Unregulated production and distribution, especially to minors, should not be tolerated; sanctions should be strict. Illegally manufactured LSD may contain harmful additives, and use of any hallucinogen by adolescents should be kept to a minimum.

PCP, however, should not be legalized. Too harmful to the user and too frequently evocative of violently assaultive behavior, the dangers of PCP are exacerbated by the longevity of its effects. The contribution to crime resulting from our efforts at suppression are most probably less than the contribution to crime and antisocial behavior that might result from possible greater accessibility. Fortunately, PCP use has been declining, largely because many users find its effects unpleasurable. Unfortunately, many former PCP users have taken up crack instead (NNICC).

Heroin: Heroin should be legalized with distribution restricted to medically certified addicts. Heroin is indeed very harmful to the user; however, our attempts at prohibition have engendered greater harm to society. Making heroin available to addicts will greatly reduce drug-trafficking-related crime but, most important to most people, it will dramatically reduce street crime. Criminal behavior is not associated with heroin addiction in England, where heroin is available by prescription (Mott). In addition, taking the profit out of heroin will reduce the number of recruits to the heroin-using population. Since there will be no financial incentive to initiate the uninitiated, the number of heroin users will fall as addicts die or become rehabilitated. Thus the psychosocial costs of addiction will also be reduced and fewer families will experience the tragedy of an addicted member.

Another advantage of legalization is that product potency could be kept within identified and safe limits and dangerous contaminants would not be present. Also, sterile injection equipment and AIDS information could be distributed along with the drug, thereby slowing the spread of disease.

Heroin could be distributed by prescription or at designated sites, but it should be free. No strings must be attached. If distribution is tied to enforced participation in a rehabilitation program or if the heroin could only be administered on the premises, the black market would continue to thrive.

The danger of making heroin readily available to addicts is that it reduces the cost of addiction and thus weakens a deterrent to experimentation. The danger is real, since, despite a greatly shrunken market, the retention of strict sanctions against extralegal distribution, and dealers' lesser ability to charge risk-compensatory prices, some heroin would remain available on the street. However, even though more individuals might be tempted to try it, the net social benefit would be great. The savings in criminal justice costs alone would be enormous.

Cocaine: Cocaine is a trickier issue. Many economists would say legalize it, regulate it, tax it and warn people of the dangers of using it. This sounds like a rational approach, as our current attempt at prohibition has not only been a costly failure, it has led to unprecedented violence on our city streets. However, like PCP, cocaine presents dangers other than those stemming from its illegality. Since it severely stresses the cardiovascular system and since its effects are of such brief duration that addicts immediately crave more, to allow them all the cocaine they demand may be to kill them. This may not be the worst outcome, as the point could be made that they are killing themselves (and others) already. What is worse is that cocaine's mood-altering properties often produce mean or violent behavior and abrogation of parental responsibility and that crack-cocaine often elicits promiscuous behavior resulting in the birth of a drug-affected baby.

Still, as long as demand remains strong, legalization with distribution restricted to certified addicts may be the best strategy. Less restrictive legalization would create more problems than it solves.

A realistic observer would find it difficult to imagine that any of this will come to pass. At first glance, such a radical policy revision appears to contradict our educational messages and could be considered a weakening of resolve. But even though more critical analysis would reconcile education and legalization, legalization would still be virtually impossible politically. The opposition to the mere distribution of clean needles to check the spread of AIDS makes that clear. Rather, we will continue to pay huge sums in tax dollars to keep the price of drugs high so that addicts have to steal what we have left in order to meet the higher prices. Drug addicts are not the only ones living in Wonderland.

Research

The objectives of drug control research are to promote more efficient drug law enforcement, to collect and evaluate data, to strengthen prevention efforts and to increase the effectiveness of treatment programs.

The first category includes the improvement of contraband detection technology and improved communication security for law enforcement operatives. According to the ONDCP, these and other law enforcement technologies are continually being upgraded.

Data collection on drug use and trends, while imperfect, has been improving. Studies are being conducted more frequently, sample sizes have been enlarged and NIDA will make an effort to reach some of the hitherto excluded populations. But the collection and evaluation of prevention and treatment data are highly inadequate and thus undermine our ability to forge effective programs (ONDCP 1991a; USGAO 1990d).

Prevention research seeks to discover why people choose to take drugs and why they become addicted.

Use-prevention research emphasizes identification of the psychosocial and behavioral factors associated with the propensity to initiate drug use. Such research has been fairly fruitful in terms of information gathering. We know, for example, that children whose parents or siblings abuse drugs or alcohol are much more likely to become substance abusers (Kumpfer). Lack of parental affection, concern, involvement and general parenting skills are associated with drug and alcohol use by children, as is coming from a broken home or one that manifests unusual levels of conflict or stress (Hundleby & Mercer; AMA). But the strongest predictor of substance abuse is use by peers (Hundleby & Mercer). Children who exhibit antisocial behavior at an early age, who become involved with the juvenile system, who are poor academic achievers and who show little interest in school are also at elevated risk, as are children who are rebellious, alienated from societal values and who have a high tolerance for deviant behavior (Kumpfer; AMA 1991). To these traits, at least with respect to addictive drugs, economists would add a preference for risk taking, an inability to accurately estimate risk, perceived low opportunity costs, a short time horizon and an inability to delay gratification. In other words, persons who take up hard drugs may be risk-taking thrill seekers who live for the moment. They may also be ill informed, unintelligent or simply arrogant.

However, even though we have been able to isolate risk predictors, even to the point of identifying a "vulnerability syndrome," there has been little practical application of that knowledge (Kumpfer). It is not enough to know the warning signs. Early warning must be met by early intervention.

Addiction-prevention research seeks to identify the biomedical, neural or genetic underpinnings of addiction, primarily with respect to the children of alcohol abusers. Investigation into the physiological aspect of addiction seeks, among other things, to identify the biomedical mechanisms that transmit heightened vulnerability and the genetic markers that indicate heightened vulnerability. Such knowledge would allow the development of preemptive intervention strategies such as genetic counseling, fetal testing, psychological counseling or pharmacological intervention. But, although such research holds great promise, little has yet been determined (Kumpfer; Schuckit 1987). More research is needed.

The objective of treatment research is to enable more effective rehabilitation therapies. Research on treatment for alcoholism has proceeded apace; but, while federal funding for drug treatment research has increased greatly in recent years, according to a scathing report by the General Accounting Office, the monies have not been well spent (USGAO 1990d).

Treatment models that effectively meet today's drug abuse challenges are needed. Yet NIDA, the agency principally responsible for drug abuse treatment research, has failed to keep abreast of the very drug use tends it tracks. As of 1990, it was still emphasizing opiate addiction and the treatment of male addicts (USGAO 1990d). Treatment modalities that are at least moderately effective in treating male heroin addiction are not effective in treating the new patterns of abuse, foremost among which is cocaine addiction. The number of cocaine addicts today greatly exceeds the number of heroin addicts, yet narcotic addiction still claims the lion's share of research funding. Another newly emerging trend is polydrug addiction. Heroin addicts, for example, are also likely to be addicted to cocaine, amphetamines, benzodiazepines or alcohol (USGAO 1990h). Also, the fact that increasing numbers of women, including pregnant women, are addicted and have special treatment needs is not being addressed (USGAO 1990d).

Since these shortcomings have been pointed out, more federally funded research has been conducted on cocaine addiction. Fundamental advances have been made in identifying the neural mechanisms by which cocaine and other stimulants produce their effects (ONDCP 1991a). These will, one hopes, allow the development of medications that can block cocaine euphoria and relieve cocaine craving.

Much more research is necessary. A great deal is still unknown about treating even heroin addiction, much less the newer patterns of abuse. Without more efficacious treatment, consequential demand reduction is stalled.

Rehabilitation

The primary goal of drug treatment is to reduce addicts' drug dependency and abuse. Some treatment programs include an increased ability to earn legitimate income, maintain a household and care for dependents as client goals (Hubbard et al.). The major concomitant social policy objective is reduction in crime. Success in achieving any of these goals would reduce social costs, thus justifying public funding of treatment programs.

Success, however, is usually limited at best. This is partly because many treatment programs are not well managed, many addicts are not amenable to rehabilitation and addiction itself is an intractable condition.

Like alcoholism, drug addiction is a disease that cannot yet be cured. Chemically dependent persons can only hope to eventually gain control over their substance-abuse problem. Many never do. The great majority of addicts relapse rapidly and frequently after treatment and experience recurring cycles of remission and relapse that often persist throughout their lives (Maddox & Desmond).

Treatment modalities include individual psychotherapy, group counseling, self-help support groups and pharmacologic intervention, often offered in combination. They may be provided on an inpatient or outpatient basis.

Many treatment centers report long waiting lists and many social service agencies report great difficulty finding treatment slots for clients, but improved access to rehabilitation programs is not enough. We need improved programs. More effective treatment will result from further research on addiction and de-addiction and more efficient utilization of existing facilities. Program effectiveness can be enhanced by longer duration of treatment, lower client-staff ratios, greater emphasis on life management skills including literacy and job training, and improved follow-up or aftercare. More effective treatment, while costly, will ultimately reduce the demand for treatment, as fewer addicts will repeatedly reenter treatment.

The case of heroin treatment best exemplifies the tenacity of addiction and the pattern of remission and relapse associated with recovery. It also demonstrates the need for further research and supports the argument for restricted legalization.

Most heroin treatment programs rely heavily on methadone, an orally administered synthetic narcotic designed to prevent withdrawal symptoms and block the euphoric effects of heroin. However, methadone also produces euphoria and may itself be addictive. Some heroin addicts are able to wean themselves from methadone and remain drug-free, at least temporarily, but others require continued methadone maintenance.

Not only is methadone addictive and inebriating, it is only partially effective as a blocking agent. Many methadone clients continue to use heroin while in treatment. A GAO study of 24 methadone maintenance programs found that in ten of the clinics over 20 percent of the patients continued using heroin after six months of treatment; in two of the clinics almost half continued use (USGAO 1990h). Indeed, methadone clinics quickly become centers of drug dealing (Calahan in Doweiko).

The ineffectualness of current heroin treatment programs is further evidenced by their poor retention rates. Of the 24 clinics in the GAO study, 10 had lost 20 percent or more of their patients before three months of treatment; 5 had lost 30 percent or more. By six months, 17 clinics had lost 30 percent or more of their clients; 9 had lost 40 percent or more (USGAO 1990h).

Even addicts who complete treatment may never have stopped using heroin; those who do stop almost invariably relapse. One of the largest follow-up studies of addicts after treatment found that 47 percent had relapsed to daily narcotic use within one year (Simpson & Marsh). By the twelfth year, 75 percent had relapsed to daily use at some point and 24 percent were currently daily users. Another major study found that 70 percent of treated addicts relapse to some level of opoid use within one month of completing treatment (Maddux & Desmond). In a five-year follow-up study, Duvall and colleagues found a voluntary abstinence rate of only 2 percent; 46 percent of the subjects were still addicted and 24 percent were involuntarily abstinent due to institutionalization (in Maddux & Desmond). Even prolonged abstinence does not portend lifelong abstinence. Maddux and Desmond found that one-third of their subjects who achieved three or more years of abstinence eventually resumed daily narcotic use.

This is not to imply that treatment is useless. Many addicts do benefit from rehabilitation. They reduce their drug use, reduce their criminal activity, find employment and enjoy a more stable family life. While individual programs vary in effectiveness, well-managed residential programs that provide comprehensive support services, low client-staff ratios and quality aftercare are the most effective. Effectiveness is also influenced by length of stay. Three months is minimal; one year or more is optimal (USGAO 1990h). Residential programs cost on average three times more per day than outpatient programs, yet are not only more effective, but are also more cost-effective (Hubbard et al.). Evaluating various treatment modalities and estimating the social cost savings resulting from crime reduction, Hubbard and colleagues concluded that money spent on residential treatment generated the greatest returns. Predatory crime was lessened by the greatest amount both during treatment and in the year following treatment. There is reason to believe that other benefits, such as increased productivity, lessened demand for social services, and fewer cases of AIDS transmission, also occur to a greater extent.

But even the best programs appear to be only moderately successful. This may be partly because their real effectiveness is obscured, obscured because the criminalization of drug use has filled treatment programs with addicts who have little desire for rehabilitation and recovery.

When drug suppression efforts make heroin less available or force its price upward, many heroin addicts turn to methadone clinics. They are not pursuing recovery. They simply need narcotics. Methadone will suffice until heroin is once again accessible. Another source of candidates with poor prognosis for recovery is the criminal justice system. In Los Angeles, 40 percent of the clients in public drug treatment programs have been remanded by the courts. In Atlanta the proportion is 33 percent, and in Boston it is 30 percent (USGAO 1991b). Even before the War on Drugs was declared, when it was still just a police action, many drug law offenders, and other offenders as well, were remanded to treatment either as an alternative to incarceration or as a condition of parole. Such involuntary admission is predictive of a poor treatment outcome. If heroin addicts were able to legally and freely obtain the heroin they crave, our rehabilitation programs, now understaffed and overcrowded, could better serve those addicts for whom recovery is a personal goal.

In short, rehabilitation is a worthy public investment, although we often expect more than it can currently deliver. When the suggested systemic reforms are made, when a pharmaceutical analog superior to methadone is found (three are currently in the pipeline but have serious limitations) and when parallel analogs have been found for cocaine and for polydrug addiction, returns will be all the greater.

The War on Drugs as currently being fought is not winnable. Given that people have always sought some form of chemical consciousness altering and that some people will always crave more than is legally or safely available, the war may never be decisively won. However, a strategy that accepts these basic realities, that retreats when the costs of advance are great and the benefits small and that attacks on those fronts where the potential for victory is greatest, maximizes force, minimizes causalities and achieves a more favorable balance of power.

3

Infectious Diseases

Contagious diseases are not often directly associated with behavior. However, the diseases that most worry public health officials today—AIDS and sexually transmitted diseases (STDs)—decidedly are.

At least one STD, syphilis, may have existed since biblical times. It once killed its victims but is seldom fatal today. AIDS, which can also be sexually transmitted, is very new and always fatal. Yet the two are linked and have provoked vociferous debates of public policy, raising emotional and ethical issues as well as legal and medical questions. For whereas it has long been widely acknowledged that a legitimate role of government is to protect its citizens against dangerously infectious agents, the advisability of proposed protective measures has often been hotly disputed. It is no different today. In spite of centuries of medical, scientific and social progress, we still have disease and we still quarrel over how to deal with it. Perhaps never more so than in the case of AIDS.

ACQUIRED IMMUNE DEFICIENCY SYNDROME

Epidemiology and Pathology

AIDS is a progressively severe weakening of the immune system that renders a person highly susceptible to certain infections and types of cancer. It is caused by the human immunodeficiency virus (HIV). HIV attacks particular white blood cells called "helper" T-cells, "helper" because they help other white blood cells produce antibodies to fight infection. It appears that HIV also directly attacks the brain.

The virus concentrates in an infected person's blood and semen. It is transmitted when virus particles or infected cells gain access to another person's bloodstream. This can occur during anal intercourse, vaginal intercourse and oral-genital contact. The likelihood of transmission is greatest if there is a tear or other opening in the mucous membrane exposed to risk. The other major routes of transmission are the sharing of needles among intravenous drug users (IVDUs), infusion with tainted blood supplies, and the prenatal passing to an unborn child or the postpartum passing to a breast-fed child by an infected mother.

The virus cannot be transmitted by a handshake or sneeze, or through food prepared by an infected person. It is not transmitted through casual contact or by activities related to living with or caring for an AIDS patient that do not involve direct exposure, such as unprotected sex. It is not transmitted by sharing beds, eating utensils or even toothbrushes with an infected person. But when the virus is transmitted it is invariably fatal.

HIV-infection is confirmed with considerable accuracy by laboratory blood tests that detect the pertinent antibodies, protein produced by the immune system in response to HIV-infection. A person who has the antibodies is said to be seropositive. Almost 50 percent of seropositive persons are diagnosed with full-blown AIDS within five years.

Persons are usually diagnosed with AIDS after suffering fever, weight loss, swollen lymph nodes, diarrhea and multiple long-lasting infections, usually of the skin and mouth. Diagnosis is also often triggered by the appearance of an opportunistic infection, one that rarely causes disease in a patient with a normal immune system but is life threatening to an AIDS patient. The most common is *Pneumocystis carinii* pneumonia. Kaposi's sarcoma, a form of cancer that is otherwise rare among young people in this country, is also common among AIDS patients.

We once thought that many HIV-infected people could remain alive and well indefinitely. Whereas some did go on to experience debilitating problems such as extreme fatigue, weight loss, fever and chronic diarrhea known as AIDS-related complex (ARC), the symptoms stopped short of full-blown AIDS. Now, however, we know that everyone infected with HIV will eventually develop AIDS. We had underestimated the latency period. It may be as long as 15 years.

The average length of time between diagnosis of AIDS and death, for all the cases reported since the disease was first identified in 1979, is 13 months, biased downward by the brief life expectancy of earlier victims. With earlier diagnosis and improved drug therapies, a victim's life expectancy has been extended. It now averages 18 months. It is still dreadfully short.

Incidence, Trends and Projections

The number of AIDS cases has grown rapidly, both as the disease has spread and as diagnosis and reporting have improved. The leap in cases in 1987, depicted in Table 3.1, is partly due to the Centers for Disease Control's (CDC) liberalizing of its definition of AIDS cases. Tables 3.2, 3.3 and 3.4 depict the distribution of cases.

Table 3.1
AIDS Cases Diagnosed by Year: United States, Pre-1981 to 1991

Year of Diagnosis	AIDS Cases
Pre-1981	85
1981	310
1982	1,110
1983	2,998
1984	6,043
1985	11,315
1986	18,423
1987	27,464
1988	33,297
1989	37,556
1990	36,633
1991 *	28,052

*Cases for 1991 are underrepresented due to reporting delays.

Source: Centers for Disease Control. *HIV/AIDS Surveillance
Report, January 1992.*

These numbers should be read with caution. They may seriously undercount
the actual number of AIDS cases. The General Accounting Office estimates
that prior to 1987, 15 percent of AIDS cases fell outside the CDC's overly
restrictive diagnostic criteria; 9 percent were still excluded after liberalization.
For this and a variety of other reasons, including restrictive testing requirements, failure to diagnose and failure to report, the GAO estimates that
a full one-third of all AIDS cases were not tabulated by the CDC (USGAO
1989b).

While undercounting exists in all categories, the GAO believes it has been
especially high among IVDUs and married men. It estimates that roughly 50
percent of the AIDS- and other HIV-related fatalities among IVDUs (who,
as of 1991, according to the CDC, constituted 23 percent of AIDS cases) were
not diagnosed as such. Rather, these fatalities were attributed to pneumonia,
tuberculosis, or other infectious diseases. The GAO also estimates that one-
third of the accurately diagnosed cases among married men are intentionally
not reported as such because of the stigma associated with AIDS.

New evidence suggests that undercounting is also great among women, who
may manifest AIDS in ways not familiar to health care professionals and not
fitting earlier CDC definitions. Recent CDC research has indicated that only
35 percent of the women who died of AIDS and related causes actually met
the official criteria and were tallied as AIDS fatalities (Knox 1990).

Table 3.2
Male Adult/Adolescent AIDS Cases by Exposure Category and Race/Ethnicity: United States, Cumulative Totals through December 1991

Male Adult/adolescent Exposure Category	Non-Hispanic White		Non-Hispanic Black		Hispanic		Total*	
	No.	(%)	No.	(%)	No.	(%)	No.	(%)
Homosexual contact	83,205	(80)	20,540	(44)	13,240	(46)	118,362	(65)
IV drug use (heterosexual)	7,017	(7)	16,798	(36)	11,083	(39)	35,048	(19)
Homosexual contact and IV drug use	7,547	(7)	3,578	(8)	1,925	(7)	13,135	(7)
Hemophilia/coagulation disorder	1,373	(1)	127	(0)	137	(0)	1,671	(1)
Heterosexual contact:**	813	(1)	3,307	(7)	548	(2)	4,687	(3)
sex with IV drug user	483		1,077		313		1,882	
born in or sex with person born in Africa or particular Caribbean countries	48		1,827		20		1,903	
sex with HIV-infected persons, risk not specified	232		383		197		813	
Transfusion	1,938	(2)	418	(1)	259	(1)	2,679	(1)
Other/undetermined	2,287	(2)	2,269	(5)	1,432	(5)	6,114	(3)
Male subtotal	104,180		47,037		28,624		181,696	
Racial/ethnic % of subtotal	57		26		16			

* Totals are greater because Asians, Pacific Islanders and Native Americans were omitted. Their percentage of the population and incidence of AIDS are both very low.
** Not all possibilities are listed.

Source: Centers for Disease Control. *HIV/AIDS Surveillance Report, January 1992.*

Table 3.3

Female Adult/Adolescent AIDS Cases by Exposure Category and Race/Ethnicity: United States, Cumulative Totals through December 1991

Female Adult/adolescent Exposure Category	Non-Hispanic White		Non-Hispanic Black		Hispanic		Total*	
	No.	(%)	No.	(%)	No.	(%)	No.	(%)
IV drug use	2,268	(41)	6,185	(55)	2,191	(50)	10,705	(50)
Hemophilia/coagulation disorder	29	(1)	10	(0)	3	(0)	42	(0)
Heterosexual contact**	1,700	(31)	3,784	(34)	1,694	(39)	7,249	(34)
sex with IV drug user	859		2,244		1,343		4,484	
sex with bisexual male	343		216		78		651	
sex with person with hemophilia	78		10		4		94	
born in or sex with person born in Africa or particular Caribbean countries	15		772		5		794	
sex with HIV-infected persons, risk not specified	303		514		236		1,065	
Blood transfusion	1,055	(19)	349	(3)	220	(5)	1,668	(8)
Other/undetermined	414	(8)	828	(7)	292	(7)	1,561	(7)
Female subtotal	5,466		11,156		4,400		21,225	
Racial/ethnic % of subtotal	26		53		21			
Total Adult/Adolescent AIDS Cases	109,646		58,193		33,024		202,921	
Racial/Ethnic % Total	54		29		16			

* Totals are greater because because Asians, Pacific Islanders and Native Americans were omitted. Their percentage of the population and incidence of AIDS are both very low.
** Not all possibilities are listed.

Source: Centers for Disease Control. HIV/AIDS Surveillance Report, January 1992.

Table 3.4
Pediatric AIDS Cases by Exposure Category and Race/Ethnicity: United States, Cumulative Totals through December 1991

Pediatric Exposure Category	Non-Hispanic White		Non-Hispanic Black		Hispanic		Total*	
	No.	(%)	No.	(%)	No.	(%)	No.	(%)
Hemophilia/coagulation disorder	112	(15)	22	(1)	26	(3)	163	(5)
Mother with/at risk for HIV infection.**	465	(63)	1,704	(92)	742	(87)	2,936	(85)
IV drug user	224		833		365		1,430	
sex with IV drug user	91		269		238		603	
sex with bisexual male	22		24		14		61	
born in or sex with person born in Africa or particular Caribbean countries	1		254		2		258	
sex with HIV-infected persons, risk not specified	30		70		40		144	
has HIV infection risk not specified	62		222		65		354	
Blood transfusion	152	(21)	65	(4)	66	(8)	289	(8)
Other/undetermined	11	(2)	48	(3)	19	(2)	7	(2)
Pediatric subtotal	739		1,844		854		3,471	
Racial/ethnic % of subtotal	22		53		25			
TOTAL AIDS CASES	110,385		60,037		33,878		206,392	
Racial/ethnic % of total	53		29		16			

* Totals are greater because Asians, Pacific Islanders and Native Americans were omitted. Their percentage of the population and incidence of AIDS are both very low.
** Not all possibilities are listed.

Source: Centers for Disease Control. HIV/AIDS Surveillance Report, January 1992.

It is also thought that a significant, though indeterminate, number of infected persons commit suicide rather than endure additional suffering. They also are not listed as AIDS fatalities.

Future counts should be more accurate, as the CDC has once again liberalized its definition of AIDS. As of January 1992, persons who are HIV infected and have a T-cell count of less than 200 per cubic millimeter of blood (the normal presence is about 1,000) are diagnosed with AIDS regardless of other symptoms. This would add an estimated 150,000 to 200,000 victims, doubling the 1991 tally, if everyone meeting that criteria were identified (Golan).

The Prevalence of HIV Infection

The number of AIDS cases alone, even if accurately tabulated, does not describe the full scope of the epidemic. For that we need to know the incidence of the AIDS virus in the population. The CDC estimates that 1,000,000 Americans are currently HIV-infected (CDC 1992d).

HIV prevalence differs among various sociodemographic groups. They include:

Male homosexuals: Most of the estimates place HIV prevalence in the 20 to 50 percent range. The rate in San Francisco may be as high as 70 percent (NRC 1989). Since blacks and Hispanics constitute a disproportionate percentage of homosexual and homosexual-IVDU AIDS cases, it is probable that their HIV infection rate also exceeds that of white homosexuals.

Intravenous drug users: Studies of heroin addicts in drug rehabilitation programs have found infection rates of up to 65 percent (Hahn et al.). There is evidence that seroprevalence among the 85 percent of IVDUs not in treatment is greater. Hahn and colleagues estimate that one-third of the country's 1.3 million IVDUs are HIV-infected, with prevalence 5 to 14 times greater among black IVDUs and 3 to 4 times greater among Hispanic IVDUs than among whites. IVDUs who are also homosexual males have somewhat higher rates but, overall, the seroprevalence rates for male and female IVDUs are about equal (NRC 1989). Seroprevalence is greatest in New York City, northern New Jersey and Puerto Rico (Hahn et al.). A study of IVDUs in San Francisco found seropositive rates among IV (intravenous) cocaine users to be more than three times greater than among heroin users (Chaisson et al.). Also, since a cocaine high is of relatively short duration, cocaine IVDUs inject with far greater frequency than do heroin users, increasing their risk of HIV infection yet more. Blacks, and to a lesser extent Hispanics, not only were more likely to inject cocaine than white drug abusers, but, among cocaine IVDUs, had two to ten times higher seropositive rates.

Hemophiliacs: Prevalence rates are reported to be 70 percent among persons with hemophilia A and 35 percent among persons with hemophilia B, uniformly distributed across the country (NRC 1989).

Prostitutes: Up to 45 percent of prostitutes are estimated to carry the AIDS virus. Rates are highest in large inner cities in which drug use is common, such as New York, Miami and Detroit (NRC 1989). Wallace found 50 percent of the IV-drug-using prostitutes in Harlem in 1987 to be seropositive (in Hahn et al.). Infection is three to four times higher in prostitutes who are also IVDUs. It is twice as high in black and Hispanic prostitutes as in whites (NRC 1989).

College students: A study of almost 17,000 college students across the country found that 0.2 percent tested positive for HIV. Most were older (over 24); almost all were men (Gayle et al.).

Military personnel: The U.S. Department of Defense estimates that in spite of policies against homosexual and drug-using behavior, 0.06 to 0.08 percent of active duty personnel have acquired HIV infections each year since 1986 (CDC 1990f). Among new recruits, seroprevalence rates among blacks and Hispanics were 6.9 and 3.0 times higher than among whites (NRC 1989).

Runaway and homeless adolescents: Clients of Covenant House, a New York City shelter for troubled adolescents, averaged seropositivity rates of 5.3 percent in 1988 and 1989. Other than male homosexual activity, the strongest risk factors were crack use, engaged in by 38 percent of the teens interviewed, and prostitution, practiced by 29 percent (Stricof et al.).

Disadvantaged adolescents: HIV screening of Job Corps students, primarily high school dropouts from inner city communities, found extremely high seroprevalence rates. The highest rates were found among black and Hispanic youths from large northeastern cities, where up to 1 in 40 21-year-olds were infected. Since these youths are considered a sentinel population, more representative of inner city youth than either military recruits or runaways, their high infection rates are alarming. This was the first study to find infection rates among females to equal or exceed those among males, indicating that heterosexual transmission is becoming more widespread in minority communities (St. Louis et al.).

Homeless persons: An estimated 20 to 30 percent of the homeless in New York City are HIV positive. Most are IVDUs (Spolar). Although increasing, seroprevalence is estimated to be lower among the homeless elsewhere.

Incarcerated persons: Tests conducted on nearly 56,000 prison inmates in 1988 and 1989 found 6.3 percent to be seropositive (CDC 1990j). Tests of 11,000 new entrants to ten state correctional systems in those same years found HIV seroprevalence rates ranging from 2.1 percent to 7.6 percent for men and from 2.5 percent to 14.7 percent for women. Overall, nonwhites had almost twice the seropositivity of whites (Vlahov et al.).

Persons tested at publicly funded testing centers: The CDC supported 63 programs that tested over 1.4 million persons in HIV counseling centers, sexually transmitted disease clinics, family planning clinics, drug treatment centers, colleges, and so forth. Although testees at some sites were undoubtedly at higher risk than others in their subpopulation, the results are still noteworthy. The percent that tested HIV positive by risk category included heterosexuals, 4.0; homosexual and bisexual males, 16.5; heterosexual IVDUs, 11.6; homosexual and bisexual male IVDUs, 17.1; and hemophiliacs, 14.0. The percent that tested positive by race and ethnicity were whites, 3.9; blacks, 5.3; and Hispanics, 8.6. As a proportion of those who tested positive, whites comprised 46.2 percent; blacks, 36.2 percent; and Hispanics, 16.9. Overall, 1 of 22 persons who sought publicly funded testing from January 1988 through September 1989 was found to be infected with the AIDS virus (CDC 1990j).

Women of childbearing age: A national sample found an estimated 1.5 per 1,000 women giving birth in 1989 to be seropositive. New York, the District of Columbia, New Jersey and Florida posted the highest rates at 5.8, 5.5, 4.9 and 4.5 per 1,000 respective births. Rates of infection among black women giving birth were 5 to 15 times higher than among white women in the same states (Gwinn et al.). A New York study estimated that 1 of every 151 younger women in the state was HIV infected in 1988, as was 1 in every 77 younger women in New York City. Among women who gave birth in New York City in 1988, seroprevalence was highest among minority women, with rates of 2.17 percent for black women and 1.46 percent for Hispanic women as compared to 0.39 percent for white women (Novick et al.). One in 22 babies born in Newark's University Hospital in mid-1989 was born to a seropositive mother (Boodman 1989b). Rates of infection are likely to be lower elsewhere, as the New York–New Jersey area has an unusually high concentration of infected IVDUs. Women who contract the AIDS virus most often do so through their own or their partner's use of contaminated needles.

Newborn babies: An estimated 1,500 to 2,000 newborns, 0.5 per 1,000 births, were HIV infected in 1989 (CDC 1990f). In New York State, which accounts for about one-third of the nation's pediatric AIDS cases, 0.66 percent of newborns tested positive for HIV antibodies in 1988, as did 1.25 percent of the newborns in New York City. The racial and ethnic distribution mirrored that of the mothers noted above. In zip code areas of high drug use, HIV antibodies were present in from 2.2 percent to 4.0 percent of newborns. About 40 percent of these infants will eventually develop AIDS; the others are only temporarily carrying their infected mothers' antibodies (Novick et al.).

The Distribution of Cases

The distribution of AIDS cases has changed and is expected to continue changing in a similar fashion (see Table 3.5). Homosexuals and whites comprise a smaller proportion of cases; IVDUs, blacks and Hispanics comprise a larger proportion. But the greatest change has been the shift to cases involving heterosexual transmission and, consequently, to women and infants. The number of stricken infants multiplied over 14 times just from 1984 to 1989 (NCHS 1991).

Minority women, accounting for 72 percent of the female cases today (NCHS 1991) are at greater risk for several reasons. They are far less likely than white women to use condoms even when aware of the risk of HIV infection (CDC 1990e). They or their sex partners are more likely to use intravenous drugs.

Table 3.5

Percentage Distributions and Projections of New AIDS Cases by Sex, Age, Exposure Category and Race/Ethnicity, United States: 1984, 1989 and 1993

Classification	1984*	1989	proj: 1993
Male	94%	90%	85%
Female	6%	10%	15%
Adult/adolescent cases	99%	98%	96%
Pediatric cases	1%	2%	**4%
White	61%	55%	43%
Black	25%	31%	38%
Hispanic	13%	13%	19%
Male homosexual/bisexual	65%	59%	51%
Male homosexual/bisexual/IV drug use	9%	7%	4%
Heterosexual IV drug use	18%	22%	28%
Heterosexual transmission	1%	4%	13%

* data for 1984 includes previous years' data.
** Includes perinatal transmission only.

Sources: For 1984 and 1989: National Center for Health Statistics. *Health United States, 1990.* For 1993: Centers for Disease Control. *"HIV Prevalence Estimates and AIDS Case Projections for the United States: Report Based Upon a Workshop." Morbidity and Mortality Weekly Report* 39, no. RR-16 (1990).

Black female IVDUs use condoms at about one-third the rate of black women who do not inject drugs (Ralph & Spigner). Male and female black and Hispanic IVDUs have much higher seroprevalence rates than white IVDUs and are twice as likely to not use clean needles (Schilling et al. 1990).

Also, the number and proportion of female and IVDU cases will continue to increase as crack addicts turn to injectable cocaine for its longer-lived high. Women (and teenagers) comprise a greater proportion of cocaine users than of heroin users. Here too, minorities will be disproportionately affected, as they comprise the majority of crack users.

The results of the screening of Job Corps students indicate that AIDS cases among minority women will be increasing rapidly. Seroprevalence rates among black and Hispanic adolescent women who were high school dropouts, the population hardest to reach, were almost as great or greater than those among males with similar characteristics from their communities (St. Louis et al.). The primary mode of transmission appeared to be heterosexual transmission.

As AIDS in women increases, so will AIDS in children. The hardest hit will be black and Hispanic children, who in 1991 comprised 78 percent of the pediatric cases (CDC 1992a). As current trends become more pronounced, thousands more babies will be born only to suffer and die. At least they, innocent to the end, are not likely to infect anyone else.

Projections

If current trends prevail, AIDS cases will continue to increase as those currently seropositive develop the full-blown disease and many more people become infected. The CDC had estimated that there will be up to 480,000 cumulative cases, including 14,000 babies, by the end of 1993 (CDC 1990f). The new T-cell count diagnostic criteria will possibly double that number.

The first 100,000 cases of AIDS were reported over an 8-year period; the second 100,000 were reported over a 2-year period (CDC 1992a). The third 100,000 cases will no doubt be reported over an even shorter interval.

The Role of Behavior and Choice

We all make behavioral choices intended to promote utility maximization. Some of those choices, like drug abuse, are misguided. They provide only fleeting gratification, bear considerable risk and generate significant costs. Those risks and costs may be greater than anticipated.

No one chooses to contract AIDS. It is a terribly painful and invariably fatal illness. Yet most victims of AIDS were exposed to the disease through behavior of their choosing—practicing unprotected sex or sharing hypodermic needles.

However, many who engaged in such high-risk behavior did not knowingly accept the risk. AIDS was not discovered until 1981.

By then HIV was well established in the gay community, yet no one was aware of it or of the danger it presented. Because of the high level of sexual activity among many gay men and their high frequency of anal intercourse (the sexual activity most conducive to HIV transmission as it more often involves tearing of the membranous lining), infection spread rapidly before transmission mechanisms were understood. This, combined with the median latency period of eight to ten years, means that the majority of the cases among homosexual men probably resulted from behavior that was not known to bear risk.

Intravenous drug users also played a critical role in spreading HIV infection before the mechanics of transmission were known. They not only spread the virus among themselves through sharing injection equipment that carried HIV-contaminated blood, but also infected their sexual partners and their offspring.

Now that AIDS and its transmission are better understood, many people strive to avoid risk-bearing activity. But all too often, those at greatest risk still take the greatest risks.

Homosexual Men

In what Becker and Joseph (p. 407) write "may be the most rapid and profound response to a health threat which has ever been documented," some gay populations have determinedly altered their sexual practices.

Surveys have found that between 50 and 90 percent of gay men in major metropolitan areas now abstain from anal intercourse (NRC 1989). Those that continue the practice more often use a condom. Martin reports that condoms were used in fewer than 1 percent of the episodes of homosexual anal intercourse in 1981, but were used in 19 percent of the episodes in 1985, 60 percent in 1986 and 71 percent in 1987. Individual men who always used a condom during anal intercourse rose from 2 percent in 1981 to 62 percent in 1987. In New York City, 80 percent of gay men either abstained entirely from or always used a condom during anal intercourse (Martin in NRC 1989).

Other high-risk practices among homosexual men, such as large numbers of partners, anonymous partners and extradomestic locations for sex, have also declined dramatically (McKusick et al.). Bath houses, sex clubs and the bathrooms of gay bars and adult movie theaters had functioned much the way shooting galleries did for HIV transmission among IVDUs. Spread was rapid, as men engaged in unprotected sex with large numbers of often unknown partners. Today most homosexual men are less promiscuous and practice safer sex.

However, while it appears that the spread of infection among gay men may be stalled, studies of gay subgroups portend otherwise. Gladwell reports that gay and bisexual men under age 30 are twice as likely to engage in unprotected anal intercourse, half of black gay men practice anal intercourse without condoms and 19 percent of men who practice safe sex eventually relapse. Also, men in nonmetropolitan areas are three times more likely than urban-area men to engage in unsafe sexual practices.

A study of largely white, college-educated homosexual men in Boston uncovered very disturbing information. The study included tests of serostatus. It ran eighteen months, ending June 1987, during which time all the study participants reduced their practice of high-risk sex. But whereas those who tested positive for HIV infection reduced high-risk behavior by the greatest amount, they also practiced it the greatest amount and continued to practice it the greatest amount. Of the men who tested seropositive and chose to know their test results, 33 percent continued to engage in unprotected insertive anal intercourse. Eighty percent of the seropositives who chose not to know their serostatus also continued the practice (McCusker et al.). Other men were thus placed in considerable jeopardy. Some of those men may now be dead.

Unfortunately, we have no incentive to offer people already HIV infected to cease dangerous behavior. Cigarette smokers, for example, can improve their health outlook by ceasing to smoke, but there is nothing comparable in this case. Altruism may have its adherents, but tangible incentives best motivate people to change their behavior.

Adolescents

Teenagers are also a high-risk group, vulnerable because of their high rates of unprotected intercourse and use of drugs and alcohol, which leads to riskier sexual behavior in all populations. Although the incidence of AIDS among adolescents is low, many patients in their twenties contracted the virus as teenagers.

Many adolescents today have a good deal of knowledge about AIDS, and overall adolescent sexual activity has changed accordingly. A survey of adolescent males that compared their sexual behavior in 1988 to that in 1979 found that teens were more sexually active but much more likely to use condoms (Sonenstein et al.). Only 20 percent of teenage boys used a condom at first intercourse in 1979; 54 percent did in 1988. Only 21 percent used a condom at last intercourse in 1979; almost 58 percent did by 1988. However, a survey of almost 12,000 high school students taken in 1990 found that only 50 percent of white males, 55 percent of black males and 47 percent of Hispanic males used a condom at last intercourse (CDC 1992e). The corresponding figures for female students were 42, 37 and 28. So while there may have been an increase in condom use over the last decade, use is still regretfully low.

As with gay men, teen sexual practices vary, and those at greatest risk of exposure to AIDS are often least likely to practice safe sex. The survey reviewed by Sonenstein and colleagues found that 66 percent of the young men categorized as low-risk used a condom at last intercourse, but only 51 percent of the high-risk group did. Most of the high-risk condom users were bisexuals. Only 17 percent of the young men who reported sex with a prostitute used a condom at last intercourse, as did only 21 percent of those who used, or had a sex partner who used, IV drugs (Sonenstein et al.). A 1985 study of condom use among sexually active adolescents in San Francisco found even more disquieting results. In a city that not only has a very high incidence of AIDS but also runs a multitude of AIDS risk reduction programs, some aimed specifically at teenagers, only 23 percent of the females (4 percent less than in 1984!) reported any condom use during the previous year. Only 49 percent of the males did. A large majority of the teenagers reported multiple sexual partners, but a mere 2 percent of the females and 8 percent of the males reported using a condom every time they had intercourse during the previous year. Yet they virtually all knew that condoms protect against the AIDS virus (Kegeles et al.).

Intravenous Drug Users

Another group at great risk, IVDUs, face exposure from both sexual contact and needle sharing.

Some researchers believe that HIV infection rates may be leveling off among IVDUs, partly because they are using injection equipment more safely. Proof that the IVDU population can be reached, in spite of low literacy and other problems, was found in Cleveland, where an intensive behavioral modification program produced significant reductions in high-risk behavior among predominantly black male street addicts. Participants reduced their use of intravenous drugs by 24 percent, shared needles 60 percent less often and increased their cleansing of needles with bleach by 86 percent (Stephens et al.). A larger-scale program in San Francisco was also successful. When it began in 1985, only 6 percent of those who shared needles reported they always or usually sterilized them with bleach. By 1987, this figure had risen to 47 percent. In 1985, fully 76 percent reported they never used bleach when sharing needles; 36 percent so reported in 1987 (in Becker & Joseph). But, while certainly an improvement, many IVDUs persisted in high-risk behavior. The prevalence of HIV infection among IVDUs in treatment increased from 10 to 15 percent during that time. It is still increasing in many communities. In Connecticut, for example, IVDU AIDS cases increased from 24 percent of the total cases in 1984 to almost 50 percent in 1989. In spite of vigorous education campaigns, only 34 percent sterilized their needles and more than half still shared in 1989 (Knox 1989).

Addicts also practice unsafe sex. The Cleveland program, successful in prompting male addicts to reduce their risky drug use behavior, had a less favorable impact on their risky sexual behavior (Stephens et al.). Female addicts are also more likely to reduce needle sharing than to adopt safe sex practices. A New York study found that only 11 to 13 percent of female heroin addicts used a condom every time they had sex in the previous three months, even though two-thirds of the participants had lost a close friend or relative to AIDS (Schilling et al. 1991). A nationwide study of 17,000 IVDUs not in treatment found that only 10 percent of the males use a condom every time during vaginal intercourse. Seventy percent never do. Of those who engage in receptive anal intercourse only 29 percent always use condoms; 48 percent never do. Only 14 percent of the female IVDUs not in treatment always use a condom during vaginal intercourse; 57 percent never do. Of those women who engage in anal intercourse, 16 percent always have their partner use a condom; 68 percent never do (CDC 1990k). This is extremely risky behavior considering the high prevalence of infection among IVDUs.

Similar high-risk sexual practices among IVDUs in treatment were found by Brown and Primm. Drawn from a population with a seroprevalence rate of 57 percent, their subjects reported that 65 percent of their sexual contacts were with non-IVDUs, yet only 13 percent ever used condoms, and then not consistently. Another study of IVDUs in treatment found that only 11 percent had used condoms every time they had sex in the previous month; 68 percent had not used them at all (Magura et al.). Most frightening, only 43 percent of those who knew themselves to carry the AIDS virus used condoms, placing their partners and possible offspring in great jeopardy. Sixty percent of those who tested seronegative did not use condoms; they placed themselves in great jeopardy. Their risk is greatest if their sex partner is also an IVDU, but it is also high if he or she is not. HIV seroprevalence can be as high as 14 percent among non-IVDUs who are sex partners of IVDUs (CDC 1990k).

The Cost of AIDS

Current Expenditures

AIDS is expensive. It is costly in terms of pain, suffering and premature mortality, fear, anxiety and grief. It costs lovers their partners, parents their children and children their parents. It is also costly in monetary terms. We spent about $10 billion on HIV-related activities in 1991. Federal government expenditures alone totalled $3.46 billion—$1.245 billion for research, $1.346 billion on medical care, $567 million for education and prevention and $305 million in income support to AIDS victims (OMB). Federal expenditures on AIDS from 1982 to 1991 totalled almost $12 billion (NCHS 1991; OMB). Since the federal government contributes approximately one-third of the total spent on AIDS, total spending during that time approached $36 billion.

Hellinger estimates that the direct medical costs of AIDS will have been $5.8 billion in 1991, with the cost of treating an HIV-infected person averaging $5,150 yearly and the cost of treating a patient with full-blown AIDS averaging $32,000 yearly (in Foreman).

Future Costs

Forecasts of the future costs of AIDS vary. Scitovsky and Rice estimated total personal care costs (drug, physician, hospital and nursing home costs) to be $8.5 billion (in 1985 dollars) in 1991. They projected an additional $2.3 billion to be spent on nonpersonal care activity (research, testing, education and support services). Winkenwerder and associates estimated federal spending on HIV-related illnesses to reach $4.3 billion in 1992 and total national expenditures to be three times that. Hellinger estimated the cumulative lifetime medical care expenses (in 1988 dollars) for all people diagnosed with AIDS in a given year to be $4.3 billion in 1990, $5.3 billion in 1991, $6.5 billion in 1992 and $7.8 billion in 1993 (Hellinger). He additionally projected that expenditures for medical care alone to AIDS patients in 1994 will total $10.4 billion for that one year (in Foreman). The GAO projects that in spite of the armed forces' policy of discharging HIV-infected persons, AIDS will cost the U.S. military and veterans' health care systems $3 billion by the end of this decade (USGAO 1990b).

These forecasts underestimate future costs for several reasons. They are based on CDC figures which, as discussed, may seriously underrepresent the size of the epidemic. Also, we are just now witnessing an explosion in heterosexual AIDS cases that could not have been anticipated, and we are just now recognizing AIDS cases in women that had not been previously identified. In addition, cost estimates of individual lifetime care may be low. For example, Hellinger estimates the lifetime medical care costs of an AIDS patient to be $75,000. But University Hospital in Newark reports the average lifetime cost of care to be about $200,000 (Boodman 1990b). Children with AIDS can be even more expensive. They and their families often require intensive social services. Their families have a high incidence of poverty, drug abuse and parental illness and incapacity; thus children with AIDS may spend their entire lives in the hospital or in medically supportive group homes or foster care. Their foster parents, understandably, fetch a premium wage. New York and New Jersey pay up to four times the usual stipend in order to recruit caretakers (USGAO 1989d). Medical costs are also great. Massachusetts spent over $80,000 on medical care for a foster-care child with AIDS just during the last year of its life (MDSS 1990a). Since the most rapid increase in AIDS has been among women of reproductive age, we can expect an escalation in pediatric cases.

The per patient medical cost of AIDS is also changing—it is increasing. The only antiviral drug yet approved for the treatment of AIDS is Azidothymidine (AZT), also known as Retrovir or zidovudine. Even though its producer, Burroughs Williams, cut the price by 20 percent in 1989 in response to congressional and AIDS activists' pressure, AZT is still very expensive. A year's supply costs between $4,000 and $7,000, depending on the dosage (Hellinger). AZT does not cure AIDS, but it can delay the onset of the disease in seropositive persons and extend life expectancy after AIDS has developed. Thus while it prolongs lives, it also increases costs as it is expensive and it extends the treatment period. Not everyone who is seropositive takes AZT, partly because of the cost (not every state subsidizes AZT for its Medicaid patients) and partly because it is not widely accessible. IVDUs in particular have less access to AZT. As AZT becomes more widely available and as infected persons begin taking it earlier after testing seropositive, costs will increase considerably. One year's supply of another drug, Aerosol pentamidine, is conservatively estimated to cost about $2,100 (Hellinger). About 35 percent of AIDS patients are currently using it; more are expected to start. As new drugs are approved, it is likely that they too will be expensive, given the nature of pharmacological research and production.

The shifting incidence of AIDS cases will also affect costs. Male homosexuals, especially white male homosexuals, are more likely to be privately insured. A Harvard Community Health Plan study found that well-insured AIDS patients see a doctor 9 times more, have laboratory tests and x-rays 23 times more and spend 153 more days in the hospital than other AIDS patients (Knox 1989). Black male homosexuals are statistically less likely to be well insured. As they are more likely today to practice high-risk sex, they can be expected to comprise an increasing proportion of homosexual AIDS cases and so may offset the rising per capita costs. But it is the proportionate shift away from homosexuals to IVDUs that will most influence costs. They are far more likely to not be in the labor force, to be unemployed or to be employed at jobs that provide little or no health insurance. Thus it is not unlikely that they will receive less care and less costly medication. Moreover, IVDUs typically come to treatment later in the course of the disease, so that treatment time is less.

Another change that acts to reduce the per capita cost of treatment is that medical care for AIDS patients today is more often provided on an outpatient basis. Care for the dying is more often provided at home or in a hospice. However, these trends may be offset somewhat by the increasing proportion of IVDU patients. They may require more hospitalization as IVDUs are more prone to secondary infections and have fewer home or community alternatives.

Even if per capita costs decrease, total costs will continue to rise as the disease spreads. And as the patient population changes, more of those costs will be borne by the public sector. In the 26 cities surveyed by the United States Conference of Mayors, wherein 56 percent of AIDS victims reside, privately insured patients are already a minority. Most patients are medically indigent, relying on Medicaid or on municipal coffers. Expenses are enormous, waiting lists are growing and providing adequate staffing, housing and services is difficult. Also, public health care facilities are less able to care for patients with other problems (USCM). San Francisco health officials estimate that caring for AIDS patients will cost its municipal hospitals and clinics almost 25 percent of their total operating budget (Garrison).

Insurance Claims

AIDS has also been very costly to the insurance industry, which, indubitably, transfers those costs to policy holders. In the mid-1980s, when the time from diagnosis to death was less than it is now, a typical AIDS victim filed medical claims of between $50,000 and $100,000. Some patients had claims of $300,000 to $500,000 (Banta). Employed AIDS victims may also collect disability benefits when unable to work in the later stages of their illness. And AIDS victims often purchase life insurance policies in large amounts after learning they are ill. Although some of the difference is due to the relatively young age at which AIDS victims die, it was found that 33 percent of the AIDS death claims were filed within two years of the policy's issuance, while only 1 percent of total death claims occur within that period (Banta).

Altogether, in 1989 alone, private insurers paid over $1 billion in AIDS-related health and life insurance claims, 71 percent more than in 1988 (Carrol).

Indirect Costs

Substantial indirect costs are also associated with AIDS. Productivity and income losses can be great as death comes early and many victims, notably male homosexuals, have above average education and earnings. Of those who died from AIDS in 1986, 57 percent were 25 to 39 years of age and 30 percent were 40 to 54. Twenty percent had one to three years of college, 33 percent had four or more years and 60 percent had been employed in the higher occupational categories (NCHS 1989c). Scitovsky and Rice estimated morbidity costs (the value of productivity losses due to illness and disability) to be $251 million in 1985, $421 million in 1986 and $2.3 billion in 1991 (in 1984 dollars). They estimated mortality costs (the present value of future earnings lost by people who die prematurely) as $2.8 billion in 1985, $4.8 billion in 1986 and $28.6 billion in 1991, using a 6 percent discount rate. Using a 4 percent discount rate (and still in 1984 dollars), they estimated mortality costs to be $3.5 billion in 1985, $6.0 billion in 1986 and $36.3 billion in 1991. These figures will increase as AIDS claims more lives. However, the rate of increase of indirect costs will be less than the rate of increase of fatalities as AIDS increasingly becomes a disease of the poor.

Public Policy Issues

AIDS is contagious and catastrophic. It is associated with lifestyles that may be considered deviant and behavior that may be illegal or, at the least, intensely personal. Therefore, the issues surrounding AIDS are extraordinarily complex and involve conflicting rights, values and demands on scarce resources.

As we have not yet found a cure for AIDS, preventing its spread is of paramount importance. Since there is not yet an AIDS vaccination, prevention involves population- and behavior-oriented approaches.

Prevention Issues: Population Measures

Population measures seek to contain contagious disease to those already infected, usually by physical isolation. Although often ineffective in controlling epidemics, the population measure historically favored has been quarantine.

A quarantine guarding against AIDS would have to include every HIV-infected person as well as those with full-blown cases. Fidel Castro is attempting just such a massive screening and quarantine in Cuba today.

In this country healthy prison inmates have filed suits demanding HIV screening and isolation of all seropositive inmates. A New York prison stirred controversy by granting early paroles to several prisoners with AIDS while, taking the opposite approach, former drug czar William Bennett wants prisoners with AIDS who threaten to infect other people after their release to have their terms extended (Banta). Judges have occasionally jailed HIV-infected prostitutes who refused to stop soliciting. Parents of healthy children, failing to realize that their children face greater danger riding in motor vehicles, exposed to tobacco smoke or simply at play than through casual contact with an infected person, have clamored to have children with AIDS kept out of the schools. We prohibit the entry of AIDS victims into the United States. (All applicants for permanent admission must submit to HIV screening; applicants for temporary admission may be tested at immigration officials' discretion.) But quarantine on a national scale in this country would be extremely unwieldy and expensive and entail massive violations of civil rights.

Attempts to isolate AIDS victims have been fraught with contention and have sparked legitimate disagreement even among sympathetic persons. The courts have frequently been called upon when AIDS victims have been denied housing, have been refused admission to schools, or have had their employment terminated. New legislation, similar to that which protects the handicapped, has been passed.

Although there may be good arguments on both sides, the law tends to favor persons with AIDS. For example, many laws today regulate employer use of HIV testing and prohibit employment discrimination based on AIDS, ARC or HIV seropositivity as long as the employee's condition does not make reasonable job performance impossible. These laws impose very real costs on employers, who may have justifiable concerns about absenteeism, attrition, health insurance costs, co-worker preference and customer preference as they afford what may be necessary and reasonable protection to infected workers.

Another controversy involves health care professionals. Following HIV transmission to five patients by an infected dentist, seven states (as of mid-1991) have enacted laws providing for screening of all health care practitioners and limiting the patient contact of those testing positive. Fifteen additional states have similar legislation pending. Many analysts would also require testing of patients. Seropositive patients and practitioners would then each be obliged to inform the other. However, mandatory HIV testing has serious limitations. It is costly, physically intrusive and a violation of the right to privacy. But more to the point, someone who is not infected at the time of the test could become infected shortly after and, even if HIV infection is present, current testing procedures may be unable to detect the presence of the sentinel antibodies for as long as six months. Thus, a negative test result does not assure absence of infection.

The population measures routinely used with sexually transmitted diseases, testing and partner notification, have also provoked controversy when suggested for AIDS. Most HIV screening is available on an anonymous basis. Many AIDS activists, primarily homosexual groups, have fought to continue that policy. They claim more people will submit to testing if their privacy is guaranteed. Protective legislation has not yet been widely enacted, and considerable tribulation may result from disclosure, given the prevailing negative opinions of the lifestyles associated with AIDS and the financial concerns of employers and landlords. Others recommend confidential reporting of HIV-infected persons in order to trace their sex partners. But while partner notification could help slow the spread of AIDS, effective tracing relies on memory, honesty and knowledge of partners' identities, any of which may be lacking. Perhaps a better argument against anonymous testing is that many who test positive do not return for their results, receive no counseling and may unwittingly infect others. The CDC estimates that over 500,000 persons in this country are HIV infected and do not know it (Golan).

Prevention Issues: Behavior Modification Measures

Behavioral remedies are more efficacious than population remedies. Population measures have serious limitations and are basically unnecessary, as AIDS is not spread by casual contact. People need only be aware of and avoid the avenues of transmission.

The first step in changing behavior is education. Only two-thirds of the nation's school districts provide AIDS education. Many do not offer it in the upper grades, where students are more sexually active. Teacher training is often insufficient (USGAO 1990a). Yet surveys indicate that our overall efforts have been effective, that most people know a good deal about AIDS and how to avoid it. This is especially true of low-risk groups; they have been most responsive in changing their behavior to reduce their risk yet more. We must expand these efforts, close the gaps and strengthen programs targeted to high-risk groups. A great variety of culturally sensitive techniques have been designed to reach our various subpopulations, but implementation has been limited (USGAO 1988). These programs must be more widely employed.

A second step is also necessary, as many people have failed to translate knowledge into less risky behavior. This involves encouraging and enabling people to reduce their risk-bearing activities. It is here that the greatest controversies have arisen and the diversity of American values have been shown in sharpest relief.

The clean needle debate: Studies have indicated that many IVDUs can be reached by AIDS education efforts and will use a clean needle when one is available. Yet in many states it is illegal to dispense needles without a prescription. Opponents of needle distribution (who, surprisingly, include the top officials of the NAACP) contend that it implies tacit approval of illicit drug use and sends the wrong message to users and nonusers alike. Some even oppose the distribution of bleach kits. Los Angeles County commissioners voted against the kits even though county public health officials urged their approval. Opponents feel that if IVDUs want to avoid AIDS, they should stop using drugs.

But proponents note that addicts face a highly inelastic demand curve for drugs. Addicts pay a high, sometimes life-threatening price for drugs as it is. The threat of AIDS does not raise the cost enough to effect a decline in quantity demanded. In other words, addicts can't "just say no." They will continue to use drugs and, in the absence of strenuous educational efforts accompanied by readily available sterile injection equipment, will continue to infect each other and perhaps also their sex partners and their children.

The condom debate: Sexual transmission, and the perinatal transmission that may follow, can be averted by proper use of high-quality latex condoms, especially if they are lubricated with the spermicide Nonoxynol-9. Yet here, too, opponents of condom distribution are concerned about the appearance of tacit approval of nonmarital sex and sending the wrong message. The Catholic Church has been an especially active opponent of condom distribution. The National Conference of Catholic Bishops issued a policy statement that claimed that promoting the use of condoms means "promoting behavior that is morally unacceptable" (NCCB p. 421). (The Church forbids condom distribution in its homeless shelters, whose populations tend to have high seroprevalence rates and include alcoholics, drug addicts and men with a propensity for violently antisocial behavior. Yet these people should be held to the high moral ground and not be given the wrong message about sex.) New York's Cardinal John O'Connor, decrying the city's anti-AIDS efforts, claims New York has been turned into "Condom City" (in Crowley & Standora p. 4).

Boston's Cardinal Bernard Law labeled the city's public school AIDS education classes "valueless" and "amoral" and has urged parents to not let their children attend because, even though the classes stress abstinence, they also recommend condom use to teens who are sexually active. The Cardinal claims the curriculum "admits of a permissiveness in sexual behavior which is not acceptable" (Law p. 10).

Whereas opponents of condom distribution take an idealistic approach, proponents have more realistic notions of human sexuality. They know people are sexually active, sometimes thoughtlessly so, in spite of known risks. One reason people frequently give for not using condoms is that they did not anticipate having sex, that it was spontaneous. Having condoms readily available may make some of those encounters less unsafe. Other reasons are that they are embarrassed to discuss it or fear their partner would rather not use a condom. Visible, active promotion of condoms would normalize their use in our society. It would reduce embarrassment and increase acceptance—and perhaps prod those who experience unplanned sexual encounters to keep one at hand. Some people, blacks in particular, report that they do not use condoms because they lessen sexual pleasure (CDC 1990e). Perhaps condoms could be eroticized so that they enhance rather than diminish pleasure. Some programs do provide colored or textured condoms; however, making the types found in adult novelty stores more available might not be a wise strategy at this time.

Proponents of condom distribution are currently gaining strength. Massachusetts, for example, is a state with a large Catholic population in which the Church exerts considerable influence. Massachusetts did not allow the sale of contraceptive devices until 1961, and was the last state to legalize abortion. Yet it has embarked on an aggressive plan to promote the distribution and use of condoms. Among other strategies, the state has urged the media to accept paid condom advertisements and to use its newly developed radio and TV spots about AIDS prevention, some of which are targeted to teens and homosexuals. The state has asked cinema owners to screen public service announcements at movies aimed at older adolescents and adults and has urged owners of restaurants, bars, clubs, theaters, liquor stores, hotels and motels to distribute condoms and AIDS prevention materials. Cambridge, Massachusetts, has gone a step further and become the nation's first municipality to enact an ordinance requiring facilities serving the public to make condoms available. (Exemptions are automatically granted upon request.)

More controversial are the issues of condom distribution in schools and prisons. Again, officials are concerned about sending the wrong message and possibly encouraging, as well as condoning, sexual activity. This is especially troublesome in prisons, as homosexual contact is forbidden. However, some school boards and prison boards have recognized that many students and inmates are indeed sexually active and that public authorities have a moral obligation to help them stay healthy.

Fiscal Issues

Public health care dollars are scarce. That AIDS may be consuming a disproportionate share rankles some observers. A backlash is building. Federal spending alone for AIDS-related activity was about $1.6 billion in 1988, a year in which AIDS deaths numbered 19,695 (NCHS 1991; CDC 1991c). Yet federal spending for cancer, which killed approximately 500,000 Americans that year, also totalled about $1.6 billion; federal spending for heart disease, which killed approximately 770,000 Americans, totalled about $1 billion (Garrison).

Proponents of spending point out that the number of AIDS fatalities, or even of AIDS cases, greatly understates the magnitude of the epidemic, given the high prevalence of HIV infection. Also, unlike heart disease and cancer, AIDS kills its victims when they are relatively young, with a great deal of life yet to experience, and is highly contagious. It is spreading not just here but worldwide. The World Health Organization estimates that 10 million persons were HIV infected in 1990 (in CO 1991b). Up to 120 million could be infected by the year 2000 (Global). Perhaps American scientific expertise can find a cure and a vaccination. AIDS research is also increasing our understanding of other viral diseases. So even though AIDS research has already been liberally funded, one could make a good case for increasing AIDS research allotments.

Treatment Issues

Inclusion in experimental drug programs and access to drugs like AZT have been another source of contention. For the most part, white gay men, well insured, articulate and politically mobilized by the AIDS epidemic, have had the greatest access to treatment. Minority and IVDU victims, less articulate and unified and sometimes more engrossed in their addiction than in their health, have had considerably less access. Infected prison inmates have sued for AZT therapy and been denied. Minority spokespeople view differential access as a civil rights issue, while gay activists feel stung by criticism for doing too good a job for their constituents.

The controversy raises unsettling issues of racism, class bias, and the value of human life. The question is partly one of money, partly one of equality versus equity and partly, perhaps, one of social self-protection. Drug therapies are expensive and, while they extend life, they do not save it. Nor do they prevent HIV transmission. They extend life expectancy but also extend costly treatment time and increase the opportunities for spreading the disease. They may also increase opportunities for criminal behavior, as drug addicts frequently finance their habits through crime.

It has been reported that hospital staff sometimes resent diverting time, effort, resources and services away from other patients for IVDU AIDS cases, in particular, since they often fail to keep appointments or to comply with treatment. Brudny and Dobkyn reported that fully 83 percent of the patients discharged from Harlem Hospital with AIDS-related tuberculosis in 1988 were lost to follow-up and did not continue treatment (in McCord and Freeman). Medical personnel are also chagrined, as addicts frequently continue to take drugs, often while still in the hospital. (Yet if ever a case can be made to provide an addict with drugs, it is when death is imminent. It is cruel to provoke the additional pain of withdrawal, especially since heroin is a powerful analgesic that would relieve much of the AIDS patient's suffering.)

If treatment cured AIDs, it would be a different matter. In that case, failure to treat would be a sentence of death. Deviant lifestyles are not capital crimes.

Another question is when to begin treatment. Should it begin immediately after seropositivity is determined and add years of expensive care, or do we wait until symptoms appear? If early intervention services had been offered to all infected individuals in 1988, it would have cost over $10 billion (Arno et al.). Would such expenditures have been justified?

We need to balance our medical and fiscal responsibilities, but we do not yet know where that balance lies.

Women and AIDS

At issue today is the recent recognition of the unique manifestations of AIDS in women, such as yeast infections and cervical cancers. Since AIDS cannot be treated until it is diagnosed, the CDC must revise its definition of AIDS to accommodate female types. Because AIDS in women had not been properly diagnosed and classified, women received treatment much later in the course of their illness. Thus the average length of time from diagnosis to death for women is seven months, compared to two years for men (Knox 1990). One hopes that the new diagnostic criteria will lead to earlier detection.

We must make a greater effort to screen high-risk women. Women with gynecological problems who could have been exposed to the virus should be routinely tested for HIV. Women need to be informed of their serostatus not just to begin timely treatment but also to receive AIDS-associated social welfare benefits, to better make critical life decisions and, most important, to prevent pregnancy.

Women who are HIV infected should not bear children. We cannot tell in utero if a baby is infected; in fact, amniocentesis may introduce the virus into a previously uninfected fetus. And AZT administered to a pregnant woman may produce birth defects. Therefore, counseling, family planning and pregnancy termination services must be available and affordable. Interestingly, a study of pregnant HIV-infected female IVDUs found they were not much more likely than their noninfected peers to elect abortion, even though they believed their babies had a greater than 50 percent chance of contracting AIDS (Selwyn et al.). Female IVDUs are frequently poor contraceptors and conceive rather haphazardly (Ralph & Spigner). Yet some HIV-infected IVDUs in Selwyn's and other samples report conceiving deliberately, even though they may have already given birth to several AIDS babies, because they want to produce a healthy child. Their children will, of course, be shortly orphaned. They will join the growing legion of AIDS orphans, infected and not, straining our foster care system who, because they are usually minority children, rarely find adoptive homes. We are not about to make pregnancy management part of AIDS control, but it is somewhat ironic that we restrict abortion and not procreation. We allow people to make choices that impose great suffering on others.

One hopes that science will come to the rescue and AIDS will become a disease of the past. In the meantime we must pursue an aggressive course of multifaceted, linguistically and culturally sensitive education, screening and counseling, specifically designed to reach our various subpopulations, especially minorities. They are at greatest risk but have been least influenced by current behavior modification efforts.

We must expand and improve our drug rehabilitation programs. Those that effectively reduce IV drug use effectively reduce HIV transmission.

We must also promote realistic AIDS risk reduction strategies, recognizing the fact that people do not always act in accordance with their own best interests. People have a taste for drugs and people are sexually active, sometimes promiscuously so.

SEXUALLY TRANSMITTED DISEASES

There are many types of sexually transmitted diseases. Some are minor, like herpes simplex II, the STD that was most in the news during the 1980s. Caused by the herpes virus, genital herpes spread rapidly, infecting an estimated 200,000 to 500,000 Americans (CDC 1990h). We can control outbreaks of the unsightly, painful sores it produces, but we do not yet have a cure. However, although there is some evidence that herpes increases women's risk of cervical cancer, the infection is not life threatening. Far more serious are the major venereal diseases, syphilis and gonorrhea, diseases that had not, until recently, been newsworthy. We had thought they were under control.

Epidemiology of Syphilis and Gonorrhea

Syphilis is caused by a tiny spiral germ, *Treponema pallidum*. It is almost always contracted through direct contact of mucous membranes during sexual activity with an infected person. In its final stages, usually many years after infection, it may attack the brain, spinal cord, heart valves and blood vessels, possibly producing syphilitic meningitis, paralysis, insanity or blindness. It had almost been eradicated in the United States by the late 1970s.

Gonorrhea, caused by a bacterium, *Neisseria gonorrhoeae*, is also spread through direct sexual contact. It involves an inflammation of the genitourinary tract that can do great damage to the reproductive system, especially women's. It can also destroy the eyes. Although the most common bacterial infection of adults, overall infection rates have been falling in recent years. However, there are two forms of gonorrhea. One, like syphilis, can readily be cured in its early stages by penicillin; the other cannot. The latter type, difficult and expensive to cure, while serious to the afflicted person, had not been particularly worrisome to public health officials, as its rate of incidence was extremely low.

With the onset of the AIDs epidemic in the early 1980s and the resultant rise in sexual health consciousness, the good news, that is, the near eradication of syphilis, the falling rates of gonorrhea infection and the low incidence of penicillin-resistant gonorrhea, should have gotten even better. And for some groups, notably gay men, it did. Gay health facilities in New York, San Francisco and Washington, D.C., reported approximately an 85 percent decrease in rectal gonorrhea and approximately a 45 percent decrease in syphilis from 1984 to 1988 (Boodman 1989a).

But aggregated data of the homosexual population obscures considerable information. STD rates among gay men have fallen largely because they have decreased dramatically among gay white men, who comprise the majority of the homosexual population. An Atlanta-area study found that while syphilis cases among white men who reported same-sex encounters decreased almost 86 percent from 1981 to 1985, cases among black men who reported same-sex encounters more than doubled (Landrum et al.). Race was not the only distinguishing characteristic. Black patients were ten times as likely as white patients to work at low-income jobs and twice as likely to have less than 12 years of education. They were not reached by or were not influenced by the massive AIDS risk-reduction efforts aimed at gay men.

Many people have failed to get the safe-sex message. Instead, they practice ever more risk-bearing sex. And STD rates have skyrocketed (see Figure 3.1).

Alarming as these figures and those to follow may be, the incidence of venereal diseases is greatly underreported, largely because they are frequently asymptomatic for an extended period. The most common early symptom of syphilis in a male is a genital sore that usually disappears without treatment within three to five weeks after infection. The female's lesion usually occurs on the cervix and so is often undetected. Symptoms of gonorrhea in a male, painful urination and a thick discharge, usually appear shortly after infection, but most women with gonorrhea never show any symptoms.

Compounding the problem of asymptomacity, STD rates are soaring in those populations with least access to and/or least interest in health care services. Consequently, the Centers for Disease Control estimates the actual 1989 incidence of new cases of preliminary- and secondary-stage syphilis to be more than 2.5 times greater than the 44,540 cases reported and the new cases of gonorrhea (both types) to be more than twice the 733,151 reported. It is estimated that as of July 1990 over 12,000,000 Americans were infected with a sexually transmitted disease (CDC 1990h).

Figure 3.1
Sexually Transmitted Diseases, Reported New Cases: United States, 1985 to 1989

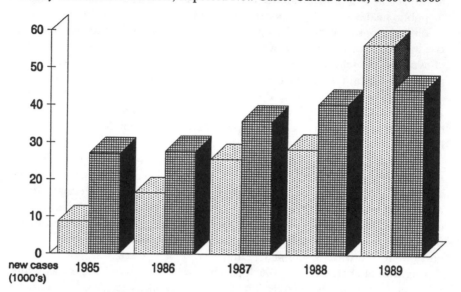

Source: Centers for Disease Control. Package of statistical tables

STD Prevalence among Various Subpopulations

Crack Users

After declining for several years, the incidence of reported syphilis in Philadelphia increased 65 percent in 1986. The increase continued in 1987 and 1988 (Rolfs et al.). The upsurge coincided with the onset of the crack epidemic.

Crack-cocaine greatly intensifies sexual arousal and incites binges of compulsive sexual activity. It is highly aphrodisiacal and, at first, very affordable. But it is also extremely addictive. So whereas the first hit is very inexpensive, the habit is very expensive. Exacerbated by the nature of a crack high—very intense but very short-lived—users' demand for the drug rapidly increases and becomes highly inelastic. Thus as their need for the drug escalates, so does their need for the money to buy it. Many women finance their supply by prostitution.

In Philadelphia, as elsewhere, authorities found many female crack addicts exchanging sex for drugs or cash. In fact, there emerged two distinct classes of streetwalker. One is the traditional hooker, blowsy and bawdy, overly made-up and flashily dressed to advertise her $20-and-up services. The other is the crack addict, dirty and disheveled, hair uncombed and eyes vacant, selling her services (much to the anger of the nonaddicted established professionals) for as little as $3. They attract numerous buyers, men willing to sacrifice quality for price, and are a significant avenue for the transmission of STDs.

In response to the alarming increase in syphilis in Philadelphia, the Centers for Disease Control and the Philadelphia Department of Public Health studied the relationship between cocaine use, sexual behavior and syphilis. Syphilis patients enrolled at a Philadelphia STD clinic were compared to a control group enrolled at the same clinic who did not have syphilis.

The researchers found cocaine use to be significantly more common among syphilis patients of both sexes. High-risk behavior such as sex with a prostitute, crack-house sex or sex with a woman on the first day of meeting were far greater among male syphilis patients than among the control group males. Female syphilis patients were six times more likely to have engaged in prostitution than the control group females and averaged 40 percent more partners in the preceding three months. The conclusion was as expected: cocaine use and the high-risk sexual behavior associated with it are serious risk factors for syphilitic infection (Rolfs et al.).

African-Americans

Disproportionately low-income, undereducated, young and black, crack users would be at a greater risk of exposure to venereal disease even without the influence of the drug. Since such statistics were first recorded, STD rates among blacks had been five to six times greater than among whites, though the differential has lessened somewhat in recent decades. However, with the introduction of crack-cocaine, although there has been a slight reduction in non-penicillin-resistant gonorrhea, the incidence of STDs among the black population has reached epidemic proportions. The rate of syphilis infection among blacks soared 22.8 percent from 1985 to 1989, at the same time that white rates fell 62 percent. The 1989 gonorrhea infection rate in black males was 45 times the white male rate (CDC 1990i).

Obviously, looking only at aggregated U.S. data obscures considerable information. Obvious too is the fact that cities with large black populations, especially those whose black population is large relative to their gay white population, will feel the impact most severely (see Table 3.6).

Some cities, notably San Francisco, San Juan and Austin, where AIDS is a serious problem, appear, on the whole, to have gotten the safe-sex message across and are experiencing decreasing overall rates of venereal disease. In the San Francisco area, however, crack and its concomitant promiscuity and prostitution are spreading so rapidly through its sizable black population that STD rates are expected to increase again. A study of 222 black teenage crack users in San Francisco and Oakland found that 41 percent had already had a sexually transmitted disease, 25 percent reported trading sexual favors for drugs or money and 27 percent of the boys had more than ten sex partners in the last year. While the teenagers said they worry about AIDS, only 59 percent reported ever using a condom, and only 23 percent reported using one in their last sexual encounter (Fullilove et al.).

Table 3.6
Antibiotic-Resistant Gonorrhea and Syphilis, Reported Case Rates per 100,000
Population: Selected U.S. Cities 1985, 1989

City	Antibiotic-resistant Gonorrhea		Syphilis	
	1985	1989	1985	1989
Atlanta	16.7	413.0	117.7	206.7
Chicago	1.6	55.0	13.5	28.2
Detroit	1.1	151.7	10.3	48.6
Los Angeles	6.5	77.1	34.2	35.2
Newark	0.0	255.0	57.1	135.6
New York City	22.0	84.5	30.3	45.9
Philadelphia	1.6	248.4	37.7	123.5
Washington, D.C.	3.2	358.0	48.6	158.4

Source: Centers for Disease Control. Package of Statistical Tables.

Risk Takers

In Washington, D.C., where drug use, primarily crack, is the single biggest predictor for venereal disease, 75 percent of the patients treated for syphilis at the Free Clinic are under 18 (Boodman 1989a). STD rates have been increasing most rapidly in adolescents, with an estimated 2.5 million teens contracting a venereal disease each year (USHR). This is no surprise, as risky sexual behavior has become virtually endemic among teenagers. A Massachusetts Department of Public Health study found that 69 percent of sexually active adolescents never use condoms or use them inconsistently. As among other age groups, drugs and alcohol are critical risk factors. Sixteen percent of the teens surveyed reported using condoms less frequently after drinking; 25 percent use them less after taking drugs (Reid). STDs among Massachusetts teens grew 10 percent a year from 1986 to 1990. Syphilis alone increased 29 percent just from 1989 to 1990. The problem in Massachusetts also is especially pronounced among minorities. The 1990 gonorrhea infection rate in Hispanic male teens was more than 15 times that in white male teens, the black male teen rate was more than 100 times greater. Hispanic male teens were almost 20 times more likely to contract syphilis than white male teens; black male teens were over 40 times more likely (MDPH 1991).

Black teens are at greater risk for several reasons. They use condoms less frequently at any age of adolescence (Sonenstein et al.). They are more sexually active at any given age and initiate sexual activity at a much younger age (Moore & Peterson). Younger persons of any race use condoms less frequently (Sonenstein et al.). And persons who initiate sexual activity at a younger age usually have a greater number of sex partners, not just over their lifetime, but also within the first several years following their first intercourse (CDC 1991e). Consequently, by their late teens 4 percent of whites but 17 percent of blacks have been infected with genital herpes (CDC 1991e).

For adults and teenagers, unprotected sex is usually a choice. Granted, their judgment, sometimes poor to begin with, may be greatly diminished by drugs, alcohol or raging hormones. Considerable pressure may be brought to bear, as many a teenage girl can testify. Women who insist on condoms may be beaten or abandoned by men whose concept of ''macho'' sex precludes their use. But for the most part, engaging in risk-bearing sex is a choice—a choice all too frequently made. Many studies reveal that condom use is minimal, especially among those who are most at risk. A San Francisco STD clinic found that 97 percent of its clients knew that regular condom use reduces the likelihood of acquiring HIV infection. All knew that the clinic dispensed condoms for free. Yet only 37 percent of the whites, 14 percent of the Hispanics and 16 percent of the blacks reported using one at last intercourse. And clinic officials felt condom use was exaggerated (CDC 1990e). As Carol Jordan, program manager for AIDS and STD clinics in the Washington area said, virtually all those who come to the clinics know how diseases are transmitted, how to protect themselves and where to obtain condoms. They just don't do it (in Boodman 1989a). So the choice is perhaps not well thought out, perhaps grounded in ignorance, but it is a choice nonetheless.

Children

It is oftentimes the most innocent who suffer the consequences of someone else's poor choice. Congenital syphilis, passed from an infected mother to an unborn child, was once a medical rarity. Now it is all too common, having increased fourfold from 1985 to 1989 (CDC 1990i). Forty percent of infected fetuses are stillborn or die shortly after birth (CDC 1988a). Survivors may suffer brain damage, blindness or other severe disorders.

Because increases in congenital syphilis lag behind increases in syphilis in women, congenital syphilis is expected to continue to increase. It will increase most dramatically in the children of urban black and Hispanic women, as they have experienced a disproportionate increase in syphilis and are less likely than white women to get prenatal care. New York City reported 779 cases in just the first six months of 1989 (''Reports''), fourteen times more than in all of 1986 (Blair). The increase is directly traceable to mothers who use drugs and do not practice safe sex. In New York, 39 percent of the syphilis babies' mothers admitted to using cocaine or crack while pregnant; only half reported any prenatal visits (''Reports'').

It gets worse. Venereal diseases, traditional evidence of sexual abuse, have also increased considerably in young children (CDC 1990i). Girls, and sometimes boys, are molested in crack houses or prostituted by their mothers whose sexual "favors" she trades for drugs or money. Crack-cocaine certainly brings out the most reprehensible in human behavior. Nowhere is it more clearly evidenced than in the suffering of children abused and made ill.

The Social Costs

Although these children bear a greviously heavy share of the cost of others' choices, society also pays a price. Except for penicillin-resistant gonorrhea, treatment in the early stages is fairly inexpensive; but sheer numbers are putting quite a burden on our already overtaxed public health facilities.

Those who fail to get treatment may be even more costly. Untreated and asymptomatic women with gonorrhea constitute a growing reservoir of carriers. Often prostituting themselves, they spread the disease still further. Persons with untreated syphilis, debilitated by the many associated illnesses, perhaps blinded, are little able to support themselves, and draw upon considerable social services. Victims of syphilitic psychoses need to be institutionalized. The expense sheet can be quite long.

STDs and AIDS

The expense sheet will grow still longer. The numbers will become larger. For the huge increase in STDs we have witnessed is only the tip of the iceberg. Incubating below the surface, already beginning to reveal itself, is an enormous increase in AIDS. The increase in STDs is more than just a signal that tens of thousands of persons are engaging in very high-risk sex. And the relationship is due to more than just the fact, true as it is, that persons with a sexually transmitted disease are much more likely to be HIV infected.

Venereal lesions provide an open port of entry for the AIDS virus. Not only do the ulcers break the skin, allowing the virus to pass through more easily, but the ulcers also attract large numbers of T-4 blood cells, the prime targets and carriers of the AIDS virus. Thus the sores concentrate the virus just at the point where it can most easily pass from person to person.

It is just beginning. The United States is just now seeing transmission of the AIDS virus similar to that in Africa: among heterosexuals and without known contacts with intravenous drug users.

However, IV drug users did play a role. Their stage, not surprisingly, was the crack house. A New York survey found that 20 percent of IV drug users also smoke crack (Kerr 1989). They introduced the AIDS virus into an arena of pathologically hyperactive sexual behavior, an arena where people engage in unprotected sex with numerous partners. They thus combined the most potent of risk factors. In San Francisco (where new HIV infections among drug addicts outnumber those among homosexuals three to one), it was found that crack use increases risk sevenfold, failure to use condoms increases risk (for women) sixfold and a high number of sexual partners increases risk of infection fivefold (Knox 1989).

It is just beginning and it is inevitable. Given the average AIDS incubation period of 8.5 years and the recent enormous increases in STDs, often accompanied by the AIDS virus and providing a conduit for its transmission, we are due for a fatal explosion. It will be largely confined to poor neighborhoods and it will be devastating to those cities already drowning in drugs and crime.

Public Policy Recommendations

The explosion is inevitable. The soaring increases in STDs in those populations with the highest prevalence of HIV infection make that clear. But we cannot be defeatists. We must make every effort to contain the AIDS explosion and minimize damage. Our strategies must include the following measures.

Educating the Public

Sex education classes and media campaigns must detail the symptoms, and lack of symptoms, of sexually transmitted diseases. They must describe explicitly the relationships between drug and alcohol use, unsafe sex, STDs and AIDS. We must make extra efforts to reach out-of-school youth and high-risk populations, using the vernacular of the targeted group.

Distribution of Condoms

Condoms must be highly accessible. Sexually active persons must be urged to keep them at hand and to use them. This is especially true of teens, who, as a group, have experienced the greatest increase in STD rates. We prefer that our youth not use drugs or alcohol, but they do. They must be told to either be prepared for or decline the unplanned sex that may follow. No one in a high-risk situation should ever have sex without a condom. Therefore, condoms should be dispensed in schools and every other appropriate place.

Testing and Treatment

We must expand STD services. Fiscal difficulties and the belief that venereal diseases were no longer a widespread threat led many cities to scale back STD clinics. We must open more and extend evening and weekend hours. School-based health clinics should provide testing. Family planning, obstetrics/gynecology and prenatal care clinics should routinely test visitors with any perceived risk. Especially strenuous outreach efforts must be made to locate and test high-risk pregnant women. Newborns in high-risk areas should be tested, as should children who have been intrusively sexually abused. Non-traditional sites such as drug treatment centers and prisons should also provide STD testing. Heavily impacted cities might follow Philadelphia's example.

It is now sending screening teams to crack houses, shooting galleries, brothels and prostitution strips (CDC 1991a).

Since venereal diseases do not carry quite the stigma AIDS does, identification should be made, interviews taken and sex partners of positives notified and tested when possible. This is standard recommended procedure.

Everyone testing positive should automatically be screened for HIV infection. Persons who test negative for an STD, but who nonetheless may have been exposed to the AIDS virus, should also be screened.

We must see that treatment is carried through. Expanded clinic sites and hours will help, but more aggressive efforts may be necessary. Many infected individuals are drug abusers or otherwise members of the underclass and often fail to keep appointments or comply with treatment.

Recognizing Prostitution

We must take a realistic approach to prostitution. Centuries of suppression and education have failed to eradicate it. Demand will always exist, and as long as there is demand, there will be supply. With the emergence of crack-cocaine and the need to finance addiction, the supply of male and female prostitutes is at a modern-day high, especially in inner cities. Price has fallen and, combined with the increased sexuality induced by crack, has resulted in a great increase in the quantity of sex for money or drug transactions.

With the high prevalence of STD and HIV infection among prostitutes, prostitution is no longer the victimless crime we may have thought. As police sweeps or jailing never did deter prostitutes and will not now, we must take prostitution out of the closet and confront the dangers openly. Sex education classes must be frank. Signs in rest rooms of facilities frequented by adolescents and adults in high-risk areas must warn of the dangers of unprotected sex with prostitutes, as should discreetly timed radio and TV spots. Television shows and films sometimes include prostitutes as marginal characters—a few well-chosen words could make the point. In fact, since American entertainment reaches such a wide audience, the industry should be mobilized to incorporate safe-sex messages in its scripts and lyrics whenever possible.

Some fault an approach that emphasizes caution rather than abstinence, but we must be pragmatic. People will continue to do what people have been doing since time immemorial. Government has a responsibility to protect public health, and although we cannot force people to make healthy choices, we can help them better appreciate their risks and better protect themselves. Failure to do so places all of us at greater risk. Failure to do so will be very expensive.

4

Racial Disparities in
Health and Mortality

Some behavioral choices clearly have such adverse effects that they shorten our lives. The Centers for Disease Control estimates that the long-term patterns of behavior known as "lifestyle" are responsible for approximately 50 percent of the mortality from the ten leading causes of death in this country (in APA). Many of those lifestyle choices are more often made by blacks, whether because of lesser education, lower income or cultural factors. The result has been shorter life expectancies among blacks than among whites.

Behavior and choice are, of course, not the only sources of disparity; other factors also loom large. These, too, will be examined, for to omit them would be to paint an unfair and inaccurate portrait of black America. They also bear important policy implications, especially as the longevity gap between blacks and whites has widened in recent years.

BLACK AND WHITE AMERICANS: FATAL DISPARITIES

Life span has long been the thermometer used to measure the health of the public. Only in this case, assuming quality of life is maintained, elevation indicates better health. We have come to expect greater longevity as one of the benefits of continued economic development. A fall in life expectancies is cause for alarm. Fortunately, this has happened only rarely. But it has happened recently.

The Department of Health and Human Services 1988 mortality statistics reveal that, while white life expectancy was unchanged, black life expectancy fell for the third time in four years (see Table 4.1). The black-white longevity gap widened, causing overall life expectancy to fall from 75.0 years in 1987 to 74.9 years (NCHS 1990a). Department Secretary Louis Sullivan blamed the falling black life expectancy rates on increased deaths from AIDS, homicide, influenza and pneumonia. The black-white longevity gap widened further in 1989

Table 4.1
Expectation of Life at Birth by Sex and Race: United States, Selected Years

Year	White			Black		
	Total	Male	Female	Total	Male	Female
1970	71.7	68.0	75.6	64.1	60.0	68.3
1975	73.4	69.5	77.3	66.8	62.4	71.3
1980	74.4	70.7	78.1	68.1	63.8	72.5
1984	75.3	71.8	78.7	69.7	65.6	73.7
1985	75.3	71.9	78.7	69.5	65.3	73.5
1986	75.4	72.0	78.8	69.4	65.2	73.5
1987	75.6	72.2	78.9	69.4	65.2	73.6
1988	75.6	72.3	78.9	69.2	64.9	73.4

Source: National Center for Health Statistics. *Advance Report of Final Mortality Statistics, 1988.*

when white life expectancy increased to 76.0 years while black life expectancy remained unchanged at 69.2 years (CDC 1992c). Manning Feinleib, director of the National Center for Health Statistics, attributes much of the racial difference to living conditions, access to health care and increasing violence and drug use in the black community (in Halpert). Blacks' greater incidence of poverty also undoubtedly played a part.

Lifestyle-Related Mortality Predictors

Poverty makes it more difficult to lead a healthy life. Shelter and diet may be inadequate. Neighborhood air quality may be poor. Life is generally more stressful.

Few people consciously choose to live a life of poverty, but people can and do make unhealthy lifestyle choices. People who are poor and less educated tend to make them more often, perhaps because of lesser understanding of the possible consequences. But more likely it is because some of those choices provide considerable utility, particularly in the very short run and particularly to persons whose long-run expectations are low.

Substance Abuse

The high, the blocking out, the comraderie drugs and alcohol often entail may provide very pleasurable, indeed euphoric, short-run benefits. The short-run costs are obviously perceived as well worth paying. The long-run costs, of which personal health problems are just a part, may be perceived (all too often inaccurately) as being so far in the long run as to be not worth discounting.

Or the long-run costs may be calculated as very low, especially if one's prospects for the future are perceived as limited (self-fulfilling prophecy notwithstanding). Yet the actual short- and long-run individual and social costs can be very high.

Although only a minority of both races use drugs, and only a very small minority use hard drugs, drug abuse among blacks greatly exceeds that among whites. The National Institute on Drug Abuse's 1990 National Household Survey found that although whites were more likely to use hallucinogens and that both races used inhalants to about the same extent, blacks' use of most other drugs was far greater than that of whites. Blacks were 30 percent more likely to smoke marijuana, 2.6 times more likely to use heroin, 3 times more likely to use cocaine and 4.5 times more likely to use crack (NIDA 1991).

These figures are all biased downward, however, by the survey's approach. Only persons in traditional households were interviewed. Overlooked were persons in prisons, group homes, residential rehabilitation programs, homeless shelters and single-room-occupancy dwellings, places where blacks are often overrepresented and whose populations engage in a disproportionate amount of drug and alcohol abuse. In the Boston metropolitan area, where blacks comprise but 6 percent of the population, they made up 33 percent of the clients admitted into substance abuse treatment centers in 1990 (Hofmann et al.). Sixty-one percent of the clients specifying cocaine as their drug of choice were black, as were 23 percent of those specifying heroin and 17 percent of those specifying alcohol.

The age-adjusted drug-induced death rate for blacks in 1988 was 2.2 times that for whites (NCHS 1990a). Blacks accounted for 41 percent of the cocaine-related deaths and 32 percent of the heroin-related death. (USDHHS 1991a).

Although whites have a higher prevalence of heavy drinking and blacks are more likely to abstain from alcohol consumption, overall black and white alcohol use levels are fairly similar (NIDA 1990). However, research has found that, while drinking levels among blacks are comparable to or less than those among whites, blacks endure more severe consequences from drinking. Black males, especially, suffer more alcohol-related diseases, social complications and dependency problems (USDHHS 1990c). One possible explanation is that among whites, heavy drinking is more likely to be a short-lived phenomena of youth, whereas among blacks, heavy drinking begins in their thirties and is more likely to continue. Problem drinking rates remain higher for blacks throughout middle and old age (Herd in USDHHS 1990c). Another possibility, one not yet well researched, is that blacks may be more biologically vulnerable to alcohol-related health problems. It has been found that similar alcohol consumption patterns among pregnant women beget graver consequences for black babies (Chavez et al.).

Whatever the reason, the 1988 age-adjusted alcohol-induced death rate for blacks was 2.7 times that of whites (NCHS 1990a).

Cigarette Smoking

Cigarette smoking produces a mild euphoria—at times a bit of a rush and brief excitation, at other times a soothing sensation. The health hazards are many and well known but are usually very long-run—perhaps, one hopes, never to be realized.

The decision to smoke is a poor one and is made most often by black men. Although the prevalence of smoking among black and white women is about the same, black men are 30 percent more likely to smoke than white men (NCHS 1991). Blacks also have a greater preference for mentholated cigarettes; 75 percent of blacks smoke menthols, consuming over three-quarters of those produced (USDHHS 1991b). Menthol imparts a cooling sensation that may mask air passage discomfort, inducing the smoker to inhale the nicotine- and tar-laden smoke more deeply. The marginal benefit is obvious to anyone with a taste for menthol; the marginal cost is not.

There are prospects for a healthier future, however. As discussed in the first chapter, smoking among young blacks is considerably less than among their elders. It is also considerably less than among young whites. The eventual result will be a greatly reduced disparity in smoking-related deaths, deaths that tend to be premature.

But today's deaths result from yesterday's choices, and black men today are 44 percent more likely to die of lung cancer than are white men (NCHS 1991).

Compounding the problem is the addictive potential of drugs, cigarettes and alcohol. Since these were analyzed in earlier chapters, it suffices to note here that the costs, direct and indirect, physical and financial, personal and social, only escalate with addiction, and that in health terms, blacks are disproportionately affected.

Crime

Cost-benefit analysis may also be applied to associating with violent persons or engaging in criminal activity, especially if it involves the high-risk–high-profit business of drug dealing. The risk itself may be euphoric, the scene charged. So not only may benefits be quite high but, for risk-takers, the risk itself is utility generating. Add the prospects of greatly increasing one's income and one's status in the subculture of drugs and violence, limited alternatives, expectations of a short and brutish life and relatively low opportunity costs if injured or imprisoned, and you just may have people making choices that pose great threat to their health but yet are perversely rational.

Homicide was the fourth leading cause of death among black males in 1988. They were killed at a rate 7.6 times greater than white males (NCHS 1991). The violence has escalated since then as crack, gang wars and the increased availability of high-powered weapons have ravaged black communities. Sometimes the victim is a perfect innocent, sometimes not. But as the bodies mount, so do black mortality rates.

Risking AIDS

Blacks were 3.4 times more likely to die from AIDS in 1990 (CDC 1991c). As discussed in the preceding chapter, that disproportion will worsen. Blacks have a higher HIV seroprevalence in every major risk category and have demonstrated a greater propensity for continued high-risk behavior.

Dietary Choices

Poor nutrition can also be deadly. The traditional black diet, with its emphasis on leafy green vegetables, poultry, fish and dried beans, is generally rich in vitamin A, iron and protein (USDHHS 1986). However, more so than that of other Americans, the diet of low-income urban blacks tends to be very high in fat, salt, sugar, calories and cholesterol. It is overly reliant on fast foods, junk foods, packaged or canned foods and fried foods, often cooked in lard. Observers believe these dietary choices are more a matter of culturally defined tastes than of lesser access to healthier foods and nutritional information or low income per se (Freedman). As a result, blacks have a greater incidence of heart disease, high blood pressure, diabetes and obesity, which is itself a risk factor. Blacks are 50 percent more likely than whites to be seriously overweight (NCHS 1991).

Black-White Mortality Differentials

While death rates from heart, liver and cerebrovascular diseases, diabetes and pneumonia have fallen considerably over the last several years for both races, blacks still oftentimes suffer and die disproportionately. Moreover, as cancer rates have increased at an average annual rate of 0.9 percent for white women and 1.2 percent for white men from 1973 to 1988, they have increased 1.2 percent for black women and 1.5 percent for black men (NCHS 1991). In addition, the five-year survival rate for all forms of cancer in 1987 was 30 percent greater for white than for black women; white men faced odds 41 percent more favorable than black men (NCHS 1991).

Blacks suffer excess mortality. In other words, holding age constant, the death rate for younger blacks is higher than for whites for most causes of death (see Table 4.2). For example, the crude death rate from heart disease is greater in whites than in blacks—that is, whites are more likely to die from heart disease. But holding age constant, blacks have a higher death rate from heart disease at every age until age 85 (NCHS 1991).

Overall, the 1989 age-adjusted death rate for blacks exceeded the rate for whites by 60 percent (CDC 1992c).

Sources of the Differentials

Attempts to explain the differential support what has been discussed here.

Table 4.2

Age-Adjusted Death Rates per 100,000 Population for Selected Causes of Death,
According to Sex and Race: United States, 1988

Cause of Death	White Male	Black Male	White Female	Black Female
All causes	664.3	1037.8	384.4	593.1
Diseases of heart	220.5	286.2	114.2	181.1
- ischemic heart disease	155.8	146.9	74.7	93.0
Cerebrovascular diseases	30.0	57.8	25.2	46.6
Malignant neoplasms	157.6	227.0	110.1	131.2
- respiratory system	58.0	83.4	24.8	24.6
- colorectal	16.6	19.0	11.5	14.9
- prostate	14.1	30.3	--	--
- breast	-	-	23.0	27.0
Chronic obstructive pulmonary diseases	27.8	26.0	14.5	10.0
Pneumonia and influenza	18.0	28.0	10.7	13.4
Chronic liver disease and cirrhosis	12.1	20.7	5.0	9.3
Diabetes mellitus	9.6	19.8	8.4	22.1
Accidents and adverse effects	49.9	69.0	18.8	22.2
- motor vehicle accidents	28.5	29.6	11.6	9.2
Suicide	19.8	11.8	5.1	2.4
Homicide and legal intervention	7.7	58.2	2.8	12.7
Human immunodeficiency virus infection	9.9	31.6	0.7	6.2

Source: National Center for Health Statistics. *Health United States 1990*.

Behaviorally related risk factors: Otten and associates determined that 31 percent of the excess mortality is explained by a higher prevalence among blacks
of six well-established risk factors: cigarette smoking, systolic blood pressure,
cholesterol level, excess weight, alcohol intake and diabetes. Adding HIV
seroprevalence would explain somewhat more.

Income and class: Although it is impossible to fully isolate the roles of culture,
income and education, the Otten group attributes an additional 38 percent
of the excess black adult mortality to lesser family income.

Information on mortality, morbidity and class in the United States is limited,
but, having examined what is available, Navarro found that class differentials
were greater than racial differentials. For example, whether class was measured
by income, education or occupational classification, lower-class persons were
more likely to die of heart disease than upper-class persons. The age-adjusted
heart disease mortality rate in blue collar workers (operatives) was 2.3 times
that in managers and professionals, whereas the black male rate was only 1.2
times the white male rate and the black female rate was 1.5 times the white
female rate.

The same was found to be true of morbidity (the relative incidence of disease).
Blue collar workers reported a morbidity rate 2.9 times greater than that of
professionals, while blacks reported a morbidity rate (only) 1.9 times greater
than that of whites (Navarro).

The differential derives partly from poverty itself, partly from the behavioral choices more prevalent among lower-income people of all races. Both are replete with risk factors predictive of premature and excess mortality.

Excess mortality is extreme in Harlem, where the average annual income is about half that of all United States blacks and somewhat less than a third that of United States whites. A review of deaths in Harlem from 1979 to 1981 uncovered an age-adjusted rate of mortality from all causes that was more than double that of United States whites and 50 percent greater than that of United States blacks (McCord & Freeman).

Cardiovascular disease accounted for 23.5 percent of the deaths in Harlem that were in excess of white deaths nationwide. Neoplasm accounted for 12.6 percent, and diabetes, pneumonia and influenza together contributed 6.7 percent. But the largest proportion of the excess deaths was directly due to violence and substance abuse. Homicide, overdoses, accidents, cirrhosis of the liver and other manifestations of alcohol and drug use were responsible for 45 percent of the excess deaths (McCord & Freeman).

Excess mortality in Harlem is doubtless greater today, as crack and AIDS have since impacted heavily on the community. As McCord and Freeman note, AIDS is now the most common cause of death among Harlem residents aged 25 to 44.

For the most part, blacks of higher socioeconomic status have better health indicators than whites of lower socioeconomic status. For example, when income is held constant, the difference in smoking rates between black and white men narrows considerably (Novotny et al.). It is the relatively lower status of blacks overall that explains some of the mortality differentials.

Residual factors and preventable causes of death: While class differentials may be greater than racial differentials, a comparison of extremely poor blacks to extremely poor whites would still reveal excess mortality. Blacks tend to have poorer health at both high- and low-income levels. In response to the 1989 National Health Institute Survey, 15.9 percent of blacks reported their health as fair or poor, compared to 8.2 percent of whites (NCHS 1990d). The disparity narrows when income is taken into account but is still distressingly apparent (See Figure 4.1).

Some of the residual excess mortality may be due to biological factors. Genetic predisposition may partly explain why, for example, black men are more susceptible to prostate cancer at every socioeconomic level (Ernster et al.).

However, while genetics may provoke greater morbidity, it does not necessarily follow that mortality should also be greater. Earlier detection and enhanced treatment could, perhaps, offset biological predisposition. Yet blacks are not only more likely to contract prostate cancer, but having contracted it, they are more likely to die from it. The black-white prostate cancer mortality ratio exceeds the black-white incidence ratio. Many of those deaths could doubtless have been prevented.

Blacks suffer considerable excess mortality from causes that need not be fatal. Blacks more often die from conditions such as tuberculosis, asthma, appendicitis

Figure 4.1

Average Annual Percent of Persons Self-Assessed to Be in Fair or Poor Health by Race, Age and Family Income: United States, 1985 to 1987

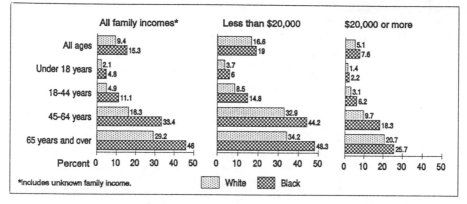

Source: National Center for Health Statistics, *Health of Black and White Americans, 1985–1987*

and cervical cancer, conditions that could be prevented or would respond to timely, appropriate medical care (Schwartz et al.). Schwartz and colleagues found the overall age-adjusted death rate for blacks from twelve such conditions to be 4.5 times greater than that for whites. Higher mortality rates may indicate a greater incidence of disease or a higher case fatality rate. Greater incidence may result from a higher prevalence of risk factors. Greater fatality may result from late diagnosis, treatment delays or the presence of other medical problems. In any case, many such deaths might have been prevented.

Environment, income and lifestyle may militate against black health. Biological factors may make blacks more susceptible to particular diseases or allow disease to pursue a more aggressive course. But together they still do not completely explain the black-white mortality gap. Most authorities attribute the remaining disparity to blacks' lesser access to health care.

Differential access to health care: In 1989, 59 percent of blacks under age 65 were covered by private health insurance plans; 17 percent were covered by Medicaid; 22 percent were not covered at all. With overall higher income and employment status, the respective figures for whites were 80, 4, and 14 percent (NCHS 1991). Thus blacks often incur higher out-of-pocket costs for medical care and have fewer choices among health care providers. Theoretically and intuitively, we would expect this to result in fewer health care contacts, far fewer of the routine examinations that are so important for early detection of potential problems, and greater delay in seeking care when ill. Research has found this to be true. The Harvard School of Public Health found that one in 11 blacks reported not receiving medical care for economic reasons compared to one in 20 whites (Blendon et al.). The number is unacceptable for whites; it is unconscionable for blacks. Considering the ultimate cost of poor health, it is also uneconomic.

Although according to the National Health Institute Survey, blacks in this country are, on the whole, less healthy than whites, whites report a greater incidence of both chronic and acute conditions. It is not clear, however, whether whites actually experience more ills or are simply more likely to report them. Blacks report seeking physicians' care for their ills less often but experience those ills (surely consequently) to a more serious degree. Blacks therefore incur more days of restricted activity, are hospitalized for longer periods and lose more days of work each year (NCHS 1990d). Private costs and social costs are that much greater.

Even after adjusting for income, age, sex and health status, blacks have significantly fewer medical care contacts during a year (Blendon et al.). According to the NHIS, the difference in physician contacts between whites and blacks who considered their health to be fair or poor was especially pronounced. This was particularly true for children and portends adverse consequences: more days of school missed and less favorable prospects for a healthy adulthood.

The place of medical care contact also differs greatly. Blacks are 31 percent less likely to see a doctor in his office, 67 percent more likely to go to a hospital outpatient department (clinic or emergency room), and 40 percent more likely to see a doctor at a clinic outside of a hospital (NCHS 1991). This is partly because fewer doctors choose to practice in inner cities, partly because of Medicaid restrictions and partly because blacks are more likely to experience the emergency trauma of violence.

Thus some analysts argue that while blacks do not necessarily have less access to health care services and the general quality of their medical care is comparable, the overall ambiance of their care is less. They might have a longer wait, in a less pleasant atmosphere, see the same doctor less frequently, experience greater impersonality of care and travel farther, often on inconvenient public transportation, to obtain care. It is not surprising, therefore, that the Harvard survey found that only 58 percent of the black respondents were completely satisfied with their health care as compared to 77 percent of the white respondents (Blendon et al.). When added to the increased likelihood of the opportunity cost of an hourly wage job and the oftentimes greater need for child care, the result is medical care whose implicit cost may be very great even if the dollar price were zero.

There is every reason to believe, as economic analysis suggests, that these greater costs lead to lesser utilization. This lesser utilization and delay in seeking care would indeed produce observable health and mortality differentials.

Public Policy Issues and Recommendations

Most of the lifestyle choice issues, notably drug, alcohol and cigarette consumption, have been covered in previous chapters. Policy recommendations to lessen unhealthy choices involved a combination of taxation (however regressive), punishment, reward, rehabilitation and education. This chapter makes the point that some of these choices are made more often by blacks, resulting in unfavorable differences in health and mortality. While some tactical measures, such as taxation, cannot be made racially specific, others, such as education, can. Just as, for example, cigarette companies target blacks in their advertising, so can we target blacks in our antismoking campaigns. We must make a special effort to reach black children and teens. Many health-threatening behaviors are habits or addictions arising from choices made when young.

The issue of poverty, a major contributing factor to poor health and one that impacts more severely on blacks, is simply too far beyond our purview to treat here. However, it bears remarking that some of the recommendations made in this volume are, in fact, poverty reduction measures. For example, policies that would lead to a reduction in drug and alcohol abuse would also lead to a reduction in poverty, for just as substance abuse is partly a result of poverty, so is it also partly a cause. Even more effective as poverty reduction devices are policy proposals yet to appear. Although their primary purpose is to relieve other problems, measures such as family planning services, teen pregnancy prevention programs, parent training classes, infant stimulation programs and early childhood education all attack poverty at its roots.

We will discuss access to health care, though not as thoroughly as the topic deserves. In short: health care must be made affordable and available to all at levels that promote the proper degree of utilization. This will be possible only with major systemic reforms.

Health Care Costs Must be Contained

Like so much else, this is easy to say but hard to do. Health care is expensive. Its cost has been growing both absolutely and relatively. Medical costs increased at an average annual rate of 8 percent during the 1980s while the overall consumer price index increased an average of 4.7 percent annually and median family income increased an average of 5 percent (NCHS 1991; USBC).

Sources of increasing costs: On the demand side, the population both grew and aged, while Americans in general demanded more and better health care services. Prices have also been driven up by the increasing demand for catastrophic care, psychiatric care and the medical care and rehabilitation associated with alcoholism and drug abuse. General inflation exerted supply-side pressure on prices. Rising malpractice premiums, resulting from multitudinous lawsuits and generous awards, also contributed. But the greatest source of increasing costs has been the new, sophisticated medical technologies, primarily in surgery, diagnostic tests and pharmaceuticals. Not only are many new procedures more costly, but they often benefit many additional patients. They are therefore performed more frequently.

These forces together generated total United States health expenditures of $666 billion in 1990, 122 percent of our GNP, the greatest in our history and the greatest of any developed nation (Levit et al.). They made the health care industry one of the nation's largest and fastest growing.

Paying for health care has become a serious problem. Most Americans under age 65 are covered by employer- or union-provided plans, but these are not without price. Health care costs to business increased more than 800 percent from 1970 to 1987, worsening overall inflation (USGAO 1990f). They increased almost 22 percent in 1990 alone for the firms surveyed by Foster Higgins, an employee benefits consulting agency. Noble Lowndes, an accounting and actuarial firm, surveyed the 15 leading health insurers and found that the expected increase in corporate health care costs for 1991 range from 24 to 34 percent. These percentages, of course, are compounded on an ever larger base. Small businesses, often unable to obtain group insurance, have borne even greater increases, 33 percent just in 1988 (USGAO 1990f). They pay 10 to 40 percent more for the same plan, when they can get it (USGAO 1989c). Many small businesses no longer insure their workers, citing insufficient profitability and high premiums. Increasing numbers of firms of all sizes are switching to copayment as a defense, touching off some of our more virulent labor-management disputes.

As out-of-pocket costs grow, family income is squeezed and more health care is forgone.

The cost to taxpayers has also increased. Spending for Medicare increased 14 percent in 1989 to a total of over $100 billion; spending for Medicaid increased 12 percent to a total of $54.5 billion, 34 percent of which was spent on the elderly (NCHS 1991). Medicaid has been a substantial burden for state governments, who pay 43 percent of its costs. Growing Medicaid payments have forced many states to curtail other important services. Medical costs truly must be brought under control.

Cost-reduction measures: Few medical cost factors are susceptible to much control. Countries that have limited doctors' fees typically experience doctor shortages. Patients have longer waits and fewer choices. Medicaid's policy of containing costs by limiting provider reimbursements has produced similar results here and is partly to blame for blacks' lesser access to health care. Also, limiting fees is economically inequitable; it imposes a selective tax on the medical profession. Health maintenance organizations have kept doctors' fees somewhat lower by promising a larger caseload. But that approach may soon reach its limits. Reducing hospital costs by early release of patients to the care of untrained family members may also soon reach its limits. Some say it has already surpassed them. Providing more professional home care as opposed to expensive hospital or nursing home care may result in genuine cost savings. But it may also backfire as the "woodwork effect" brings people into the system who would not have otherwise sought care. The cost of pharmaceuticals could perhaps be contained, although interference in the market seldom produces desirable results. We do not want to discourage research and development of new drug therapies (which may be better funded through tax subsidies), but neither should we pay exorbitantly high prices for drugs made by American companies that are sold abroad for a much lower price.

Alternative means of reducing costs may be more feasible. Malpractice awards could be capped. The government could underwrite malpractice insurance for selected practitioners similar to its insurance of the banking system. Duplicate or unnecessary tests could then be better avoided. All unnecessary care must be avoided. Kennedy estimates the cost of such care to be $18 billion a year. Studies of selected surgical procedures by the Rand Corporation found that 15 to 40 percent were unnecessary and potentially harmful (Kennedy). Greater responsibility could be shifted to midlevel practitioners such as nurses, midwives and physician assistants. The supply of practitioners at all levels could be increased through recruitment, training, scholarships and other financial assistance. Government-supported financial incentives could induce more health professionals to practice in underserved, low-income areas. Greater emphasis should be placed on preventative care; it is almost always cost-effective. Individuals should be provided economic incentives to healthy lifestyles. Stokes suggests linking health and life insurance premiums and deductibles to behaviorally modifiable risk factors, such as alcohol use, cigarette smoking and cholesterol levels, where modification would reduce health risks. Greater efficiency in provision of care and utilization of resources may be achieved through regionalization of the hospital system. Costs could be kept down through less duplication of expensive equipment. Greater specialization would be encouraged, promoting economies of scale.

Health care should also be rationed. While we want greater access, access should not be unlimited. However, rationing should not be dependent, in most cases, on ability to pay. Some should be based on the relationship between the supply of the desired service and the "merit" of the prospective recipient. For example, alcoholics should not be first in line for liver transplants. Organs are in short supply, transplantation is expensive and there are persons waiting who are not responsible for their liver damage. Rationing can also be based on a cost-benefit approach that distinguishes between procedures that enhance the quality of life and those that simply prolong it, perhaps beyond its welcome. The greatly disproportionate share of health care dollars spent on patients in their last year of life (as reported by Lubitz and Prihoda) indicates that many useless procedures are being performed on terminal patients. Other patients may survive but at a grieviously reduced level of existence. The elderly would, of course, be most affected, but others would also. Accident victims kept alive at great expense and in great agony and children born severely damaged, saved only to live lives of terrible disability, should be treated humanely, not heroically. The issue is obviously not merely fiscal; it is ethical and involves the quality of life and the right to do as nature intended—to die. But, whereas financial considerations should not be foremost, neither should they be overlooked. Resources are limited; society has many needs; and we have already witnessed a major redistribution of income to the health care industry.

Everyone Must be Insured

Many are not. Senator Edward M. Kennedy claims that 40 percent of the United States population had no coverage or inadequate coverage in 1991. The 1989 Current Population Survey found that over 13 percent of the total U.S. population had no insurance coverage. Non-Hispanic whites comprised a majority of the uninsured, although they had the lowest rate, 10 percent. Almost 20 percent of non-Hispanic blacks, 40 percent of Mexican-Americans, 16 percent of Puerto Ricans and 20 percent of Cuban-Americans had no insurance (in Treviño et al.). Most minorities that are insured are covered by private policies; the remainder are covered by Medicaid. Puerto Ricans and blacks are most likely to be insured by Medicaid, with rates of 33 and 23 percent respectively. By contrast, only 4.5 percent of whites are Medicaid recipients.

Although imperfect, Medicaid does pay for health care. Access may be limited, ambiance may be less, but care is provided. The uninsured are far worse off. Some of the cost of their care is shifted to the insured through higher charges (and thus higher premiums) but much of it is out-of-pocket. Therefore much of it is forgone. Many studies have shown that uninsured persons have far fewer health care contacts. Hadley and colleagues also found that uninsured hospital patients, compared to the privately insured, were far less likely to undergo high-cost or high-discretion procedures. Uninsured patients were 50 percent less likely to have normal results on various tissue pathology reports and had a 44 to 124 percent higher risk of in-hospital mortality. Although some of the differential may be due to lifestyle differences (uninsured persons tend to be low income and may more frequently engage in health-risking behavior), much of the differential is undoubtedly due to their coming to treatment later. They cannot afford care.

One of the ironic inequities of our system is that we spend billions of public dollars on health care for people who no longer work or who never did work but spend very little on those who do. Fully 72 percent of uninsured adults are members of the work force; 28 percent work full-time, full-year (USGAO 1989c). Their industriousness is rewarded by their ineligibility for Medicaid.

Uninsured workers are more often young, unmarried and less educated and low income. They are disproportionately black and Hispanic and likely to be employed by small firms or in the service sector. Their employers either provide no insurance or require a large employee copayment. Again, minorities are most adversely affected as, having larger families and lower incomes, payments are often beyond reach.

Almost everyone agrees that the time has come for reform of the system and extension of coverage. Universal health care is both desirable and inevitable. The question is one of form. President Bush's plan departs the least from current practice, relying on market-based reform to make health care insurance affordable. It seeks to lessen insurance premiums by, among other things, regulatory reform to reduce administrative costs and the inclusion of small businesses in larger risk pools. The President's plan also includes major malpractice reform but its cornerstone rests on tax policy. The plan provides a health insurance tax credit for low-wage workers (which would take the form of a negative income tax for those whose tax liability is less than their insurance premiums, to a limit) and restores income tax deductions for health care premiums to middle-income earners. Most plans, however, such as the Kennedy plan and the Pepper Commission plan, require employer coverage of all full-time workers, with public funds providing for the low-income uninsured. Under the Kennedy plan, known as HealthAmerica, employers would either provide basic health insurance to their employees or would pay 7 percent of their payroll to the federal government to fund comparable public insurance coverage. AmeriCare, as the public insurance portion would be called, would be a joint federal-state program replacing Medicaid, and would insure all Americans not covered by Medicare or employer-provided insurance. The Physicians' Proposal and the Health Security Partnership are more radical, calling for a single national plan and abolishing private insurance. All the proposals have merits and drawbacks. Those that would end private coverage would meet great resistance from the insurance lobby. Those that mandate employer coverage must provide for serious cost containment, if not cost reduction, and provide special assistance to small businesses. Otherwise it will further reduce profitability, raise prices, reduce American competitiveness and exacerbate the shift to part-time employment and offshore production.

Each of the proposed plans is expensive. The Pepper Commission plan is estimated at over $66 billion annually (CHAUS). Kennedy's HealthAmerica is estimated to cost employers over $100 billion a year, with government spending to increase by $6 billion in the first year, and more thereafter (CHAUS; Erlich).

United States Comptroller General Charles Bowsher has testified that we could provide health care to all Americans without increased expenditures if we adopted the key features of the Canadian system. Relying on a single source of payment, uniform reimbursement rules and systemwide spending control, the Canadian system is highly cost-effective. It reduces the need for insurance record keeping, thereby reducing operating expenses for doctors and hospitals. The Ministry of Health determines each hospital's operating budget, motivating hospital administrators to contain costs. As a result, Canada provides quality health care to all her citizens, yet her per capita spending is 23 percent less than that of the United States (USGAO 1991a).

The General Accounting Office estimates that implementation of the Canadian system would save the United States $3 billion annually *after* meeting the increased demand for health care that would result (USGAO 1991a).

The system does have some shortcomings, however. Choices are limited, waits can be long, and advanced procedures are less readily available. Too great a reduction in price to the individual leads to overutilization of the system, increasing costs and creating bottlenecks. Interfering too greatly with profit taking reduces supply and lessens innovation. For most Americans, other nations' systems represent a step backward. But for the many now largely shut out of the world's finest health care system, they would be a blessing. Whether the high-quality care now enjoyed by the well insured can be made available to all at prices the nation can afford remains to be seen.

In the meantime, as the debate rages, poor people, largely minorities, are dying at excessive rates. Some of those dying are children.

INFANT MORTALITY RATES

Infant mortality, the death of a child less than one year of age, has long been a major public health concern. It has caused even greater concern in recent years for two reasons: the falling relative position of the United States internationally, and the growing disparity between the races.

U.S. Infant Mortality Rates

Even though American infant mortality rates (IMRs) have fallen a great deal during this century, our relative position has deteriorated dramatically. In 1918, the United States ranked sixth out of 20 countries reporting comparable data; by 1986, we had fallen to 13th out of the original 20 countries, and 22nd out of all those reported by the World Health Organization. Ahead of us were almost all of Western Europe plus Canada, Hong Kong, Singapore and Japan (MTF).

In 1975, the total U.S. IMR stood at a historical low of 16.1 deaths per 1,000 live births. The figure for white babies was 14.2; for black babies it was 26.2 (NCHS 1991). Even though these rates were almost half what they had been twenty-five years earlier, our relative position indicated we still had needless infant deaths, especially among blacks. Thus the Surgeon General, in a 1979 report, set a standard for improving infant survival rates in the 1980s. The goal was an overall IMR of 9.0 with an IMR no greater than 12.0 for any ethnic or racial groups by 1990 (NCHS 1990e).

We may meet some of those goals. National data for 1989 indicates a total IMR of 9.8, the lowest ever recorded in the United States. The rate for white infants was 8.2; however, the black rate of 17.7 is still distressingly high. The gap between the races has increased for, whereas rates for both black and white babies have fallen, those for white babies have fallen considerably more. In fact, from 1988 to 1989, when the white IMR fell by 4 percent, the black IMR actually increased 0.6 percent (CDC 1992b). Recent city statistics suggest that the disparity, in spite of considerable effort to reduce it, has increased further.

The contrast between the American IMR and that of other affluent nations reflects our comparative distribution of pregnancies. These lead to an unfavorable distribution of birth weights. Birth weight is closely associated with an infant's chance of survival. A low-birth-weight (LBW) baby, one that weighs less than 2,500 grams at birth, is 40 times more likely to die in the neonatal period (the first 28 days after birth) than a normal-weight baby and five times more likely to die in the postneonatal period (28 days to one year after birth). A very-low-birth-weight baby (VLBW), one weighing less than 1,500 grams, faces far greater risks (MTF).

The United States has developed sophisticated, effective and expensive technology for saving LBW babies. However, as LBW is still related to 70 percent of the infant deaths in this country, our medical advances are apparently not enough to compensate for our excess LBW deliveries (MOD).

Infant Mortality Rates, Low Birth Weight and Racial Disparities

The racial disparity in IMRs is rooted in differential incidence of LBW. In 1988, 5.7 percent of white babies were LBW; 0.9 percent were VLBW. The respective rates for black babies were 12.7 and 2.7 (NCHS 1991). Disorders relating to short gestation (prematurity) and low birthweight are the leading cause of death for black infants, accounting for 15 percent of their deaths in 1989. Black babies were 4.5 times more likely to die from such disorders than white babies and their risk of dying within the first year of life was 2.3 times greater (CDC 1992b).

Role of Prenatal Care

Common wisdom attributes most of the birthweight differential to black women's lesser access to adequate prenatal care (PNC). PNC is a key predictor of birth weight. Though the causal relationship may be more apparent than real, research by the March of Dimes indicates that a woman who has about 13 prenatal visits has only a 2 percent chance of having a LBW baby (MTF).

In 1988, among white mothers who delivered full-term infants, the percentage that were low birth weight was 2.2 percent for women who initiated care in the first trimester; 3.4 percent, the second trimester; 3.9 percent, the third trimester; and 7.8 percent for those who received no prenatal care. In comparison, among black mothers who carried to term, the proportion of low-birth-weight deliveries was 5.2 percent for women who initiated care in the first trimester; 6.3 percent, the second trimester; 6.6 percent, the third trimester; and 13.3 percent for those who received no prenatal care. (CDC 1991g).

As noted earlier, black women are more often poor and more likely to be insured by Medicaid or not at all. Fewer obstetricians and hospitals are willing to handle Medicaid maternity patients, largely because of the increased discrepancy between their costs and Medicaid reimbursements and the greater possible malpractice liability of high-risk cases. (Poor black women with or without adequate PNC are at greater risk.) Budget cutbacks and the closing of municipal hospitals have raised additional barriers to low-income women. Sara Rosenbaum, program director of the Children's Defense Fund, said,

"The great majority of poor women understand the need for prenatal care and actively seek it out, but often have to wait weeks or months to get a doctor's appointment. In some cities, a pregnant woman has to be heroic just to get an appointment at a public clinic" (in Pear p. 5).

However, important as access to adequate care is, utilization of existing facilities is just as much so. City after city, many of which have established outreach programs of PNC in low-income black neighborhoods, report the difficulty of getting women to come for care or to keep follow-up appointments.

Yet the racial disparities cannot be fully explained by the disparities in prenatal care. Monitoring fetal development may detect or forestall the occasional major problem, but, for the most part, prenatal visits serve primarily to remind the woman to take proper care of herself. It may be that most women who seek PNC already do. Thus the value of PNC per se may be overstated. Other factors are also important.

Role of Marital Status

Single mothers, more apt to live in poverty, often lacking in sound family and social support, have a much higher incidence of LBW babies. Of the black babies born in 1988, 63.5 percent were born to unmarried mothers; the white rate was 18 percent (NCHS 1991).

Role of Maternal Age

Teenagers are much more likely to give birth to LBW babies. Their eating habits are often poor and they are far less likely to seek early and adequate PNC. Whether due to denial, embarrassment, lack of understanding of its importance or lack of knowledge of where to find it, 46 percent of pregnant teens do not receive PNC during their first trimester, 9 percent wait until their third trimester and 4 percent do not receive any PNC at all (NCHS 1991). Black women are more than twice as likely as white women to be teenage mothers (NCHS 1991).

Role of Biological Factors

Age–birth-weight charts reveal an increase (and, ultimately, a decrease) in average birth-weight that corresponds to each additional year of the mother's age with such regularity that exogeneous factors such as nutrition and PNC do not alone explain it. Something endogeneous, that is, biological, must be at work.

The same regularity is evident in the age–birth-weight charts when a racial distinction is made. But, although the progression (and regression) in birth weight is similar, the difference in absolute values between the two is startling. At every maternal age the average birth weight of black babies is much lower than that of whites—so much so that the lowest average-birth-weight white infants, those born to mothers under 15 years of age, weigh more than the highest average-birth-weight black infants, those born to women 20 to 24 years of age (USHR).

In a study of women in Chicago, Collins and David found that the same is true even when the mother's education and income are taken into account. Black women with college degrees and family incomes over $40,000 are more likely to give birth to abnormally small babies than are young white high school dropouts with family incomes of less than $10,000. The authors, prominent specialists in perinatal epidemiology and neonatology, regard some undefined legacy of poverty as the likely explanation. But perhaps there is simply a genetic tendency on the part of black women toward lower-birth-weight babies.

Genetics may be a very important factor. It may partially explain why, although Puerto Rican rates are somewhat higher, overall Hispanic IMRs are lower than those of non-Hispanic whites (USHR). With an incidence of poverty three times that of whites (USBC), Hispanic women face the same obstacles as blacks in obtaining PNC, with the oftentimes additional barrier of language difference. As with blacks, 39 percent do not get first-trimester PNC (compared to 21 percent of whites) and they are more likely than blacks or whites to get very late or no PNC (USHR). Teenage mothers account for 16 percent of their births, unmarried mothers for 33 percent (USBC). Yet, except for the case of Puerto Ricans, whose incidence of LBW deliveries is roughly in between that of whites and blacks, the Hispanic LBW rates are only slightly higher than those of whites (USHR). And as mentioned, their IMRs are the lowest of all.

When biological predisposition is coupled with the exogenous risk predictors of poverty, teenage and single motherhood and lesser access to PNC, it is not surprising that black women tend to have LBW babies and higher rates of infant mortality. The increasing relative difference is due, in part, to the increasing proportion of black mothers in groups at high risk for low-birth-weight deliveries (i.e., women less than 20 years of age, with fewer than 12 years of education, or with late or no prenatal care). The increase in the absolute number of low-birth-weight infants reflects the increasing number of births to young unmarried white and black mothers and to mothers receiving late or no prenatal care (CDC 1991g).

The New Element

A 1987 study conducted by the Philadelphia Perinatal Society found that in one low-income black neighborhood one in five women failed to get adequate PNC, 16 percent of the babies were LBW, 14 percent had mothers 17 years of age or less and 85 percent had mothers who were not married. The IMR was 30 per 1,000 live births. The situation was even worse in many other poor black neighborhoods—more than one in four women received little or no PNC, and IMRs were as high as 42 per 1,000 live births (Fitzgerald 1989a).

The findings were frightening. The city had targeted various outreach programs to just these women, and free PNC was available at 29 city-funded sites. Yet the proportion of women failing to get adequate PNC was the highest since the city began keeping such statistics. IMRs were also at their highest.

What made the lethal difference was crack-cocaine, the repercussions of which were just beginning to be felt in Philadelphia. The Perinatal Society study found one in six new mothers (citywide, more in many neighborhoods) admitting to cocaine use while pregnant. Of the cocaine-using mothers, 71 percent had minimal or no PNC in spite of the fact that 80 percent were on Medicaid and free care was readily available (Fitzgerald 1989b).

The problem is even more dramatically illustrated by the experience of the City of Boston. Concerned about an increase in IMRs from 9.6 per 1,000 live births in 1981 to 10.1 in 1982, the first such increase in nine years, Boston formed a Task Force on the Prevention of Low Birth Weight and Infant Mortality. The task force found that black IMRs were twice that of whites, Hispanic rates were in between, and rates for teens were consistently higher than for older mothers. It also found that babies born to poor women, who were less likely to have had adequate PNC, were 1.5 times more likely to die than those born to higher-income women. Babies born to women who had no PNC had IMRs ten times greater and LBW rates five times greater than babies whose mothers had adequate PNC.

Though the state supported 20 Maternal and Infant Care Centers (MICCs) as well as numerous other public health centers, the number was insufficient. Also the Women's, Infants' and Children's Supplemental Food Programs (WIC) as well as Family Planning Services did not reach all who were eligible.

Following the task force's 1985 recommendations, Massachusetts, already one of the most generous in social welfare expenditures, embarked on a comprehensive program to aid women in need. The state initiated "presumptive eligibility" of all low-income women not enrolled in Medicaid. This meant that health care providers were to assume all poor women were eligible for benefits and provide care during the application period, to be reimbursed later. Also included were various outreach programs, expansion of MICC and WIC, and targeting of additional funds to low-income pregnant teens. PNC was made more available and free to all low-income women.

But even as these measures were being put into place, the crack epidemic hit Boston. Figure 4.2 depicts its impact.

The results were as one would expect. LBW deliveries and IMRs for white babies fell. For black babies they soared. In 1988, Boston's overall black IMR approached 25 deaths per 1,000 live births, three times that of whites. It was 37 in one neighborhood, 88 in another (BDHH). LBW deliveries and IMRs also rose for Boston's Hispanic women, who were increasingly using heroin as well as crack (BDHH; Nardone & Steriti). Births to teens, especially very young teens, also increased dramatically, as did the proportion of teen births that were LBW (BDHH).

The 1990 Massachusetts Task Force on Infant Mortality called for yet more outreach, greater expansion of programs and enhanced detoxification and rehabilitation services for pregnant drug-addicted women. In addition, the city, for the first time, directly hired obstetricians to serve low-income women and

Figure 4.2
Trends in Adequacy of Prenatal Care by Maternal Race: Massachusetts, 1980 to 1988

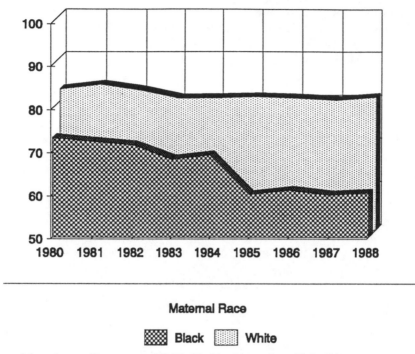

Maternal Race

▓▓ Black   ░░ White

Source: Massachusetts Department of Public Health. *Advance Data: Births 1988.*

put pressure on local hospitals to greatly expand clinic facilities and hours and to take other measures to serve low-income women. Boston University and Boston City Hospital initiated midwife training programs in response. But it will be an uphill battle. Preliminary figures for 1989 in Boston revealed that the black-white infant mortality ratio was very close to four to one (McNamara).

Crack has such a devastating and multifaceted effect on an infant and the social costs are so very great that it will be examined more thoroughly in the chapter on children at risk. Since the discussion here centers on differential mortality rates, it will simply be said that use by pregnant women increases IMRs by an estimated factor of three (Plaut & Kelley) and increases the likelihood of sudden infant death syndrome five to ten times (NAPARE). And that, although crack use is found in many sociodemographic groups, it has been running rampant through many poor black communities. Indeed, crack use among pregnant women has inflated black IMRs to such horrifying heights that public health officials now refer to Boston's black neighborhoods as "death zones"— not because of homicide or AIDS or drug abuse per se, but because babies die.

Public Policy Issues and Recommendations

The reduction of infant mortality rates is not an Olympic event. We want our babies to survive for reasons other than our world standing. However, an examination of why American rates compare unfavorably to those of other industrialized nations provides guidelines as to possible remedies.

Our situation differs in the following respects.

* We have a greater proportion of teen births.
* We have a greater proportion of unmarried mothers.
* We have a far greater proportion of black women, who not only tend to have lower-birth-weight babies, but also have higher rates of pregnancy.
* We do not have a comprehensive, cohesive system of health care in general or of gynecological-obstetrical care in particular.

Therefore, specific steps must be taken.

Family Planning Services Must Be More Readily Available

Prevention is always cost-effective. It is also less expensive socially and psychologically. Since the earliest and least costly prevention is at the source, before conception, we need a more extensive and accessible system of family planning services. Teens, single women and poor women, who have the highest incidence of LBW babies, are most likely to use publicly funded family planning services (NCHS 1990f) and to have far more unwanted pregnancies (NCHS 1985).

The publicly funded family planning system we now have, helter-skelter though it is, provides contraceptive services for about 4.5 million mostly high-risk women. Without these services there would be an estimated 1.2 million additional unintended pregnancies each year and over 500,000 additional births (Forrest and Singh). IMRs would only be greater.

Federal and state governments spend approximately $400 million annually for contraceptive services (and save, according to the Alan Guttmacher Institute, an approximate $1.8 billion on services that would have to be rendered to those women who would otherwise give birth). The statistics tell us we need to spend more. Yet we are cutting back. Federal money for family planning was made available primarily through Medicaid and Title X of the Public Health Service Act. However, Title X, one of whose original sponsors in the early 1970s was Congressman George Bush, has not been reauthorized. Bowing to fundamentalist and antiabortion pressure, the Reagan and Bush administrations opposed Title X spending and made it extremely difficult for any family planning clinic that presents abortion as an option to receive Medicaid funding. Then in May 1991, the Supreme Court decided that the government may forbid federally funded family planning clinics from offering abortion advice, even if continued pregnancy endangers the mother's life. Brushing aside both a women's legal right to an abortion and a doctor's First Amendment right to talk freely with patients, the Court forced thousands of clinics to choose between not discussing abortion (even if the patient asks) and losing a major (perhaps vital) portion of their funding. Unless Congress takes remedial action, many clinics will close or greatly curtail their services. Just as free speech has suffered a serious blow, so will women and children. More babies will die. Many will survive to lead a life of deprivation or abuse. Poverty's grip on women will tighten. Social costs will escalate.

Deficit-ridden state and local governments are also cutting back family planning services and teen pregnancy prevention programs. This is no way to balance a budget. It is cost-ineffective on every level. Savings in public medical costs alone are estimated to be $4.40 for each $1 spent in contraceptive services to the typical clinic patient (Forrest & Singh). Savings in income support and social services are greater yet.

We must expand family planning services, not cut them back. Contraceptive and pregnancy termination services must be made equally available to all women. As it now stands, they are least available to those women at greatest risk and most in need.

Prenatal Care Must be Accessible to All

We must do more to make PNC available and affordable, since women do become pregnant, intentionally or not.

Insofar as we do not yet have a universal health care plan, all states must institute "presumptive eligibility" for low-income women not yet enrolled in Medicaid. Eligibility is a reasonable assumption, as Congress has recently expanded Medicaid coverage of pregnant women significantly. Whereas, if we deny care to pregnant women because they do not have Medicaid cards, we risk losing them from the system altogether. It will, of course, be the highest-risk women who are lost.

Medicaid payments must fully cover reasonable expenses so more providers will be willing to treat Medicaid patients. Failure to do so thus far has led to a reduction in the supply of care.

Private health insurance must make maternity coverage available and affordable for all women, married and single. Almost 10 million women of reproductive age have no insurance at all. Over 5 million such women are insured under plans that do not provide maternity coverage, largely for financial reasons (USGAO 1990g). State insurance commissioners should pressure insurance companies to reduce the current costly premiums for maternity benefits. (They must also push for inclusion of routine gynecological exams and mammograms.)

We could go further and do as East Germany had done—pay women to keep PNC appointments.

Every Woman Must be Educated about the Need for Care

We must target black women of all ages and incomes. They must be informed of their greater risk of LBW babies and their greater need to monitor their diet and vitamin intake.

We must target teens. Sex education classes must stress the need for early PNC and a nutritious diet. Prenatal counseling can be made available and vitamins can be dispensed at school-based clinics. Prenatal exams could be made more readily available at school or community clinics.

The media could be used more effectively. Low-income women watch television more than Americans generally; teens listen to the radio more. Prenatal advice should be incorporated into current programming. Public service messages such as the March of Dimes Be Good to Your Baby before It Is Born series should be more widely aired.

Outreach Efforts Must be Extended to Poor and Single Women

Many cities have developed outreach programs in the form of Mom Mobiles, traveling PNC clinics that encourage follow-up at full-scale clinics. These have been helpful, though patients' follow-up is often lacking. Many cities have instituted door-to-door canvassing to locate pregnant women and bring them into the PNC system. This too has been helpful.

These together with a system of mentoring could be quite effective. Women, minorities in particular, could be trained (perhaps as part of a welfare-related employment training program) to act as a big sisters/godmother to high-risk women and their babies. Medicaid now covers pre- and postnatal visits to high-risk women, as they have proven to lessen LBW deliveries and reduce IMRs. Indeed, all parties would benefit and it could ultimately lessen public expenditures.

Neighborhood-based clinics staffed by nurse-midwives could make PNC easier to get and less costly to provide. They would be less intimidating than the scale and bureaucracy of hospital-based clinics.

We need to train more nurse-midwives. We need training facilities and full-support scholarships for interested low-income women. We should recruit trainees, again perhaps as part of a welfare-related program. We could make preparatory training available in high schools and produce numerous beneficial results even if few participants go on to higher study. In the meantime, we should relax immigration standards for midwives. This would be especially beneficial in non-English-speaking neighborhoods. (Recent Asian immigrants are another group that is reluctant to use existing facilities.)

Addicted women are the most difficult to reach and bring to care, and they bear the babies most in danger. Their case is examined more thoroughly in the following chapter. Here we will note that even with the best technologies and the expenditure of perhaps hundreds of thousands of dollars, many of their babies are lost. Those that survive often face such severe physical and intellectual handicaps that one must ask if simple reduction in infant mortality is necessarily a laudable goal. There surely are more humane and socially productive ways our financial and health care resources can be used. It is not that these babies should die (though that may not always be the worst case, given their pain, incidence of AIDS and likelihood of suffering child abuse). They should never have been conceived. Our emphasis with addicted women should be on pregnancy prevention. But if they do get pregnant and abortion is unavailable or undesirable, addicts need guaranteed access to PNC, which is often denied because their addiction imposes greater costs and risks, and priority access to rehabilitation, which is often denied because their pregnancy imposes greater costs and risk.

The demand and supply measures suggested here would, if successful, result in a lower client price for prenatal care and much greater consumption of services by high-risk women. IMRs should decline. But such measures may not be enough. Lowering the IMR is going to take imagination, commitment and money. The reduction of infant mortality rates may not be an Olympic event, but the elimination of racial disparities may be an Olympian feat.

5

Children at Risk

The terrible costs of others' unhealthy choices are often borne by children. This was evidenced in previous chapters by the accounts of babies stricken with AIDS and children made ill by environmental cigarette smoke. However, in these cases, as in most of those described earlier, harm was inflicted indirectly, even inadvertently. This chapter continues the discussion of endangered children but focuses on those who suffer as a direct result of someone else's behavior. That someone is often the child's mother.

Injury may be inflicted during any stage in the child's development: in utero, postpartum, or well into the youngster's childhood. Except in some instances of physical abuse or neglect, harmful behavioral choices are rarely made with the intent to injure a child. The mother may want to enhance her short-run utility function, perhaps by drinking or taking drugs, and may be ignorant of the potential harm to her child. She may want to avoid pain, such as that provoked by withdrawal from an addictive substance. Or no actual choice may be made—rather, the behavior is a spontaneous eruption, a response to temper, stress or impulse. In any case, the damage may be quite severe and long lasting. And costly.

This chapter will examine two risk arenas, places where a child should be most secure and protected, places of great potential harm: the womb and the home.

THE UNBORN CHILD

There are dozens of ways a woman may jeopardize her unborn baby—cleaning a cat's litter box, eating unwashed fruit or undercooked meat, gardening without gloves, contracting chicken pox, taking Accutane to treat acne or suffering unrelieved psychological stress. Although most risks can be avoided if a woman is aware of them, some arise from addictive behavior and thus are very difficult to avert or reduce.

Cigarette Smoking

Prevalence and Short-Term Consequences of Prenatal Smoking

Smoking during pregnancy can have profound effects on the developing fetus. It increases the risk of spontaneous abortion by 70 percent and of perinatal death (death of a late-term fetus or infant less than seven days old) by 25 percent. Babies whose mothers smoked while pregnant are 36 percent more likely to be born prematurely and 98 percent more likely to be low birth weight (USDHHS 1989b). Babies born to nonsmoking women whose fathers smoke during the mothers' pregnancy are at twice the risk of LBW as babies born into homes in which neither parent smokes (in Cook et al.).

Most people understand something of the dangers. A 1985 NCHS health interview found that 74 percent of American women knew that smoking during pregnancy increased the chance of miscarriage, 80 percent knew it increased the likelihood of low birth weight, 66 percent knew about stillbirths and 70 percent knew it often precipitated premature births (Fox et al.). Yet despite their awareness of the risks, 32 percent of all women in that year, including those who gave birth, were smokers. Only 21 percent of the delivering smokers quit when they learned they were pregnant; 36 percent cut down. The prevalence of smoking among pregnant women was 77 percent of the prevalence of smoking among women in general and varied inversely with age, income and education (USDHHS 1989a).

Fewer women smoke today. We do not know what proportion of women smoked during pregnancy, but in 1987 (the most recent year for which age- and race-specific data are available), 26.1 percent of women aged 18 to 24 smoked, as did 31.8 percent of women aged 25 to 34. The respective rates for white women were 27.8 and 31.9; for black women they were 20.4 and 35.8 (NCHS 1991).

State data are more recent and more specific. In Massachusetts 18.6 percent of white mothers, 16.3 percent of black mothers, 10.9 percent of Hispanic mothers and 2.4 percent of Asian mothers reported smoking during pregnancy in 1988. Those who smoked had twice the incidence of LBW deliveries as nonsmoking women (MDPH 1989). The data do not reveal how often cigarette smoking was combined with risk factors such as young age, alcohol or drug use; however, the two-to-one LBW ratio is what researchers have been finding for the last 25 years.

The state of New Hampshire did examine additional factors, although drug use was not among them. Reviewing all births in the state from 1987 through 1989, it found that 40 percent of teenage mothers, 52 percent of mothers with less than 12 years of schooling and 43 percent of mothers whose income was below 150 percent of the poverty level smoked during pregnancy, as did 48 percent of unmarried mothers and 48 percent of those who had late or no prenatal care (SCHS 1991b). It also found maternal smoking to be a far greater predictor of low birth weight than maternal age, education, income, marital status or adequacy of prenatal care. Smoking also reduced birth weight by the greatest amount, 7 to 12 ounces, compared to the 3 or 4 ounces attributed to other risk factors. Also noteworthy, considering the current interest in prenatal care, is that New Hampshire mothers who smoked and began PNC in the first trimester had higher rates (7.3 percent) of low-birth-weight deliveries than nonsmoking mothers who initiated PNC in the third trimester or who received no care (6.0 percent) (SCHS 1991a).

Five major studies of births in the United States, Canada and Wales found that 21 to 39 percent of the incidence of LBW was due to maternal cigarette smoking (USDHHS 1989a). Research has also shown that smoking cessation during pregnancy can partly reverse the reduction in infant birth weight (Hebel et al.).

A 1988 NCHS study of pregnant women in Missouri found infant mortality rates (IMRs), adjusted for age, income, education and marital status, to be 15.1 per 1,000 subjects for white nonsmoking mothers, 18.8 for white mothers who smoked less than one pack per day and 23.3 for white mothers who smoked more. The respective IMRs for black mothers were 26.0, 32.4 and 39.9. It was estimated that if all pregnant women in this country stopped smoking, the number of fetal and infant deaths would be reduced by approximately 10 percent. About 4,000 fewer babies would die (USDHHS 1989a).

Investigating 1988 mortality, the Centers for Disease Control attributed the deaths of 2,552 children less than one year old to cigarette smoking. Most involved respiratory difficulties; 702 were classified as sudden infant death syndrome (SIDS) (CDC 1991b). A study of Swedish women found that, holding all other factors constant, maternal smoking greatly increased the incidence of SIDS. Compared to not smoking, smoking up to nine cigarettes a day doubled the risk of SIDS; smoking more than nine cigarettes tripled the risk (Haglund & Cnattingius).

Longer-Term Effects

Studies detailed in *Prenatal Smoking and Childhood Morbidity* (NCHS 1987) have traced the adverse consequences of maternal prenatal smoking on children for years after birth. Holding mothers' race, income and education constant, young children whose mothers smoked during pregnancy were perceived to be in poorer health, were confined to bed by illness more often and suffered more chronic conditions, especially respiratory problems. Those whose mothers smoked heavily (more than 16 cigarettes a day) were significantly worse off than those whose mothers smoked less (NCHS 1987). However, since the mothers probably continued to smoke, much of this distress might have been due to the children's inhalation of environmental smoke.

Although most of these effects appeared to be transient, that is, they diminished as the children grew older, other research has found that teenagers whose mothers smoked during pregnancy were, on average, shorter and more likely to have reading disabilities (NCHS 1987).

The fact that the adverse consequences of maternal smoking are so well known yet so many women continue to smoke while pregnant is a telling indication of the strength of nicotine addiction. It also indicates that many women do not find their baby's decreased well-being too high a price to pay to smoke. Only a large increase in the monetary price of cigarettes will significantly reduce their consumption and lessen the probability of an adverse outcome to their pregnancies. There is no better argument for a higher cigarette tax.

Alcohol Consumption

When a pregnant woman drinks, the alcohol passes swiftly through the placenta to her unborn baby. Because its underdeveloped organs cannot break the alcohol down as quickly as can an adult's, the baby's blood alcohol content is higher than its mother's. But the baby is not merely drunk; it is severely jeopardized. Drinking during pregnancy greatly increases the risk of miscarriage, stillbirth and death in early infancy. Heavy drinkers are two to four times more likely to have a miscarriage between the fourth and sixth month of pregnancy and two to three times more likely to lose their baby in the perinatal period than are nondrinkers (MOD).

The 1985 NCHS survey cited earlier found that 84 percent of American women associated heavy drinking during pregnancy with increased risk of adverse outcomes. However, many respondents did not know what form those adverse outcomes take. Most knew of the increased mortality risk, but only 55 percent had heard of fetal alcohol syndrome (FAS). Seventy percent of those thought the syndrome represented alcohol addiction in the affected newborn; only 24 percent correctly identified it as a set of birth defects; only 13 percent knew the effects were permanent (Fox et al.).

Effects of Prenatal Drinking

The effects are serious. Babies with FAS suffer both pre- and postnatal growth retardation; they oftentimes never catch up to other children. They have heads and brains that are abnormally small and experience varying degrees of mental retardation. Victims of FAS often have facial malformations such as narrow eyes, a short nose, thin upper lip, absent upper lip crease and underdeveloped jaws. They may have defects of the heart or other major organs. They have weak immune systems and react poorly to stress. They are often jittery, poorly coordinated and unable to concentrate, and they often manifest multiple behavioral problems. Physical malformations diminish as the FAS child passes into adolescence and adulthood, but intellectual disorders persist, and maladaptive behaviors often increase in magnitude and severity (Streissguth et al.).

Not all the children of women who drink prenatally are so profoundly affected. Both the number and severity of symptoms exist on a continuum. The full syndrome, in which all the symptoms are present, afflicts only babies whose mothers drank heavily during pregnancy. Children who exhibit fewer or less severe symptoms are diagnosed as suffering fetal alcohol effect (FAE). FAE children manifest more subtle cognitive-behavioral deficits. Longitudinal studies suggest that these psycholinguistic disorders, learning and attention deficits and behavioral problems persist through the child's school-age years (USDHHS 1990c). Thus all FAS and FAE children, not just the severely retarded, pay the price of their mother's prenatal drinking throughout their entire lives. Even those mildly affected may have educational or other disorders that lessen their earning capacity and their opportunities for a full, rewarding life.

Prevalence of FAS and FAE

The March of Dimes estimates that about 5,000 babies, about one in every 750 births, is born with FAS in the United States each year. Abel and Sokol estimate the number of FAS babies to be closer to 7,000. Abel estimates that another 21,000 babies are born FAE.

FAS has surpassed Down's syndrome as the leading cause of mental retardation (Abel). But unlike Down's syndrome, it is a tragedy that is entirely preventable.

There is a great variance in the prevalence of the syndrome among the various subpopulations.

Women who drink alcoholically while pregnant, an estimated 3.2 percent of pregnant women, have an estimated incidence of 59 FAS babies per 1,000 live births (Abel & Sokol). As their incidence of FAE babies is four times that (Abel), approximately 30 percent of the babies of women who drink very heavily during pregnancy suffer life-long debilitating consequences. Heavy drinkers are also more than twice as likely to have a LBW baby as light drinkers ("Alcohol"). Light drinkers do not have FAS babies; however, they may have an FAE baby, especially if they drank in the early weeks after conception when they may not have known they were pregnant.

It is the racial and ethnic differentials that are startling. The prevalence of FAS babies among Native Americans is a shocking 29.9 per 1,000 live births. Among blacks it is 6.0; among whites, 0.9; among Hispanics, 0.8; and among Asian Americans, 0.3 (Chavez et al.). Studies show that on some Indian reservations up to 25 percent of the children suffer from FAS or FAE (Krauthammer).

Much of the disparity can be attributed to differential incidences of alcohol abuse. But not all of it. The risk factors (such as threshold doses, critical periods of consumption and patterns of drinking) seem to vary in effect on both an individual and a group basis. Numerous genetic and maternal variables may determine which infants are damaged by their mothers' heavy drinking during pregnancy. Although we have not yet been able to identify the risk drinkers, several studies have shown that even when mothers' drinking habits are fairly similar, black infants are particularly susceptible to injury (Chavez et al.).

The Social Costs of FAS and FAE

Just as the afflicted children pay the price of other's drinking behavior, so do we all. The estimated economic costs of FAS were $1.84 billion in 1988 (USDHHS 1990a). Slightly more than ten percent was for medical treatment. The rest was for residential care and support services for persons made mentally retarded from prenatal alcohol exposure. Binkeley estimates the total lifetime economic costs of one FAS child to be $1.4 million (in Streissguth et al.).

Society also bears considerable costs for those less severely impaired. FAE children often need special education classes, speech therapy and other rehabilitation. They sometimes exhibit unusually severe temper tantrums, negative moods, phobias and difficulties with sibling relationships that may portend antisocial adult behavior. This is in addition to their lesser productivity as workers.

Perilous as maternal cigarette smoking and alcohol consumption may be to the health of a fetus, these are not the greatest hazards an infant may face today. Although the dangers still exist, especially as those women who continue to smoke or drink may be more severely addicted or more resistant to educational efforts, increased public awareness of health risks has resulted in a decline in both smoking and drinking among most American subpopulations. Although smoking among women, especially among young white women, has not declined as much as we would like, fewer women smoke today. Also, fewer women are heavy or moderate drinkers; more abstain or drink only lightly (NCHS 1991). Better yet, it is estimated that the number of pregnant women who consumed alcohol fell by 38 percent just from 1985 to 1988 (Serdula et al.).

More serious and more widespread today is the problem of fetal exposure to illicit drugs.

Drug Abuse

Heroin

When we worried about pregnant women and drug use in earlier years, heroin was the drug that most concerned us. Heroin users are more likely to miscarry or deliver prematurely. IMRs among babies who have been prenatally exposed to heroin are three times higher, and their risk of SIDS is also greatly elevated (Kumpfer). Heroin-affected babies are small for their gestational age, and may suffer the pain of withdrawal (Chasnoff 1988). They experience retarded growth and display intellectual and developmental deficits that may persist into later childhood (Kumpfer).

However, the number of heroin-affected babies is not large. During the peak years of heroin use, the late 1960s, about 3,000 to 5,000 heroin-affected babies were born each year (Besharov). One reason is that relatively few women use heroin. Although decidedly a conservative estimate, the NIDA Household Survey on Drug Abuse found that only 0.8 percent of the population had ever used heroin and less than half of the users were women (NIDA 1991).

Also, heroin is not strongly related to pregnancy. Males are often impotent when under the influence and users of both sexes are likely to fall asleep when high. Heroin users are either scrambling to obtain the drug or lethargic once they have it. Sex is not a high priority.

Cocaine

Cocaine is another story entirely. Over 11 percent of the population admits to some cocaine use; 1.4 percent admits to using crack (NIDA 1991). NIDA also found that 9 percent of females have used cocaine at some point; 0.8 percent have used crack. Among black women, the figures are 7.5 percent and 1.8 percent. These numbers, however, understate the incidence of crack use among black women of childbearing age in many inner-city neighborhoods. The great majority of cocaine-affected babies are black.

Perhaps because it is most often smoked rather than injected, the shift to crack as the drug of choice has been especially pronounced among women, who have joined the ranks of the addicted in unprecedented numbers. In New York State in 1987, mirroring the national picture, 24 percent of addicts on substances other than cocaine were women, but women made up 34 percent of the crack addicts (in Kerr 1988).

Women may also prefer crack because it greatly intensifies sexual pleasure and heightens sexual arousal. Users have greatly increased sexual drive and stamina. Men can maintain erections for hours.

Crack users tend to have little interest in personal maintenance such as obtaining food and practicing hygiene. It appears they also have little interest in birth control. Unprotected sex is virtually a hallmark of crack-cocaine use. The result has been an increase in sexually transmitted diseases and AIDS and also in pregnancies among the addicted. In Massachusetts over 60 percent of the pregnant women entering substance-abuse treatment in 1990 specified cocaine as their drug of choice (Nardone & Steriti).

Magnitude of the Problem

Estimates of the national incidence of cocaine-exposed babies vary. The ONDCP estimates that 100,000 cocaine babies are born each year (in USGAO 1990e). The National Association for Perinatal Addiction Research and Education estimates that 375,000 drug-exposed babies are born each year, most of whom have been exposed to cocaine (in USGAO 1990e). A 1988 NAPARE study indicated that if drug screens were conducted on all delivering women, 11 percent would prove positive (in Besharov).

Available figures are imprecise, and doubtlessly low, because we do not have a rigorous standardized protocol for testing newborns for drug exposure. One problem is that testing is performed at the discretion of the doctor or hospital.

They will generally test if the mother admits to drug use, appears addicted or had no prenatal care (PNC) or if the infant exhibits obvious symptoms of drug exposure. Studies have shown that the mother's race and socioeconomic class strongly influence the decision to test (Garcia). Thus white middle-class babies who may have been exposed to cocaine in utero are less likely to be tested and identified. Secondly, most hospitals administer only toxicology tests that detect the presence of cocaine in the infant's urine. These tests can detect cocaine only if the mother used the drug within two to four days before the baby's birth. Few hospitals test meconium, the infant's first stool, which would allow the detection of cocaine use during the third trimester. No tests as yet reveal cocaine use earlier in pregnancy, but routine testing of meconium would provide significantly more accurate information.

What is clear is that the number of drug-affected babies is great and growing explosively, doubling each year in many cities. The New York City Health Department estimated that births to drug addicted mothers increased 3000 percent from 1978 to 1988 (in French). It estimated over 7,000 such births in the city in 1989 (in Besharov). In Los Angeles County the number of drug-associated fetal deaths increased over 600 percent just from 1985 to 1987 (Besharov). Fifteen percent of all babies born to district residents in Washington, D.C., in 1988 were estimated to be drug affected (Besharov). At Howard University Hospital in 1989, 20 to 30 percent of delivering mothers voluntarily admitted to drug use. Howard director Haynes Rice said the actual usage was probably closer to 50 percent (in Gilliam). Other Washington hospitals report that 40 percent of delivering mothers in 1989 were drug addicts, quadruple the figure of a year earlier (in Abramowitz). A large urban hospital in Detroit that used meconium analysis to detect prenatal drug use in 1989 found 42 percent of the infants born there to be drug exposed (USGAO 1990e). The list goes on.

Effects of Prenatal Cocaine Consumption

Cocaine has a direct physiological impact on the fetus that could itself be fatal. It retards blood and oxygen flow to the fetus and can precipitate placental detachment, spontaneous abortion or premature labor (Chasnoff 1987). This is well known within the drug subculture, where women deliberately go on crack binges to bring about abortion or, if uncomfortable in later pregnancy, to induce or speed up labor (Brown in Besharov). Cocaine could cause a baby to suffer a cerebral infarction (stroke) or a cardiovascular accident in the womb or shortly after birth (Chasnoff 1988). Other possible effects of cocaine exposure, coupled with the mother's malnourishment arising from the appetite-suppressant qualities of the drug, are almost as life threatening.

Cocaine-exposed babies are up to eight times more likely to be LBW than their drug-free peers (USGAO 1990e). Also, holding mothers' race and socioeconomic status constant, cocaine-exposed babies are 16 times more likely to be born preterm and ten times more likely to be small for their gestational age. (Chasnoff et al. 1989). As discussed earlier, the mothers typically get very little prenatal care. A study of births in ten major urban hospitals conducted by the General Accounting Office in 1989 paints the picture very clearly. Figures 5.1, 5.2 and 5.3 illustrate the findings. However, interpretation must be tempered by the knowledge that only urine toxicology tests were used to determine cocaine exposure. Thus only those babies whose mothers used cocaine shortly before their births were classified as cocaine exposed. Many babies not so classified may have been subjected to the damaging effects of cocaine earlier.

Surviving cocaine-affected babies are not necessarily the fortunate ones; they are severely distressed. Chasnoff found possible congenital deformities to include missing middle fingers, missing small intestines and cardiac, digestive system, central nervous system, genital and kidney malformations as well as muscular and respiratory abnormalities (in Revkin; Chasnoff 1988). They are irritable, hypersensitive to light, sound and touch, have sleep disorders, tremors of the hands and feet and motor control deficits, and cry almost all their waking hours. They often experience very painful withdrawal symptoms that peak at

Figure 5.1
Estimated Percent of Drug-Exposed Infants and Infants Not Identified as Drug-Exposed Born to Mothers Receiving Inadequate Prenatal Care: Four Observed U.S. Urban Hospitals, 1989

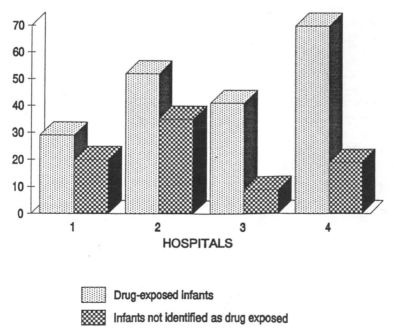

▦ Drug-exposed Infants

▨ Infants not identified as drug exposed

Source: United States General Accounting Office. *Drug-Exposed Infants: A Generation at Risk.*

Figure 5.2
Estimated Percent of Drug-Exposed Infants and Infants Not Identified as Drug-Exposed Born Low Birth Weight: Four Observed U.S. Urban Hospitals, 1989

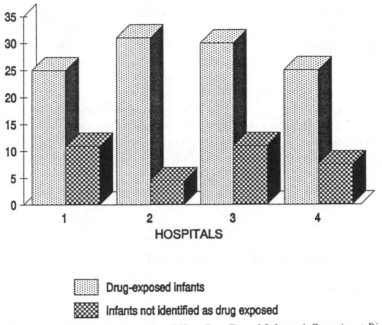

HOSPITALS

░░ Drug-exposed infants

▓▓ Infants not identified as drug exposed

Source: United States General Accounting Office. *Drug-Exposed Infants: A Generation at Risk.*

three weeks of age but may last as long as six months. They may emit a constant high-pitched scream and are very difficult to console (Chasnoff 1987). Their small head size is predictive of poor developmental outcomes. Their cognitive functioning and motor control may be permanently impaired (Chasnoff et al. 1986). They are much more likely to be infected with syphilis or the AIDS virus because of their mother's sexual behavior. And, as will be discussed shortly, they suffer abandonment, abuse and neglect to a horrifying degree. All as a result of someone else's behavioral choice.

The Social Costs of Drug-Exposed Infants

Society too pays the price, and it is a steep one.

The short-run medical costs of LBW deliveries are typically $14,000 to $30,000 (USGAO 1990e). Since cocaine-exposed babies tend to be very small and very premature, they frequently need neonatal intensive care, which can run to $3,000 per day (Gibbs). Inner-city hospitals report that their facilities are operating at above capacity, with 50 to 70 percent of the babies in their neonatal intensive care units cocaine affected (Revkin; Gilliam). The average

Figure 5.3
Estimated Percent of Drug-Exposed Infants and Infants Not Identified as Drug-Exposed Born Premature: Four Observed U.S. Urban Hospitals, 1989

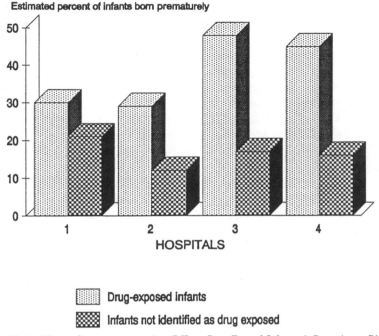

Source: United States General Accounting Office. *Drug-Exposed Infants: A Generation at Risk.*

cost of neonatal intensive care for the smallest babies at Stanford University Hospital is $160,000; nationally we spend $2.6 billion on neonatal intensive care each year (Thompson). The National Drug Control Budget allocated $5.9 million to the care of crack babies in 1991. The same amount has been requested for 1992 (ONDCP 1991b). However, most of the costs of care for cocaine babies have been and will continue to be paid by Medicaid. Of the 50 costliest Medicaid cases in Massachusetts in 1990, 19 were babies, many of whom were born prematurely and whose mothers had little or no PNC. Prenatal drug exposure was probable. The average cost of treating the babies was $361,461; the most expensive case cost $655,889 (MDPW). Most of the children will continue to require extraordinary care.

Many babies are too unhealthy to return home; many don't have a healthy home to which they can return. Many are abandoned in the hospital. Known as "boarder babies," they may remain for over a year, unable to experience the bonding and environmental stimulation essential to normal development. Haynes Rice of Howard University Hospital says a 245-day stay is not unusual for an abandoned baby, and costs $250,000 (Gilliam). The National Drug

Control Budget provided $9.6 million in 1991 to assist abandoned infants; the same amount has been requested for 1992 (ONDCP 1991b).

Many cocaine-exposed babies (26 to 58 percent of those in the GAO study) go directly into foster care. Many enter foster care later, after an unsatisfactory stay with the mother or other relative. Basic foster care can cost as much as $8,000 a year. Specialized foster care that provides medical monitoring can cost $36,000 (USGAO 1990e).

Researchers at the University of California at San Diego found that 25 percent of drug-exposed children had developmental delays and 40 percent experienced neurologic abnormalities., As the children grew older, their language, cognitive and fine motor skills did not develop normally to the extent that they are expected to have difficulties functioning in a school environment (in USGAO 1990e). Another researcher has estimated that 42 to 52 percent of the children exposed to drugs and/or alcohol will require special education services (USGAO 1990e). The extent of services and their costs will depend upon the severity of impairment. The Florida Department of Health and Rehabilitative Services estimates that the total service costs to age 18 for each drug-exposed child that suffers significant physiologic or neurologic impairment will be $750,000 (USGAO 1990e).

No one knows how many cocaine-affected children will be entering the school system. The crack epidemic was in its early stages when the 1991 kindergarten class was born. But it is clear that the number of these children will be taking a quantum leap. Studies have shown that drug-exposed children may soon comprise 40 to 60 percent of inner-city school populations (Henry). Many may need special education classes that are beyond the scope of those currently in place. The Los Angeles Unified School District has begun a special program for preschool children that were mildly impaired by drug exposure. It costs $17,000 per year per child. (USGAO 1990e).

If we do not yet know the midrange expenses, we surely cannot estimate the long-range costs. We do know that they may involve, in addition to medical care, foster care and special education, expenditures for psychological and physical therapies, vocational training and rehabilitation, welfare and the criminal justice system as well as diminished productivity and diversion of scarce social resources.

The Role of Choice

All this expense, all this suffering take place because some women chose to use cocaine, conceived irresponsibly and would not or could not secure an abortion.

This should not be happening. None of what has been described here should be happening. It is all preventable, although prevention can be very difficult to realize. People make choices. Economists assume those choices are rationally made—that is, they are made freely and with a full understanding of all the associated costs and benefits. They assume that behavioral choices that no longer generate benefits in excess of costs will no longer be made.

This assumes a great deal. It assumes people have knowledge of both long- and short-run costs, knowledge that they may not possess. It assumes a level of maturity and intellectual capacity to make consumption and other behavioral decisions, attributes that they may not possess. It ignores the addictive elements of some of those choices and the fact that many who make those choices fail to accurately estimate their propensity for addiction.

Compounding the problem is the fact that pregnancy is often unintended or unexpected. There is also a time lag between conception and awareness of pregnancy. Thus women may indulge in substances that are harmful to their babies before they suspect they are pregnant. This is especially common among crack-cocaine users, most of whom also smoke and drink alcohol (Chasnoff 1988). Because crack disrupts a woman's menstrual cycle, users may be well into their pregnancy before they realize it (Chasnoff 1987). They are used to missing their periods. So much for perfect information on the part of the consumer.

In any event, terrible harm is being perpetrated on thousands and thousands of babies before they are even born. Terrible costs are being imposed on them and on society as a whole. And in the case of drug abuse, the situation is only getting worse. Increases in social service and social capital expenditures should ideally result in positive net investment—that is, we should progress, improve our social well-being and enhance our socioeconomic production function. Instead, we are spending considerably more just trying to stay in place, and we are failing to do even that.

Public Policy Issues and Recommendations

Education

Change starts with education. It must start with education. Campaigns to reduce cigarette, alcohol and drug use must place greater emphasis on the hazards of prenatal consumption. Surveys show that while most people do understand the dangers, significant numbers do not. Warning labels on alcoholic beverages should be like those on cigarettes: prominent and explicitly informative. We must use every media form, including signs in bars, as well as educational, medical and social service contacts to provide hard facts on the harmful, possibly lethal, effects of using hazardous products during pregnancy. Television and radio stations must be encouraged to include pregnancy endangerment topics in their news, talk and magazine-format shows. The point must be stressed that there is much we do not know about dose-thresholds and which babies will be affected. Although some substance abusers may have healthy babies, others should not view that as an indication that their babies will also be born healthy. The odds of giving birth to an unhealthy child may be slim, but the consequences could be dreadful. We must also make the point that cigarette, alcohol and drug use are best stopped before pregnancy. But if not, cessation during pregnancy can avert or ameliorate some of the worst outcomes.

Prevention

We need to develop behavior modification programs that are suitable for pregnant women.

Smoking cessation programs should be more available, with both day and evening hours. Additional clinics could be opened in public health centers, women's shelters and schools. Pregnant women should be urged to attend and given priority. Pregnant students should be required to attend.

Women who are heavy drinkers should be urged to avoid pregnancy until they are sure they can stop drinking and remain alcohol free at least for the duration of the pregnancy.

If an alcohol-abusing woman does get pregnant, abortion should be a feasible option. Full Medicaid funding should be reinstated. As of 1992 only 14 states and the District of Columbia subsidize abortions for Medicaid-eligible women. Federal funding is available only if the health of the mother would be endangered by carrying the baby to term. The health of the baby should also be considered. This is not a contradiction. Life should be a blessing, not a punishment. We would not subject a mass murderer to the sort of tortures we routinely inflict on severely troubled infants, who may not survive, in any event, or who may survive only to live a life of severe physical and intellectual disability.

If a heavily drinking woman chooses to carry to term, she must be urged to seek help. Alcohol detoxification and rehabilitation programs should be made more accessible and more affordable. The Alcohol, Drug Abuse and Mental Health Services (ADMS) block grant to the states should be increased and the ADMS Women's Set-Aside should be increased from the current 10 percent. Expanded services should be targeted to pregnant women. Outpatient and residential programs for substance-abusing women must provide child care for those women who would otherwise be unable to participate.

The dangers of drug use during pregnancy should be made clear. Most occasional users are easy to reach and find it easy to desist. Drug addicts, on the other hand, are very difficult to reach and to rehabilitate.

Again, our emphasis with addicts should be on pregnancy prevention. We must fully fund family planning clinics and begin vigorous pregnancy prevention outreach programs. Given that addicts are poor contraceptors, we cannot expect them to rely on techniques such as condoms or birth control pills that require their active participation. Their minds are on other things, notably procuring drugs and getting high. And a woman need be remiss only once. While interuterine devices (IUDs) have higher overall failure rates than birth control pills, they may be more reliable for drug addicts, as their use is entirely passive. However, IUDs can induce painful hemorrhaging or other problems. Far better are the new birth control technologies currently available in parts of Europe and Asia but not yet widely available here: hormonal injections and implants that secrete hormones to suppress ovulation. The implant, known as Norplant, is effective for five years and is just now becoming available in the United States on a limited basis.

Although many addicts would doubtless welcome such an advance, some observers fear a possible civil rights violation when a drug addict of diminished judgment is asked to accept an implant which she herself could not remove. Others claim addicts must be encouraged to accept an implant. If an addict's judgment and ability to make and implement contraceptive decisions are diminished, so is her ability to bear and rear children.

It was concluded in Chapter 2 that drugs will probably not be made legally available to addicts, even on a highly restrictive basis. However, if they are, the temporary trading of reproductive capability for free, clean and available drugs may not be a bad bargain. As it is, crack-addicted mothers have been known to barter their children's diapers, formula, food, food stamps and sexual "favors" for drugs. Perhaps a better trade can be arranged. Perhaps we could simply pay these women to accept an implant.

This is not China. We do not impose Draconian measures, thank goodness. They only lead to Tiananmen Square. Rather, the mechanism of a market economy can be used to everyone's advantage. Innocent creatures should not be born only to pay the terrible price of another's poor lifestyle choice. Society should not have to pay.

But addicts do get pregnant. Women steeped in drug use should, as should all women, have access to affordable abortions.

Prenatal Care and Rehabilitation

Addicts who continue their pregnancy require especially good prenatal oversight. Since many have little interest in prenatal care, outreach efforts must be intensified. Many cities are just now establishing PNC centers for addicts. More are needed, as traditional PNC centers often turn away pregnant addicts because they lack drug treatment capacity or they wish to avoid patients that are high risk and would consume a disproportionate share of their limited resources. They would, understandably, prefer to devote those resources to women who would be more likely to follow the prescribed regimen and produce a healthy outcome—in other words, to utilize their resources where they will generate the greatest return.

Substance-abusing pregnant women also need treatment for their addiction. Yet most drug and alcohol treatment programs categorically exclude pregnant addicts because they lack obstetrical expertise, fear treatment medications would endanger the fetus, or fear possible liability resulting from a malpractice suit should the pregnancy's outcome be poor.

Some regard this as simple sex discrimination. At this writing, the first such discrimination case is before the courts, brought by the American Civil Liberties Union on behalf of three women who were denied drug or alcohol treatment because of their pregnancy by various New York hospitals. Others see this exclusion as reasonable and would have treatment centers specifically designed for pregnant women. Several cities and states are currently establishing such centers. Greater emphasis is being placed on outreach, care and rehabilitation of pregnant addicts. But it will take time and considerable resources. The General Accounting Office estimates that 280,000 pregnant women were in need of drug treatment services in 1990. Less than 11 percent received care even though the National Drug Control Budget provided $32.6 million for the treatment of pregnant addicts (USGAO 1990e; ONDCP 1991b). Almost $46 million was provided in 1991, and another $52.4 million has been requested for 1992 (ONDCP 1991b). However, this too will likely prove insufficient.

We must develop treatment models that suit women's needs, primarily the need for child care. Very few rehabilitation centers, residential or outpatient, provide child care facilities. Most were established before the current crack epidemic for single male heroin addicts, who often had a history of antisocial behavior. Residential programs that accepted female patients often required them to place their children in foster care or with relatives for up to two years. That alone would dissuade many women from accepting admission when a slot opened. We need to prioritize pregnant and postpartum women. We need programs that allow mother and child to live together in a supportive, therapeutic, drug-free environment that, not incidentally, provides parenting training as well.

We need to develop crack-specific treatment technologies along the lines of methadone, a pharmacologic substitute for heroin. Methadone has been useful in treating pregnant heroin addicts. Babies born to mothers on methadone are still distressed and suffer withdrawal, but it is less difficult for them, as methadone is clean and less harmful to the fetus. They are also less exposed to hepatitis and the AIDS virus, as their mothers no longer use needles that may be contaminated. We do not yet have a methadone analog for crack, and crack is far more addictive than heroin.

We must also be realistic about rehabilitation. In New York, 45 percent of the enrollees in traditional therapeutic drug communities drop out in the first 90 days; only 10 to 15 percent complete the programs. Only 77 percent of those who do complete the programs significantly reduce their drug use (Plaut & Kelley). In Massachusetts, 50 percent of the women in substance abuse rehabilitation programs drop out (Nardone & Steriti). And in many cities, outreach programs specifically designed for pregnant crack addicts report dropout rates of 50 percent or more. St. Petersburg program director Shirley Coletti repeats a familiar refrain when she tells of the extreme difficulties of working with crack addicts as opposed to heroin addicts or alcoholics. Maternal instincts can overpower heroin and alcohol so that mothers can often stay clean at least through pregnancy. Not so with crack. It apparently destroys virtually all maternal instincts (in Revkin). Yet women on crack continue to get pregnant. So we must continue our rehabilitative efforts.

Legal Measures

Many advocate a tougher approach. Efforts to criminalize prenatal drug use are gaining momentum. Judges have incarcerated pregnant addicts to disallow their continued drug use. District attorneys have charged addicted women whose children died shortly after birth with manslaughter and indicted mothers whose babies were born drug affected on the charge of delivering controlled substances to a minor.

Several states have amended their child neglect laws to include children born with FAS or who test positive for illicit drugs. Minnesota mandates the reporting of drug-abusing pregnant women to the criminal justice authorities. Oklahoma mandates reporting the birth of a chemically dependent child to social service agencies. Legislation pending in Oregon would remand custody of children with positive toxicology tests to juvenile court, which has jurisdiction over child abuse cases. Legislation pending in California requires manslaughter charges and imprisonment for women whose illicit drug use causes the death of infants born alive. The measure also guarantees amnesty from drug charges for women who seek prenatal care and give birth to drug-free babies. Another bill submitted to the California legislature establishes drug treatment services and expanded PNC for pregnant addicts. It also penalizes women who refuse care. A bill before the Illinois legislature requires twice the maximum prison term to anyone delivering illicit drugs to a pregnant woman and requires pregnant addicts to participate in treatment programs.

The urge to take punitive action is understandable, especially when confronted by women who are repeatedly warned about their drug use, refuse treatment and continue to take substances harmful to their babies. It is especially understandable in the case of repeat drug-endangered pregnancies. Crack may be relatively new, but there are women who have already had three or four crack babies. An estimated 25 percent of drug-exposed newborns have siblings who were also fetally exposed (Besharov).

Although these laws are well intended, they can be unfair and ineffective. Prosecuting pregnant addicts for their drug use will only drive them from the health care system and the PNC their babies desperately need. Some pregnant addicts do not seek PNC and deliberately elude outreach efforts for fear of prosecution. They sometimes deliver at home, refusing emergency care for their sick newborns. Certain prosecution would only heighten that fear and further jeopardize endangered babies.

Automatically removing a child from its mother's custody just on the basis of a positive toxicology test violates the mother's right to due process. It may also result in the placement of a baby into an overburdened foster care system when its interests may be better served in the care of its mother. Positive results may indeed be indicative of maternal impairment and neglect, but they alone are not enough evidence. Additional screening is necessary to determine parental fitness.

Furthermore, it is unfair to prosecute pregnant women for their drug use or to remove their children (if their well-being is not otherwise threatened) when so few treatment programs are available to pregnant addicts, family planning funds are being cut and access to abortion is restricted. Obligating doctors to report drug-abusing pregnant women interferes with the doctor-patient relationship and violates a woman's right to the confidentiality of her medical records.

Still, hospital staff may have good cause to believe a newborn will face imminent danger if it is released to a substance-abusing mother. About half our states allow hospitals to hold such infants against parental objections, pending formal legal intervention. All states should have such laws. Children are entitled to protection. The question is when such entitlement begins.

Prosecution of women who prenatally exposed their babies to harmful substances often fails in court because state criminal statutes do not usually classify the fetus as a person. The issue of pregnant drug abusers inevitably evokes the dilemma of women's rights versus fetal rights. Unfortunately, this often becomes part of the abortion debate with prochoice forces arguing that recognition of fetal rights diminishes women's rights and antiabortionists insisting that the unborn child deserves protection. Perhaps the dilemma will be resolved, legally if not morally, when impaired children start bringing lawsuits against their substance-abusing mothers for injury and loss resulting from improper prenatal care.

In any event, the two sets of rights should not be irreconcilable. Women should have the right to abort, but if they choose to give birth, their babies should have the right to a healthy start. Women should have the right to reproductive choices, to privacy, to freedom from unwarranted government intrusion into their lives and to certain lifestyle choices. However, those rights have their limits, and those choices should not inflict extreme adversity on someone else. We prohibit smoking in public places so as to not impose costs on others. We forbid driving while intoxicated to protect others. Yet it is legal to smoke and drink while pregnant.

We do not want "pregnancy police" monitoring pregnant women's diets, overseeing their exercise, telling them what work they can do and how long they must sleep. But we do want to do something. The costs are just too great. Society must have rights as well.

THE CHILD AT HOME

A child's home should be a haven of nurturing love, comfort and happiness, a refuge where a child grows in physical and emotional health, encouraged, guided, supported and sheltered. But such is not always the case. For some children home is not all it should be. Rather, it is where they are hit, kicked or punched, rejected, ridiculed or raped. For others it is worse. It is a place of unspeakable cruelty, a place where they are burned with cigarettes, held on a hot stove, immersed in scalding water, whipped with belts, battered until their bones are broken, forced to service their mother's paramours and starved, drowned, burned or beaten to death.

Following the lead of Gary Becker, economists sometimes analyze children as commodities, one good out of many consumers may buy. After allowing for unintended pregnancies and unwanted infertility, the "children as goods" analysis makes sense. Children are costly, provide considerable utility and compete with houses, cars and vacations for adults' income, time and effort. However, one look at a battered child and all concepts of consumer rationality evaporate, all notions of behavioral choice become abhorrent. Economists do not analyze insanity. Economists do not analyze evil.

There is good news. There has been a significant change in attitudes about harsh and abusive treatment of children over the last several years. Fewer people yell at or spank their children; more families have adopted benign, constructive, nonphysical forms of discipline; fewer parents support corporal punishment in schools (Bernier).

But while the less severe forms of abuse have declined, the most severe forms have increased in number and in degree.

Child Abuse and Neglect: Types, Incidence and Family Characteristics

Child maltreatment is generally divided into four major types: physical abuse, sexual abuse, neglect and emotional maltreatment.

Physical Abuse

Physical abuse is nonaccidental bodily inquiry inflicted on a child by its caretaker. It involves willful cruelty and may arise from unjustifiable or unlawful corporal punishment. Fatal when extreme, the rates of homicide and undetermined-injury death are 8.8 per 1,000 infants and 3.1 per 1,000 children age 1 to 4 (USHR).

The average age of a child reported as physically abused is 5.3 years, with the most severe abuse usually inflicted on younger children (AAPC 1986). Older children are less likely to be reported as they are more likely to run away or move in with friends or relatives when subject to abuse.

Parents who physically abuse their children are more volatile and manifest more psychological and interpersonal difficulties than parents who commit other forms of abuse. Children who are abused physically are not only subject to more bodily harm, but exhibit more social and educational difficulties than children who suffer other forms of abuse (Daro). Home life is violent and chaotic.

Sexual Abuse

Sexual abuse is the sexual victimization of a child. Compared to the victims of other forms of maltreatment, victims of sexual abuse are predominantly female (75 percent of reported cases), generally older (average age 8.1 years, although 25 percent of the victims are under 5), and are more often victimized by someone other than a parent (AAPC 1986). Slightly more than 50 percent of reported sexual abuse cases involve the child's natural parent or stepparent; however, most of the other offenders are known to the victim (Daro).

Families in which we find sexual abuse run the full socioeconomic spectrum. Since the perpetrator is almost always male, such families are more likely to be two-parent households and thus of higher income than families engaged in other forms of abuse (Daro).

Sexual abuse varies by degree of severity, duress and duration of abuse. According to the 1988 Study of National Incidence and Prevalence of Child Abuse and Neglect, 45 percent of the children who were sexually abused in 1988 experienced genital molestation, 32 percent intrusion and the remaining 23 percent "other" or "unknown" sexual abuse (USDHHS 1988). Sometimes the abuse is violent in nature and occurs in families that are also physically abusive and have a long history of public agency involvement. But it most frequently occurs in families that appear normal to outsiders (Daro). In this case the abuse is usually nonviolent, with the father obtaining compliance through assertion of his parental authority or by playing on his daughter's need for love and acceptance. The mother may also consent, explicitly or tacitly, usually because consent is easier for her and less disruptive to the family. The abuse may be continuous or episodic, or may be a single event occurring only once, perhaps when the perpetrator was drunk or on drugs. It is harmful to the child in any context. While reactions vary, sexually abused children may be withdrawn or self-destructive and have low self-esteem and troubled interpersonal relationships.

Neglect

Neglect is defined as failure to provide adequate food, shelter, clothing, medical care or supervision to a child in one's care. It may involve intentional drugging, promotion of delinquency, expelling the child from the home or abandonment. Educational neglect, which may involve failure to enroll the child in school or allowing chronic truancy, is sometimes categorized separately.

Neglect is rarely willful. Rather, it is the result of inadequacy and inability to cope.

Neglectful parents are more likely to be poorly educated, nonwhite, single mothers who receive Aid to Families with Dependent Children (AFDC). They typically are socially isolated, that is, they have no supportive network of family and friends (Daro). Codega characterizes neglectful mothers as infantile, apathetic, impulse-ridden and sometimes also mentally retarded or psychotic. Over half are substance abusers (Hartley).

Although most neglectful mothers are extremely poor, most extremely poor mothers are not neglectful. In a major study holding women's age, race and income constant, Zuravin found the most significant difference between neglectful and nonneglectful mothers (other than the maltreatment itself) to be that neglectful mothers are twice as likely to be depressed and that they are extremely poor contraceptors. She found that neglectful mothers had twice as many unplanned pregnancies and twice as many children. They had their first child at a younger age, spaced their first two children more closely together and had children by more fathers. Zuravin also found that neglectful mothers were 3.2 times more likely not to use contraceptives. Of the women Zuravin interviewed who did not want another child, 55 percent of the neglectful mothers versus 21 percent of the nonneglectful mothers did not use contraceptives at last intercourse. Moreover, 55 percent of the neglectful mothers continued to have one or more unwanted children after they were involved with child protective services. Kadushin found 7 percent of neglectful families to have between 7 and 13 children (in Codega).

The average age of a neglected child is 6.4 years (AAPC 1986). Studies comparing them to children subjected to other forms of abuse found them to be lowest in self-esteem and self-confidence (in Daro). Neglected children have higher frequencies of personality damage, developmental immaturity and cognitive deficiencies, especially in language development (Hartley). They are often apathetic and withdrawn, and their physical growth may be arrested, sometimes fatally (Bernier).

Emotional Abuse

Emotional abuse is maltreatment of a child by its caretaker that is nonphysical in nature, although it also includes torturous restriction of movement and close confinement, such as tying a child to a bed or locking him in a closet. For the most part, emotional abuse consists of overtly hostile or rejecting treatment or habitual verbal assault such as yelling, swearing, ridiculing, scapegoating, belittling or threatening assault or abandonment. The National Incidence Study included a separate category of emotional neglect. This involved marked inattention to the child's need for affection or attention, spouse abuse in the child's presence and encouraging or permitting drug or alcohol use by the child.

Emotional maltreatment is not unique to single-parent families of low income and limited education. Three-quarters of the victims are white; their average age is 8.5 years (AAPC 1986). Emotionally abused children may be withdrawn and suicidal or they may be aggressive, violent and impulsive. They show signs of feeling unloved, inferior, inadequate, fearful and anxious (Bernier).

Other Abuse

Other forms of abuse include exploitation and caretaker absence or incapacity. The former involves forcing or coercing a child into performing activities for the benefit of the parent or guardian that are beyond the child's capacities or that are illegal or degrading. The latter includes caretaker absence due to hospitalization or incarceration and inability to provide adequate care for the child because of physical or emotional illness or substance abuse.

Incidence of Abuse and Neglect

Table 5.1 relates the incidence of child maltreatment reported to child protective agencies in selected years. Table 5.2 relates the distribution of maltreatment.

A few qualifications are in order: (1) The increase in incidence over time is largely a result of increased reporting arising both from greater public awareness and expansion of state reporting mandates; (2) although approximately 40 percent of the reports are confirmed by child welfare personnel, this does not mean that abuse did not occur in the remaining 60 percent of the cases, but only that confirmation was not then possible; (3) child welfare experts are certain that the vast majority of child maltreatment cases go unreported, that reported cases represent "only the tip of the iceberg" (USDHHS 1988 p. 2-1).

Underreporting is most likely in sexual abuse cases. Visible scars are usually absent and disclosure usually depends on the victim. Victims may keep the abuse secret because they may feel partly responsible, have a strong emotional tie with the perpetrator or fear no one would believe them. Surveys have found that one-fifth to one-third of all adult females experienced some kind of sexual abuse as a child (Bernier). The incidence of emotional maltreatment is also difficult to estimate, both for lack of physical evidence and because not all states require that it be reported. Over 60 percent of the families in treatment for other forms of abuse were found to emotionally maltreat their children as well (Daro). Physical abuse is also often unrecognized, despite our heightened awareness. Bernier contends that only one in seven injury cases serious enough to warrant hospitalization is accurately identified as the result of abuse. Child abuse fatalities also go unrecognized. Although each year over 1,200 deaths are confirmed as attributable to child abuse or neglect, with 75 percent of the victims one year of age or less, a study conducted by the National Committee for the Prevention of Child Abuse found that many deaths that appear natural,

Table 5.1
Number and Rate of Child Maltreatment Reports: United States, Selected Years

	1976	1980	1984	1986	1987
Number of child maltreatment reports (1000's)	669	1,154	1,727	2,086	2,178
Rate per 1000 children	10.1	18.1	27.3	32.8	34.0
Number substantiated					871,200

Source: United States House of Representatives Select Committee on Children Youth and Families. *U.S. Children and Their Families: Current Conditions and Recent Trends, 1989.*

Table 5.2
Percent Distribution of Child Maltreatment by Type and by Age, Sex and
Race/Ethnicity of Child: United States, 1986

Type of Maltreatment*	Percent Distribution
Physical injury	
- major	3%
- minor	14%
- unspecified	11%
Neglect	55%
Sexual abuse	16%
Emotional maltreatment	8%
Other maltreatment	8%
Age	
0 to 5	43%
6 to 11	33%
12 to 17	24%
Sex	
Male	48%
Female	53%
Race/ethnicity	
White	67%
Black	18%
Hispanic	11%
Other	4%

* Percents for type of maltreatment add up to more than 100 as children may be reported for
more than one form of abuse.

Source: United States House of Representatives Select Committee on Children, Youth and Families.
U.S. Children and Their Families: Current Conditions and Recent Trends, 1989.

for example, deaths from drowning, pneumonia or SIDS, are in fact homicide.
The NCPCA estimates that over 5,000 children die from maltreatment each
year, half from battering and half from lack of food, medical care or supervision (in Bernier).

Characteristics of Maltreating Families

Although child maltreatment, especially sexual abuse, can be found in any
socioeconomic stratum, certain characteristics appear with greater frequency

in maltreating families. The National Clinical Evaluation Study (NCES), examining the clients of 19 family treatment projects throughout the United States, found that maltreating families had extraordinarily high frequencies of financial difficulties, substance abuse, physical violence between adult partners, sexual performance problems, social isolation and mental illness (in Daro). Holding income, race and ethnicity constant, maltreating families were larger, experienced more marital disruptions and were more likely to be female headed. The mother was more apt to be unmarried and experience greater turnover of partners. The National Incidence and Prevalence Study found no significant relationship between a child's race or ethnicity and maltreatment but it did find family size to be a factor. Families with four or more children had higher rates of all forms of maltreatment, especially physical abuse and neglect. Their children were five times more likely to lose their lives as a result of maltreatment than were children of smaller families. Just as shocking were the study's findings with respect to family income (see Table 5.3). Children from lower-income families experience not only a greater incidence of maltreatment, but also suffer more severe injury and impairment (USDHHS 1988). Estimating prevalence (the percentage of children abused during their youth) as opposed to incidence (the percentage of children abused during any one year), Garbarino conservatively concluded that 30 percent of low income children are abused at some time.

Table 5.3
Maltreatment Rates per 1,000 Children by Family Income: United States, 1986

Type of Maltreatment	Income Less Than $15,000	Income $15,000 or More
All maltreatment	54.0	7.9
All abuse	19.9	4.4
Physical abuse	10.2	2.5
Sexual abuse	4.8	1.1
Emotional abuse	6.1	1.2
All neglect	36.8	4.1
Physical neglect	22.6	1.9
Educational neglect	10.1	1.3
Emotional neglect	6.9	1.5
Fatal injury/impairment	0.03	0.01
Serious injury/impairment	6.0	0.9
Moderate injury/impairment	30.9	5.5
Probably injury/impairment	5.4	0.9

Source: United States Department of Health and Human Services. National Center on Child Abuse and Neglect. *Study Findings: Study of National Incidence and Prevalence of Child Abuse and Neglect: 1988.*

The Role of Substance Abuse

Alcohol and drug abuse have long been risk factors for child maltreatment. Sever found alcohol abuse to be a factor in 71 percent of the sexual abuse cases he investigated (in Daro). A Massachusetts Department of Social Services study, supporting similar studies elsewhere, found alcohol abuse to be closely associated with physical child abuse, particularly when an alcohol-abusing male was present in the household. Drug use, particularly cocaine, was found to be more predictive of neglect and was more often a problem in female-headed households. The department also reported greater severity of injuries to young children when drugs or alcohol were involved (MDSS 1989).

Crack-cocaine use is responsible for the explosion in child maltreatment cases we are witnessing today. Too recent to be tabulated on a national basis, crack's impact is revealed by city and state data. Boston's child abuse rates increased 17.4 percent in 1988 and 15 percent in 1989 (MDSS 1990a). Maltreatment reports supported by investigators climbed 19 percent in 1989 and 27 percent in 1990 (MDSS 1991). Child abuse in Philadelphia increased 30 percent in 1988 alone (Enda). In Washington, D.C., the cases of child maltreatment severe enough to warrant criminal prosecution jumped 34 percent in 1988 and an astounding 135 percent in 1989 (OPPE). In California, total child maltreatment cases climbed 45 percent from 1987 to 1989 (SCDSS 1990). These increases are not due to improved reporting. They are all due to the increase in substance abuse, notably that of crack-cocaine. In Boston, 64 percent of the child maltreatment cases in 1988 involved substance abuse (MDSS 1989). In Philadelphia it was 68 percent (Enda). In Washington, D.C., as in California, the figure was almost 90 percent (Besharov; SCDSS 1989).

Crack's contribution to negligence is often evident at birth—in the tens of thousands of drug-affected babies and in the thousands of boarder babies. Other infants may be abandoned by their mothers to social service agencies, relatives or strangers or left in doorways or in trashcans. Children living with crack-addicted mothers are often severely neglected, living in filth, lacking even minimal care, begging for food from neighbors if old enough, starving if not. Sometimes left alone for days, they are usually removed from the home when brought to the attention of child welfare workers.

Children residing with crack-addicted caretakers are also at great risk of physical battering. Crack is a mean drug, and crack users often become violent and dangerous. The abuse they inflict is especially severe. In New York City, 73 percent of the child maltreatment fatalities in 1987 resulted from drug use, up from just 11 percent in 1985 (Kerr 1988). In Boston, a crack addict beat his girlfriend's three-year-old son to death by whipping him 277 times with a belt. In an ironic twist of justice, he was convicted on the lesser charge of manslaughter, rather than murder in the first degree. The defendant claimed that crack caused him to hallucinate that worms were emerging from the boy's body—and he was killing the worms, not the boy. A psychiatrist convinced the jury that it could have been true (Wong).

Cocaine-affected babies are especially vulnerable to abuse. They are in pain; they cry and wail. They are overly sensitive to stimuli, difficult to get to sleep when awakened and difficult to console. Cocaine-affected babies would be a trial to any caretaker. To a crack-addicted parent they are a nightmare, and the result is all too often what one would expect.

Children living with crack addicts are also subject to other forms of abuse. They are often sexually abused in notoriously orgiastic crack houses. They are sometimes sold as prostitutes by their mothers, who need money for drugs. Anecdotes also abound, related by medical and child welfare personnel, of infants who are administered cocaine by their mothers to stop their crying and of older children who are given crack to smoke because it is easier for their mothers to give them drugs than to feed them (Barnicle). Three-month-old babies who were not born drug addicted are brought to urban hospitals for detoxification; eight-year-olds are turned into junkies. Young children die from overdoses of crack (USGAO 1990e).

The larger social effects are even more devastating. As crack use has been concentrated among poor minority women, a whole generation of children of color is at risk. Women are the lynchpins of minority families. Those families are losing much of their underpinning, and their children are paying the price. So is society.

The Costs of Child Abuse and Neglect

Every topic covered in this volume bears costs that are multifaceted. Most of the costs are externalities falling under the rubric of social costs. But when the costs are imposed on children, the human costs are so very pronounced they warrant special emphasis.

The Human Costs

Numerous studies have documented the effect of maltreatment on children. The National Clinical Evaluation Study (NCES) described in Daro is the most comprehensive. In its evaluation of maltreated children under thirteen years of age the study made the following findings:

- Approximately 30 percent suffered chronic health problems.
- Approximately 30 percent displayed cognitive or language disorders.
- Approximately 22 percent had learning disorders requiring special education.
- Approximately 50 percent had been disciplined at school for misconduct or poor attendance.
- Approximately 50 percent suffered severe socioemotional problems such as low self-esteem, lack of trust, or low frustration tolerance.
- Approximately 14 percent engaged in self-mutilative or self-destructive behavior.

Other researchers found significant relationships between maltreatment and mental retardation, cerebral palsy, schizophrenia, multiple personality disorders, physical disabilities, central nervous system damage and severe developmental delays.

The NCES found that the difficulties of abused and neglected children intensify over time, that maltreated adolescents had a wider range of problems and a larger number of severe disorders (in Daro). Its evaluation of maltreated adolescents revealed the following:

- Twenty-five percent had severe drug or alcohol problems.
- Forty percent engaged in self-destructive behavior.
- Seventeen percent attempted suicide.
- Sixty-seven percent performed poorly academically.
- Sixty-seven percent had extraordinarily high rates of status offenses such as truancy, incorrigibility and running away.

Studies cited by Bernier found that 72 to 90 percent of the juveniles incarcerated as delinquents had been previously reported as abused or neglected. Alfaro traced 5,136 children reported to New York authorities for suspected abuse or neglect during 1952 and 1953 in order to determine later contacts with the courts. He found that 50 percent of the families reported for maltreatment had at least one child who was taken to court as delinquent or ungovernable. The rate of referral for juvenile delinquency and incorrigibility was five times greater among children reported for abuse than among the general population of adolescents from similar socioeconomic backgrounds. Alfaro also found that maltreated adolescent offenders had a much greater propensity commit violent crimes than nonmaltreated offenders (in Garbarino). In addition, Boyer and Fine found that girls who had been sexually abused had extraordinarily high rates of teenage pregnancy.

Abused children continue to pay the costs as adults. Their costs include higher drug and alcohol dependency, recurring physical and mental health problems, lessened ability to form satisfactory relationships and income loss due to reduced productivity. Many are permanently consigned to the economic underclass. Many are institutionalized because of severe retardation or criminal conduct.

Incarcerated men, particularly violent offenders, experienced a very high incidence of physical abuse in their childhood. Sex offenders were subject to a high incidence of physical and sexual abuse. Prostitutes suffered extremely high rates of sexual abuse and, while seldom imprisoned, often lead lives of danger, degradation and self-hate. Women who were abused as children frequently take up with men who continue the abuse.

These human costs translate into social costs.

The Fiscal Costs

The monetary costs of maltreatment are extremely high and may continue throughout the victim's lifetime.

The immediate costs of protecting maltreated children include the costs of prevention, investigation, intervention and treatment. Federal and state child protection expenditures totalled $3.5 billion in 1987 (Daro). The Massachusetts Department of Social Services alone spent $415 million for child protective services in 1990 (MDSS 1990a). It still was not enough to adequately protect children-at-risk in Massachusetts.

We spend a great deal on foster care, but it is still insufficient. Massachusetts, reflecting the national average, places 18 percent of the children confirmed as maltreated in foster care. The mean length of placement is 2.0 years; the median length (a more representative figure) is 1.4 years (Felix). One year of basic foster care costs from $3,000 to $8,000. The AAPC estimates that we spent $1.7 billion for foster care in 1989, but that if we had provided care for all the children confirmed as maltreated who would have clearly benefitted, foster care would have cost $7 billion (Alsop).

It is also very expensive to provide quality treatment for maltreated children and their families. The cost of the 19 demonstration projects examined by the NCES averaged $12,700 per case, in 1983 dollars (Daro, modified). This figure did not include foster care, treatment for substance abuse or program start-up costs such as rent and equipment. Neither did it include food, money and clothing distributed to clients, which, along with housing and job search assistance, greatly increase the cost of treating many families, neglectful families in particular. Moreover, these were model programs funded by the federal government, of a quality often unaffordable to states.

Three percent of the children confirmed as maltreated suffer major physical injuries. The average length of a hospital stay for children with a bone fracture is 5.2 days. If only half the children who were severely injured in 1987 stayed 5.2 days in the hospital at an average daily rate of $540 (USBC) the cost would have been $91.7 million. If, as Bernier maintains, only one in seven children who are seriously injured as a result of abuse is correctly identified as such, the actual hospital bill would have been $641.9 million. Additional costs include X rays and other lab work, follow-up care and possibly years of physical therapy.

The average annual cost of juvenile detention in 1987 was $27,400 (USBC). If only 10 percent of the 522,720 adolescents abused that year were incarcerated for just one year it would have cost $1.4 billion, excluding police and court costs.

In addition, society incurs the costs of institutionalizing children made retarded by severe beatings, medical care for children with cerebral palsy resulting from serious head injuries inflicted by an abusive parent, special education for children with maltreatment-related cognitive disorders, and prosecution and incarceration of severely abusive caretakers.

Some of these costs, notably mental health, physical therapy and institutionalization, may continue into the victim's adulthood. Other costs of child abuse and neglect shift. They are transferred to the adult criminal justice system, the income support system, the health care system and the social service system, which, among other things, provides vocational rehabilitation and therapeutic services for alcohol and drug abusers, the mentally ill, and battered women.

Intergenerational Costs

The cost of a childhood of abuse is also visited upon the next generation. Kaufman and Zigler estimate that 30 percent of abused children grow up to be abusive parents, carrying the dysfunctional and violent patterns of their childhood into relationships with their children and spouses (in Gelles). Studies tracing the intergenerational pattern of abuse have found up to 90 percent of abusing parents to have been abused as children (Bernier). The cycle of abuse, suffering and costs is continually reinitiated. That cycle must be broken.

Public Policy Issues and Recommendations

It is a cliche to say that our children are our future. But it is true nonetheless. They represent assets of great potential value; they are our stock of future human capital.

We need to produce healthy, competent, socially responsible workers and citizens. But what we sometimes produce instead are physically, intellectually, neurobehaviorally or emotionally impaired individuals. Their lives may be brief and filled with pain. They may survive but never be self-sufficient. They may be only costly liabilities, diverting resources from more productive endeavors.

This is not Nazi Germany. We are not about to exterminate "useless eaters" (as Hitler defined the mentally retarded and severely handicapped). But we do have a legitimate mission to protect our interests and produce capable individuals. We also have a legitimate mission to prevent and relieve human suffering when possible.

It is possible to prevent the suffering described here. Since it is behaviorally related, it is a matter of inducing behavioral changes. That, of course, is easier said than done. Our best efforts at prevention, intervention and treatment often fail.

Policy Goals and Their Effectiveness

The underlying purpose of our child welfare programs is both to protect children and to strengthen families. Intervention and treatment strategies are designed to prevent further maltreatment and to enhance the family's functioning as a safe and supportive entity. In the more serious cases, children are removed from the home; however, the goal is to reunite the family as soon as feasible.

Since dysfunctional parental behavior can take such diverse forms, child protective strategies must also. Included are infant stimulation programs, therapeutic day care, psychiatric therapy and household management training.

The NCES found that the least costly strategies are often the most effective. Hot lines, Parents Anonymous groups, parent aides, lay therapy and parent education classes were not simply more cost-effective in producing positive outcomes, they were often more effective. The higher cost of individual counseling provided by social workers or psychiatrists was not warranted, as client impact analysis found they did very little to modify dysfunctional behavior. However, the costs of family and group counseling, sometimes provided by lay people or formerly abusive parents, were found to be far outweighed by the benefit of improved outcomes.

But just as we must face the realities of substance abuse rehabilitation, so must we face the realities of parent-maltreater rehabilitation. Positive outcomes are possible only in a minority of cases, generally where maltreatment is less severe and shorter-lived. The comprehensive, expensive federally funded demonstration projects (which would cost the states about $30 billion to replicate for 1,000,000 maltreating families) resulted, at best, in a reduced propensity for maltreatment in about half the families they served (in Daro). Recidivism rates were very high.

Parents who physically abuse their children seldom change their behavioral patterns. Over 50 percent of the child abuse fatalities each year involve children who had been or were still under social service agency protection (Daro & Mitchell). Treatment models targeted to families at risk of being physically abusive are far more effective. However, it can be difficult to identify those families and bring them to counseling. They may have to recognize themselves and seek help. Media promotion of Parents Anonymous and child abuse hot lines can be helpful in these cases. But once severe physical abuse has occurred, it is extremely difficult to prevent reoccurrence.

Neglectful mothers are most resistant to intervention and rarely show sustained improvement in caring for their children. Early recognition and attendance to the problems of maternal depression and large, closely spaced families may reduce the incidence of neglect. But given our limited social resources, early recognition can be difficult. For many families it is already too late. And, although we have the pharmacological means to treat depression, the prevalence of mental illness and low intelligence observed in neglectful mothers makes the prognosis for overall lasting progress poor. The NCES found that 66 percent of the neglecting mothers in their sample continued to be neglectful throughout their treatment (in Daro).

The National Clinical Evaluation Study also found that 75 percent of those who emotionally maltreated their children continued to do so while in therapy. Habits of attitude and speech are especially difficult to break (in Daro).

Recidivism rates were far lower among the sexual abuse sample, most of which involved father-daughter or stepfather-daughter incest. The perpetrators often admitted their guilt and assumed responsibility for their actions. Sexual abuse continued in only 20 percent of the cases in the NCES sample. But other studies suggest that this high rate of compliance may not be sustained over time.

Almost 60 percent of the families in the NCES study engaged in multiple forms of maltreatment (in Daro). These families were found to experience a greater number of functioning problems than families involved in a single form of maltreatment. They also had significantly greater rates of reincidence during treatment and significantly greater propensities for future maltreatment.

The NCES also found that maltreating parents who were substance abusers were significantly less likely to benefit from treatment. Both their own functioning and their parenting showed little improvement.

Our dual mission of protecting children and maintaining families may be laudable, but given the poor rate of positive treatment outcomes, it may be unduly optimistic. We may seek to keep families together too often or reunite them too soon, as evidenced by the 500-plus annual fatalities among children who had been under agency supervision. All else equal, children do best with their families. But for maltreated children, all else rarely is equal. No one thrives in a chaotic, deprived or violent atmosphere. Perhaps more children, especially those of repeat or multiple offenders or of substance-abusing offenders, should be raised in alternative environments. Some people are simply not fit to be parents and never will be.

Removing the Child from Danger

When only one member of a household maltreats a child, which is not uncommon in cases of sexual abuse or battering, legal intervention can sometimes successfully remove the perpetrator from the home, allowing the child to remain with the nonabusive parent. Otherwise, we must recalculate the liabilities of outside care and act swiftly to remove children from dangerously dysfunctional environments. Treatment programs that work for less placement, through in-home visits, therapy and other relatively less costly strategies, save money and disrupt the family less. But they do not do enough to prevent reabuse or to rehabilitate children. For all its trauma and deficiencies, children in foster care have been found to engage in less problem behavior and to show significant developmental improvement (Kent).

Right now our foster care system is seriously overburdened. We have no room for many children in critical need of placement. We must recruit and train more foster parents. We need to raise their salaries as in any labor market in which there exists excess demand. People who take in drug-affected babies require yet more training and should receive greater compensation. Their work is demanding, and they are in short supply.

Since we have a shortage of foster parents and since many children require more attention than foster parents can provide, we should consider the advantages of institutional residences, not Dickensian orphanages but modern, nurturative, development-oriented group homes. Institutional settings *can* be warm and supportive. Perhaps a comprehensive system of long-term residential facilities, costly though they may be, would ultimately save money on reform schools and prisons.

We should also make adoption more feasible. More adoptions should be subsidized, especially of older children and children with behavioral or medical difficulties. We should move more swiftly to terminate parental rights when a newborn is left unclaimed in the hospital. A mother who abandons her baby has essentially abrogated her rights. We should also terminate the rights of parents whose behavior continues to seriously endanger their children. Difficult though it may be to find adoptive homes for troubled children, it is less difficult when they are younger. And they would have suffered that much less damage.

Intervention before the Fact

Much of our prevention efforts have been designed, none too successfully, to prevent reincidence of abuse and neglect. Perhaps we could realize a greater return on our child protection dollar if we put more emphasis on the prevention of initial child abuse and neglect. Effective programs can take many forms.

Education: Again, change begins with education. Neglect may stem from simple ignorance of a child's needs. Abuse may stem from unreasonable expectations or lack of self-control. Therefore students, parents and parents-to-be in areas where teen pregnancy and child maltreatment rates are high should have parenting education. They must learn about children's physical, emotional and cognitive needs at various stages of development and the behavior that is reasonable to expect at various ages. They must learn household and child management skills, including appropriate, nonviolent methods of discipline. They must also learn to control their own anger and stress.

Much of this training can be provided in schools. Students who are not parents can work together with student parents and their children. (One hopes that the nonparents will appreciate the demands of child rearing and delay their own parenthood.) Other high-risk parents, reachable through the WIC program, can also be enrolled. Providing off-school-hours babysitting in exchange for participating in parenting classes might increase the mothers' incentive to attend. The non-parent students could babysit. Everyone would benefit.

Home visiting: Parents can also be taught at home. Home visiting has been found to show such dramatic results that Medicaid will now pay for home visits to high-risk mothers and their infants. Studies have shown benefits ranging from higher birth weight, less malnutrition, higher IQs, better school performance and less maltreatment of children in families that were visited as compared to similar families that were not visited. In a follow-up study of 18-year-olds who had home visiting services as preschoolers, Schweinhart and Weikart found them to have lower dropout and arrest rates than their peers who received only center-based services. They were less likely to be mentally retarded or welfare dependent; they were more likely to be employed or in college. It was estimated that $3 to $6 of public funds was saved for every $1 spent. And in addition to the estimated $28,000 average saving (in 1981 dollars) on special education, crime and welfare, each participant was expected to pay $5,000 more in taxes (in USGAO 1990g). Hornicke and Clark found that abusive or potentially abusive families are more likely to complete a treatment program that includes home visiting. Only 26 percent of home-visited families drop out, as compared to 50 percent of the families receiving only center-based services (in USGAO 1990g).

The federal government funds home visiting programs through various project grants or block grants to the states. However, much of the at-risk population is not reached. A Medicaid-supported program would reach more potentially maltreating families. But as of 1990, only 24 states provided Medicaid-funded home visitation. All states should participate. The program should also be extended to high-risk families with older children. Many states do take advantage of the Child Abuse Prevention, Adoption and Family Services Act of 1988, which provides 25 percent matching federal funds for home visits to families where abuse or neglect has already occurred. It funds good programs, and some families do benefit. But for many other families help comes too late.

Respite services: Crisis and respite care services are immediately beneficial and preventative for high-stress, high-risk families. Most states do now offer respite care, but most of the services are utilized by parents of the mentally retarded. While it is true that parents of retarded, handicapped or other special needs children are often overburdened and that such children suffer a disproportionate share of maltreatment, respite services should be expanded to reach more specifically maltreating or potentially maltreating families.

Volunteer foster care placement serves a similar purpose. However, even before the crack epidemic overwhelmed their foster care systems, many states cut back on their voluntary placement programs. State officials felt that parents who simply wanted a vacation from their children took advantage. Some probably did. But for many families on the brink, such relief was undoubtedly prophylactic and lessened their propensity for abuse. Four months of voluntary, preventative foster care is far less costly than two years of involuntary care (plus treatment) after abuse has occurred.

We also must devote additional resources to child care. We need more infant stimulation programs, early childhood education and developmental day care. These provide children the intellectual and social skills they may not learn at home, skills vital to academic success and to a healthy, productive adulthood. Such programs also reduce the incidence of child maltreatment by providing mothers respite from child care and freeing them to work, thereby relieving some of the stresses that may lead to abuse.

Financial support: Since poverty, especially extreme poverty, is strongly associated with severe physical abuse and neglect, some feel that simply increasing income supports will greatly reduce the incidence of child maltreatment. That may be helpful. However, the fact that most low-income and very low-income parents do not abuse or neglect their children indicates that poverty itself is not a cause of maltreatment. The stress of poverty provides fertile ground for abuse and neglect, but they do not necessarily follow. As mentioned earlier, maltreating low-income parents, especially neglectful parents, differ from nonmaltreating low income parents in many ways. They are more likely to be clinically depressed, psychotic, mentally retarded or extremely apathetic and unmotivated. They are also more likely to be substance abusers and experience violent mood swings. Until these characteristics are remediated, if they can be remediated, increased income will not improve parenting. Neither would these parents derive much benefit from job training programs designed to enhance self-esteem and responsibility and endow recipients with marketable skills. Zuravin also found that whereas neglectful mothers have little interest in planning their lives, their lack of financial planning and inability to make wise consumption decisions is especially pronounced. Rather than simply increasing their income, training in money and household management would be more effective.

Family planning services: Family planning and pregnancy termination services, important to all women, are vital to the three high-risk groups: teenagers, substance abusers and neglectful mothers.

Few neglectful mothers are teenagers, but almost all neglectful mothers began their families as teens. They were among the youngest of teen mothers and had additional children in more rapid succession. In their twenties, mired in poverty and with several children to care for, they were overwhelmed and experienced what therapists term "delayed-risk syndrome." Therefore we must focus pregnancy prevention efforts on girls from high-risk areas before they approach their teens and redouble our efforts to prevent subsequent births to teen mothers.

As mentioned earlier, substance-abusing women must be provided with birth control technologies that require no effort or planning on their part. The same is true of neglectful mothers. Also, sterilization procedures must be made immediately available to women who want them. The current red tape and inadequacy of our publicly funded women's health care system often forces a women to wait six months or more for a tubal ligation. By that time the substance-abusing or neglectful mother is often once again pregnant.

We must also consider the feasibility of empowering our courts to order birth control implants in the more intractable cases—substance-abusing, neglectful or abusive mothers who make no effort at rehabilitation or exhibit no greater parental responsibility. Although such power is fraught with the potential for misuse, allowing unfit women to continue giving birth may result in far greater injustice—to vulnerable young creatures, born only to suffer, and to society, which pays the price. That the implants can be removed lessens the danger of judicial abuse and may provide the incentive for reform some women need.

Improved reporting and follow-through: We must strengthen and enforce our mandatory reporting laws. The National Incidence Study estimates that two out of three maltreated children known to professionals such as police, teachers and medical personnel, who are required by law to report their suspicions to child protection agencies, are not reported (USDHHS 1988). Failure to report is currently a misdemeanor; prosecution is rare. (However, successful lawsuits been brought by representatives of abused children against authorities who failed to report evidence of maltreatment.)

We must thoroughly investigate all reported maltreatment and not dismiss allegations too quickly.

Effective prevention and intervention are costly. But failure to adequately protect our children is far more costly. Child welfare expenditures are an investment that can generate very high returns. Indeed, they are an investment we cannot afford to forgo.

6

Teenage Pregnancy and Childbearing

Pregnancy is not a contagious disease. It doesn't foul the air. It is not responsible for traffic crashes or fatal fires. Nor does it lead to street crime. Pregnancy is not an illness and is rarely harmful to a woman's health. If the woman receives adequate prenatal care, eats properly and does not endanger the fetus by smoking, drinking or taking drugs, the outcome is usually a healthy baby. When the baby is wanted and cherished and cared for, the outcome can be quite desirable.

Teen pregnancy, then, is not a public health problem in the sense of other issues discussed in this volume. But on the scale in which teen pregnancies and births to teen mothers occur today, it poses a very real threat to the health of the body public. Teenage childbearing has stretched our health care resources, challenged our ability to provide affordable housing, increased the burden on our school systems and made a significant reduction in poverty nearly impossible. It has contributed to our alarming high school dropout rate, to the swelling numbers of single-parent households and to the unconscionable numbers of children living economically, emotionally and intellectually impoverished lives. Consequently, it has contributed to the growth of the underclass by enlarging the ranks of the unemployable and the criminal. It imposes extreme and far-reaching costs on society. And in fact, the conditions for a positive outcome cited above are often not met, and teenage pregnancy frequently results in a less than desirable outcome. Yet, teen pregnancy prevention programs notwithstanding, it can be said that our public policies actually encourage teenage girls to give birth.

INCIDENCE, TRENDS AND DEMOGRAPHIC CHARACTERISTICS

Despite improved contraception and the availability of safe, legal abortions, 488,941 babies were born to teenage mothers in 1988; 10,588 of those babies were born to girls under the age of 15. Boys under 15 fathered 376 children, while 110 children were born of parents who were both less than 15 years of age. One-quarter of teen births were to mothers who already had one or more children (NCHS 1990b).

Sexual Activity and Contraceptive Use

Sexual activity has been increasing among teenagers of all ages and races, and the age of sexual initiation has fallen dramatically (see Tables 6.1 and 6. 2).

In 1988, 32 percent of white females had had sexual intercourse by age 16; 46 percent were sexually active by age 17. Among black females, the respective proportions were 46 percent and 69 percent (USHR). The corresponding figures for white males were 47 percent and 59 percent; for black males they were 70 percent and 90 percent (Sonenstein et al.). In 1987, 15 percent of white females, 26 percent of black females, 15 percent of white males and 39 percent

Table 6.1

Percentage of Women Aged 15 to 19 Years who Reported Having Had Premarital Sexual Intercourse by Age and Race: United States, Selected Years

Race/Age	1970	1975	1980	1985	1988
All races					
15	4.6	9.8	16.7	20.0	25.6
16	20.3	18.9	26.8	30.4	31.8
17	32.3	36.6	35.5	41.7	51.0
18	39.4	49.1	56.2	53.2	69.5
19	48.2	63.9	66.9	70.7	75.3
Overall	28.6	36.4	42.0	44.1	51.5
White					
15-17	17.2	21.6	26.7	30.3	34.4
18-19	41.4	54.9	60.5	61.0	72.6
Overall	26.7	35.4	41.4	43.1	50.6
Black					
15-17	32.8	32.0	41.4	36.6	48.4
18-19	66.8	79.0	78.3	82.5	75.6
Overall	46.0	50.8	58.1	55.4	58.8

Source: Centers for Disease Control. "Premarital Sexual Experience among Adolescent Women— United States, 1970–1988." *Morbidity and Mortality Weekly Report.*

Table 6.2

Percentage of Metropolitan-Area Males Aged 17 to 19 Years who Reported Having Had Premarital Sexual Intercourse by Age and Race: United States, 1979 and 1988

	1979			1988		
Age	All	Black	Nonblack	All	Black	Nonblack
17	55.7	60.3	54.5	71.9	89.7	68.0
18	66.0	79.8	63.6	70.6	80.1	68.7
19	77.5	79.9	77.1	87.8	97.8	86.0
Overall	65.7	71.1	64.5	75.5	87.7	73.0

Source: F. L. Sonenstein, J. H. Pleck and L. C. Ku. "Sexual Activity, Condom Use and AIDS Awareness among Adolescent Males." *Family Planning Perspectives* 21, no. 4. (1989).

of black males had engaged in intercourse before reaching their fifteenth birthday (Moore & Peterson). Sexual activity is even more prevalent among urban youth, and the age of their sexual initiation is younger. A 1989 survey of tenth-graders in the Philadelphia school system found that two-thirds were sexually experienced and that 29 percent had had intercourse before reaching 12 years of age (in Mezzacappa). A 1981 study found the average age of first intercourse for urban black males to be 11.8 years (in Armstrong 1990a). Current information drawn from a large sample is needed for a good many reasons but will not be available for some time. The Bush administration squelched a major USDHHS survey for fear that it would encourage teen sexuality.

Such a survey would find that teens are more likely to use contraception today, especially condoms, as much in response to the AIDS epidemic as from a desire to avert pregnancy. As depicted in Table 6.3, unmarried urban adolescent males were far less likely to forgo birth control at first intercourse in 1988 than they were in 1979. Their condom use at first intercourse increased from 20 percent overall in 1979 to 54 percent in 1988 (Sonenstein et al.). However, a 1990 CDC survey found that only 49 percent of all high school males used a condom at last intercourse, while only 40 percent of all high school females used one (CDC 1992e).

Contraceptive use in any given year increases both with the age of the teen and with his or her sexual experience. The longer a teen has been sexually active, the more likely he or she is to contracept (Moore & Peterson). Table 6.4 depicts the practice of birth control during adolescents' then-recent sexual encounters but, unfortunately, both Tables 6.3 and 6.4 also illustrate the large number of teenagers at risk of conceiving a child. Black teens and younger adolescents incur the greatest risk.

Table 6.3
Percentage of Never-Married, Sexually Active Metropolitan-Area Adolescent Males who Used No Contraception or an Ineffective Method at First Intercourse by Age and Race/Ethnicity: United States, 1979 and 1988

	1979			1988			
Age	All	Black	Nonblack	All	Black	White	Hispanic
All Ages	71.1	76.8	69.8	37.8	50.6	33.9	42.8
<12	-	-	-	74.5	73.0	70.8	88.2
12-14	76.9	83.1	74.0	48.3	57.1	44.6	53.0
15-17	69.4	64.7	69.9	31.6	33.8	30.6	36.0
18-19	51.9	46.1	52.3	16.3	62.6	15.1	11.4

Source: F. L. Sonenstein, J. H. Pleck and L. C. Ku. "Sexual Activity, Condom Use and AIDS Awareness among Adolescent Males." *Family Planning Perspectives,* 21, no. 4. (1989).

Table 6.4
Use of Birth Control in Last Four Weeks or Last Several Times Adolescent Had Sex by Race and Gender: United States, 1987

Frequency of use	Females		Males	
	Black	Nonblack	Black	Nonblack
Every time	44.5%	77.9%	26.3%	71.4%
Most of the time	11.3%	5.7%	22.2%	9.2%
About half or some of the time	15.3%	3.5%	27.1%	4.4%
Never	28.8%	13.0%	24.4%	15.0%

Source: K. A. Moore and J. L. Peterson. *The Consequences of Teenage Pregnancy.*

Pregnancy, Abortion and Childbirth

More than one teenage girl in ten gets pregnant each year; 84 percent of their pregnancies are unintended (Armstrong & Waszak). Pregnancy rates among teens have increased a great deal in recent decades, despite their more frequent use of birth control, primarily because more teens are sexually active. However, the increasing availability of legal abortions had, until recently, allowed a reduction in the percentage of teens who gave birth each year and in the absolute number of babies born to teen mothers. Thus in 1974, 9.9 percent of teenage girls became pregnant, 2.7 percent had abortions and 5.8 percent gave birth; whereas by 1985, 11 percent became pregnant, 4.4 percent had abortions and 5.1 percent gave birth. In 1974, 29 percent of teen pregnancies were medically terminated; by 1985, 42 percent were terminated (Moore).

However, as shown in Table 6.5, birth rates to teen mothers have been increasing since 1986. The increase has been especially pronounced among younger teenagers. The birth rate for teens 15 to 17 years of age increased 6 percent just from 1987 to 1988, while the rate for teens aged 18 to 19 increased only 2 percent (NCHS 1990b). In Massachusetts, births to teens 12 to 15 years increased 23 percent from 1985 to 1988, while births to teens aged 16 and 17 increased 10 percent and the number of births to older teens was unchanged (MDPH 1989). These figures are especially disturbing because women who give birth at younger ages proceed to give birth to more children and in more rapid succession then women who delay childbearing. Women who first give birth at age 16 or younger are more than twice as likely to have a second child within two years than are women who wait at least until age 22 to have their first child (Armstrong & Pascale). Younger mothers are also more likely to be unmarried and thus have higher rates of welfare dependency.

The increase in teen births is partly due to the increase in sexual activity among younger adolescents, who, as noted, are less likely to practice contraception.

Table 6.5
Birth Rates per 1,000 Women in Specified Group by Age and Race: United States, Selected Years

Race/Age	1970	1975	1980	1985	1986	1987	1988
White							
10-14 years	0.5	0.6	0.6	0.6	0.6	0.6	0.6
15-17 years	29.2	28.0	25.2	24.0	23.4	24.1	25.5
18-19 years	101.5	74.0	72.1	70.1	69.8	68.6	69.2
Black							
10-14 years	5.2	5.1	4.3	4.5	4.6	4.7	4.8
15-17 years	101.4	85.6	73.6	69.8	70.0	72.9	76.6
18-19 years	204.9	152.4	138.8	137.1	141.0	142.2	150.5

Source: National Center for Health Statistics. *Advance Report of Final Natality Statistics, 1988.*

There may also have been an increase in noncontracepted sexual activity among teens of all ages, but this is not likely. Rather, the increase in teen births is probably also due in part to the fact that although legal abortions may be available, they have become less accessible.

Most states have rescinded Medicaid funding for abortions, a decision that impacted most heavily on adolescent women, as their incomes are lower, and more states have enacted parental notification laws. Withdrawal of public funding may require the teen or her family to save to pay for an abortion. By the time they raise the funds, if they ever do raise the funds, the pregnancy may be so advanced that abortion is no longer an acceptable alternative. A similar outcome results when an adolescent is too embarrassed or afraid to tell her parents she is pregnant or is so intimidated by the judicial bypass procedure some states offer that she delays until it is too late. The legal process itself is time consuming.

These restrictions may explain why the ratio of legal abortions to live births among teens under 15 fell by 23 percent just from 1987 to 1988 and fell by 4 percent among women 15 to 19 (NCHS 1991). Both the withdrawal of public funding and the imposition of parental notification laws have increased the cost of an abortion and, like any other service, as its price rises less of it is utilized. This, of course, is precisely the intention of the antiabortion lobby. However, if antiabortionists carefully examined the consequences of teenage childbearing, many might reconsider their position.

By Demographic Characteristic

Black teens are twice as likely to become pregnant as white teenagers (Moore). White teens are more likely to abort their pregnancies, but because of their higher pregnancy rates, black teens as a group have higher rates of both abortion and birth (Joyce; Ezzard et al.). A study of pregnant teens in New York City found that abortion rates were highest among pregnant white adolescents, followed by black, then by Puerto Rican and lastly by non-Puerto Rican Hispanic teens. The percentage of pregnancies aborted decreased with the age of the mother and increased with her socioeconomic status. Teens from low socioeconomic status families were more likely to get pregnant, less likely to abort and more likely to give birth outside of marriage. This was true even though abortions in New York are accessible and funded by Medicaid. Even though, all else equal, abortion rates are greater when funding is available, Medicaid-eligible teens were more than twice as likely to carry their babies to term than were teens who had to finance their abortions themselves (Joyce).

In 1988 nearly 1 in 4 black non-Hispanic births, 1 in 10 white non-Hispanic births and 1 in 6 Hispanic-origin births was to a teenage mother. Among U.S. Hispanics, babies born to teen mothers comprised 17 percent of Mexican births and 21 percent of Puerto Rican births but only 6 percent of Cuban and 8 percent of Central and South American births. Among Native Americans, the proportion was nearly 1 in 5, but among women of Chinese and Japanese ancestry, the proportions were only 1 in 100 and 3 in 100 respectively (NCHS 1991).

Black adolescents are not only more likely to give birth than white adolescents, they are also more likely to have additional children while in their teens (see Table 6.6). They also have a greater tendency to have yet more children when they enter their twenties. Although the rates are low for both races, black women 20 to 24 years of age are four times more likely than white women to give birth to a fourth child and six times more likely to give birth to a fifth, sixth or seventh child (NCHS 1990b). The discrepancy would be shown to be even greater if data on non-Hispanic whites versus white Hispanics were available. The fact that Hispanic women, 95 percent of whom are classified as white, have children younger and in greater number and are more likely to be unwed mothers biases the white birth rates depicted in these tables upward. As of 1988, Hispanics constituted 13 percent of the white population aged 10 to 19 (USBC, modified).

By Marital Status

The proportion of teen births to unmarried mothers has increased alarmingly from 30 percent in 1970 to 48 percent in 1980 and 66 percent in 1988 (Moore; NCHS 1990b). Although the proportion of births among unwed black teens has historically been far greater than among unwed white teens and is still growing, the rate among white teens has increased much more rapidly, reducing the discrepancy between the two groups. By 1988, 53.5 percent of the white women aged 15 to 19 that gave birth were unmarried compared to 91.2 percent of similarly aged black women (NCHS 1990b). (Further details are provided in Table 6.6.)

Table 6.6
Birth Rates per 1,000 Women in Specified Group and Percent to Unmarried Mother by Age of Mother, Live-Birth Order and Race of Child: United States, 1988

Live-birth order	White: Age of Mother			Black: Age of Mother		
	10-14	15-17	18-19	10-14	15-17	18-19
Total	0.6	25.5	69.2	4.8	76.6	150.5
First child	0.6	22.7	51.7	4.7	92.4	92.4
Second child	0.0	2.5	14.7	0.1	12.5	42.3
Third child	0.0	0.2	2.5	0.0	1.8	12.7
Fourth child+	0.0	0.0	0.3	0.0	0.2	3.1

Percent births to unmarried mother

	87%	71%*	58%*	99%	97%*	88%*

* Unweighted average of percentage for each age.

Source: National Center for Health Statistics. *Advance Report of Final Natality Statistics, 1988.*

Such specific information is not available for other groups, but the proportion of all births occurring to unmarried mothers in 1988 among other American subpopulations tallied as follows: total Hispanics, 34.0 percent; Mexicans, 30.6 percent; Puerto Ricans, 53.3 percent; Native Americans, 45.6 percent; Chinese, 4.3 percent; and Japanese, 8.6 percent (NCHS 1991). The overall proportion of births to unwed mothers among whites (including Hispanics) was 17.7 percent, among non-Hispanic whites it was 14.9 percent, and among blacks it was 63.7 percent (NCHS 1990b).

Married teens more often choose to carry to term than unmarried pregnant teenagers. But among married teenagers, blacks, followed by Puerto Ricans, are most likely to obtain an abortion (Joyce).

THE CONSEQUENCES OF TEEN CHILDBEARING

The trends that have been identified here and the numbers that have been presented are, by any standard, detrimental to our national well-being. The costs are enormous and growing. The implications are ominous.

The Health Costs

Pregnant teenagers are at higher risk of serious medical complications including anemia, pregnancy-induced hypertension (toxemia), cervical trauma and premature delivery than older women during pregnancy, and the maternal mortality rate for mothers under age 15 is 60 percent greater than for women in their twenties (Armstrong & Pascale). In fact, the overall maternal mortality rate is 12 times the overall death rate of women having abortions and 21 times that of women who secure an abortion in their first trimester (NCHS 1991, modified).

Approximately 13 percent of all teen pregnancies end in miscarriages or stillbirths (Armstrong & Pascale). Adolescents more often have preterm deliveries, and their babies tend to be small for their gestational age. Mothers less than 15 years of age are 125 percent more likely to give birth to a low-birth-weight baby than mothers 25 to 29 years old, and women aged 15 to 19 are over 50 percent more likely (NCHS 1990b). As discussed in Chapter 4, low-birth-weight babies often have severe congenital problems or other difficulties that may persist indefinitely and that may result in serious developmental lags. They may need neonatal intensive care, which can total tens of thousands of dollars or more, and they may need years of specialized therapy thereafter—if they survive. Children born to mothers under the age of 18 are twice as likely to die in their first year of life than children born to mothers over 20 (Armstrong & Waszak).

Part of the difficulty is due to the notoriously poor traditional teenage diet. Part of it appears to be genetic, as age–birth-weight charts reveal an extremely regular progression in birth weight to ages 24 and 25, followed by a regular regression (USHR). This pattern is true of both black and white mothers, the only difference being that black women give birth to babies of significantly lesser weight at every maternal age. The apparently genetic tendency of black mothers to bear smaller babies also accounts in part for the low average birth weight of babies born to adolescents, since black women are disproportionately represented among teen mothers.

The higher prevalence of cigarette smoking among pregnant teens compared to older pregnant women is also a contributing risk factor (SCHS 1991b). The New Hampshire study referred to in the preceding chapter found that cigarette smoking by women during pregnancy is the foremost risk predictor of low birthweight (SCHS 1991a).

Another important factor is the failure of pregnant teens to obtain adequate prenatal care. They may be afraid or embarrassed or may deny the evidence of their bodies. They may be unknowledgeable about where to find affordable care or ignorant of the need for proper medical supervision. Whatever the reasons, only 46 percent of teens obtain prenatal care in their first trimester as compared to 60 percent of women in their late twenties and 64 percent of women in their early thirties (NCHS 1990b). Eight percent come to care in their third trimester, and 4 percent never receive prenatal care.

When they do obtain care it is frequently paid for by Medicaid. Approximately one-third of the teens who give birth become AFDC recipients and automatically eligible for Medicaid, so at least that number receive Medicaid-funded maternity care. The actual number is probably far greater, as Medicaid eligibility requirements for maternity benefits are deliberately lenient.

The cost borne by Medicaid for a birth to a teenager 14 or younger has been calculated as $3,494, the costs for 15 to 17 year olds is $3,224 and for 18 and 19 year olds it is $2,696, exclusive of pediatric care (Armstrong & Waszak).

Most poor and near-poor children up to age six are also now eligible for Medicaid benefits even though their family income exceeds that allowed for AFDC receipt. While this may be expensive, it is an encouraging development in terms of child health.

The Personal Consequences of Too-Early Family Formation

The birth of a child can occasion profound rapture and joy. Rearing a child can be the source of life's greatest delights, an infinite wellspring of love, pride, pleasure and fulfillment. But, as every parent knows, rearing a child, even under the best of conditions, is an extremely demanding task. It demands time, labor and tremendous self-sacrifice. It is a 24-hour-a-day responsibility. When the circumstances of parenthood are less than optimal the burden can be crushing.

Teenage parents, more so than others, may find the demands of child rearing virtually overwhelming. Often unprepared to parent or provide, they struggle with the work, the cost, the stress and the restrictions child rearing places on their lives. The strain is all the greater when a woman raises her children alone.

Lesser Family Income

The National Research Council estimates that for each year a first birth is delayed, the family income when the mother reaches 27 years of age is greater by $500. Thus every year a first birth is delayed (up to age 20), the chance of a woman and her family having an income below poverty level is reduced by about 22 percent (NRC 1987). The Children's Defense Fund reports that women who first give birth as teens have about half the lifetime earnings of women who first give birth in their twenties (in Armstrong & Pascale). And three major national surveys found the incidence of poverty among families begun by a teen birth to be 20, 50 and 60 percent greater than families of mothers who gave birth to their first child at a later age (in Furstenberg et al.).

By family structure and race/ethnicity: Since the great majority of adolescent women who give birth are unmarried or, if married, are more likely to divorce and to divorce sooner, it is instructive to compare incomes of female-headed households to that of married couples.

Almost 55 percent of the households headed by women with children under age 18 lived on a less than poverty level income in 1987, compared with fewer than 8 percent of married couples with children that age. More than 60 percent of the households headed by women with children under six lived in poverty, whereas fewer than 10 percent of married couples with children under six were poor (USBC). Young single mothers confront even higher poverty rates. More than 70 percent of households headed by women under age 25 lived in poverty in 1987 (Armstrong & Pascale).

The average income of female-headed households with children in 1988 was $11,865; for married couples with children it was $38,164. Among whites, married couples' family incomes were almost twice the $17,672 of female-headed households. Black married couples enjoyed incomes three times the $10,657 of black female-headed households, and Hispanic married couples earned 2.5 times the $10,687 accruing to Hispanic female-headed households (USBC).

Since minority women have higher rates of unwed births and since their marriages are more likely to end in separation, divorce or widowhood (after adjusting for age), far more minority households are female headed. In 1988, 28 percent of black households and 16 percent of Hispanic households were headed by women in contrast to 7 percent of white households (USBC). Because the prevalence of female-headed households is greater among minorities and because minority women tend to have a larger number of children, more minority children live only with their mothers. Altogether, 21 percent of the children under 18 lived with just their mother in 1988; for whites, blacks and Hispanics the respective proportions were 16, 51 and 27 percent. Only 39 percent of black children lived with two parents (USBC). These numbers have frightful implications. They are all the more worrisome, as the proportion of mother-only households has more than doubled since 1970 and continues to increase.

This change in family structure partly explains the growing proportion of children living in poverty. In 1987, 20 percent of all children were poor, in contrast to 15 percent of all children in 1970. The 20 percent represents 15 percent of white children, 45 percent of black children and 39 percent of Hispanic children (USBC). More recent data will show an increase in numbers that are already chilling. That increase will surely be due as much to the increase in unwed teen births as to the 1990–1991 recession.

Welfare Dependency: Approximately one-third of teenage mothers receive public assistance upon their maternity (Armstrong & Waszak). Teen mothers who do not receive welfare initially may enroll later if the fathers of their children fail to provide, their families withdraw support or they are encouraged to apply for benefits. Over 80 percent of teenage single mothers who head their own families are welfare dependent for some period of time (Danziger). A teen mother who marries has a higher probability of needing public assistance than a married teen who delays childbearing (Armstrong & Waszak).

Women who enroll in welfare as teen parents are likely to remain on welfare longer than other women, not because of their teen parenthood per se, but because they tend to have personal characteristics associated with longer duration of welfare recipiency: little work history, less schooling, young children, having never been married, having lived in a mother-only welfare-dependent household as a teenager, and being of the black race (O'Neill et al.). The fact that teen mothers tend to have little or no work history and less schooling than women who enter the welfare system at a later age renders them less likely to exit the system through work. Available jobs are likely to be low paying, with little or no benefits. Their opportunity costs of remaining on welfare, even if Medicaid benefits were continued, are therefore less. Indeed, considering job-related expenses and taxes, their net disposable income may be reduced by working. Working may then be "irrational," at least in the short term, particularly for black teen mothers, who may confront an even lower potential wage and who tend to have more children. Their earnings would have to support a larger family and, unlike welfare benefits, wages do not increase with family size. The desire to work may also be reduced by the presence of young children, as their mothers may prefer to remain at home with them. Young children decidedly increase the cost of working because of the need for child care.

Lesser schooling also decreases a woman's chance of leaving welfare through marriage. Because schooling is a proxy for socioeconomic status it may be positively related to the income of a prospective husband, even to the possibility of finding a husband. Black women, disproportionately represented among teen mothers on welfare, are also less likely to exit the system through marriage. As O'Neill and colleagues speculate, this may be partly a reflection of the lower earnings of black men relative to white men or the more rapidly declining ratio of black men to black women with each additional year of age. It may also reflect the cultural mores of the black community, which attaches less of a stigma to single parenthood and to welfare recipiency than the white community does.

Women who grew up in welfare-dependent households are also more likely to find the practice condoned and so feel less of an urgency to become financially independent. Finally, unmarried mothers stay on welfare longer because they typically receive less financial support from a male partner.

Marriage, divorce, and child support: Although marriage rates have fallen among adolescent women, even among pregnant adolescent women, many do marry. The majority of teen mothers, in fact, are married within three years of their baby's birth (O'Connell & Rogers). The teen mother who marries can be expected to have a higher income than those who remain single, especially if her husband works, is older, or enjoys the support of his family. However, the negative financial consequences of too-early family formation do not disappear. Teenage parents, married or not, endure lower socioeconomic status, at least throughout young adulthood, than their peers who delay parenthood (O'Connell & Rogers).

Teen marriages also have a higher risk of failure than marriages between older partners. Only 13 percent of marriages involve women under the age of 20, but 32 percent of divorces involve women who were teenagers when they married (USBC). Lindsay reports that at least 60 percent of teen marriages end in divorce within five years (in Armstrong & Pascale).

It has been well documented that divorce frequently results in a substantial loss of income for a mother and her children. Many are pushed into poverty. Women who first give birth as teens are at greater risk of falling into poverty following divorce because their former husbands tend to earn lower wages and the household has less property to distribute. Reviewing Wisconsin data on the economic characteristics of divorcing women, Nichols-Casebolt and Danziger found that women who had ever been teen mothers suffered great disadvantage. Compared to women who were never teen mothers, they were younger, had lower income, were less likely to be employed and more were likely to be on AFDC at the time of their divorce. Their households were almost 50 percent less likely to have property to distribute and, when there was property, its mean value was less than half that of the older mothers' households. Fewer divorcing teen mothers were awarded child support. When support was awarded, the mean award granted women who had been teen mothers was substantially less; such mothers with one child were awarded $174 monthly on average; those with three children were awarded $320 on average. Comparable awards to women who were never teen mothers averaged $241 and $430. These disparities are largely a function of the shorter marriages of young mothers and partly a function of their relatively young age at divorce in that their household had less time to accumulate either human or physical assets. The lesser support awards reflect the court's assessment of the ability of the father to pay. Men divorcing women who had been teen mothers are younger, more likely to be unemployed and, if employed, earn substantially less than men who married women who deferred childbearing (Nichols-Casebolt & Danziger).

Single women who bore children as teens are even more disadvantaged in terms of child support compared to women who bore their children later. First, paternity must be established and, as Danziger and Nichols-Casebolt found in Wisconsin, fewer than 20 percent of unwed mothers pursue adjudication. When paternity has been legally established, single mothers are no less likely to be awarded child support, but their awards are typically lower and a much smaller proportion of their support payments are ever received. Fathers in paternity suit cases typically pay 42 percent of their legal obligation; fathers in divorce cases pay, on average, 56 percent. Not an outstanding performance, in either case.

Truncated Education

The lesser ability of teen parents to provide is only partly due to their youth. Their lesser financial wherewithal frequently persists and is largely a function of their educational disadvantages.

Each year over 40,000 teenage girls drop out of school because they are pregnant (Armstrong & Waszak). Pregnancy is thus the leading cause of dropping out among adolescent females. Although pregnant teens more frequently remain in or return to school today, they are still educationally disadvantaged because all women are staying in school longer. By the mid-1980s, according to Upchurch and McCarthy, the high school completion rate for teen mothers was 56 percent, three times what it had been in the 1950s; but the high school completion rate for all women had increased to 89 percent (in Armstrong & Waszak). Women who give birth before age 18 suffer lifelong deficits in schooling contrasted to women who defer childbearing until the completion of high school (Leibowitz et al.).

Teen fathers also suffer an educational disadvantage. Only 39 percent of males who father children as teenagers receive their high school certification by age 20, compared with 86 percent of male teens who do not, and teen fathers are only half as likely to complete college as their peers who delay fatherhood (in Armstrong 1990a). Thus teen fathers are typically less able to provide for their children throughout their lives.

It would be fallacious, however, to infer causality from these figures. For, while premature parenthood may restrict one's educational opportunities, there is another phenomenon at work. That is that teenagers who become parents are generally less academically proficient than their peers who delay parenting.

Whether white, black or Hispanic, teenage girls who have below-average basic skills are six times more likely to give birth than teenage girls of the same race or ethnicity who have average or better skills. White, black and Hispanic teen boys with lesser basic skills are three times more likely to father children than their peers who are more academically proficient (Pittman). Girls who are enrolled in school at the time they conceive are more likely to elect an abortion than those who have already dropped out, and of girls enrolled in school at conception, those with higher grades more often choose to abort (Leibowitz et al.). It would therefore appear that teens who become parents might have had fewer options and lower earnings even without the added burden of childrearing. Once they have children, of course, they invariably face greater restrictions on their ability to improve their stock of human capital. However, enhanced motivation should not be dismissed as a possible countervailing force.

Parenthood may be more prevalent among low achievers, since failure to succeed in school may encourage some adolescents to drop out and seek personal fulfillment through parenting. Academic failure reduces teenage girls' earning potential, as they well know, and therefore reduces the cost to them of having children. That is, they incur a lower opportunity cost when they stay home to rear children rather than participate in the labor force. If parenthood immediately increases their income, whether through marriage, child support or welfare, this may (not irrationally) appeal to a teenager confronted with few options, not highly motivated to pursue success, and not fully appreciative of the demands of parenthood. It may also be the case that poor academic achievers also are poor contraceptors, less informed about fertility and risk, less able to delay gratification and less able to chart or follow through on an optimal life plan.

Less Positive Outcomes for Their Children

Although many teen parents do an exemplary job of parenting and many children of teen mothers thrive, enjoy their childhood and go on to lead productive lives, many do not. In addition to the aforementioned health risks that children of teen mothers face, they are also at greater risk of lower intellectual and academic achievement, social-behavioral problems and problems of self-control (Hofferth in NRC 1987). They are also at greatest risk of maltreatment (Daro). And they are most subject to family instability (Danziger).

Although research on the relationship between youthful maternity and child development is scant, the evidence indicates that children of teen mothers have a lower level of cognitive functioning and lesser intelligence as measured on standardized tests. Children born to adolescent women are more likely to be behind grade, to need remedial help and to drop out (NRC 1987). How much of their intellectual disadvantage is directly related to their mothers' young age at birth is not known. Some of the deficit no doubt derives from the teen mother's relatively poor education and her subsequently lesser ability to verbalize well and to provide essential age-appropriate intellectual stimulation. Some is no doubt a function of the poverty that often accompanies adolescent childbearing. Poverty's inherent limitations are further compounded by the low-income child's increased likelihood of living in a disadvantaged neighborhood and attending a poor-quality school.

Poverty is also a risk predictor of poor health, as was discussed in Chapter 4. The low-income child, whose diet may not provide adequate nutrition, is more often ill, yet has fewer health care contacts and, consequently, misses more days of school (NCHS 1990d). A far smaller proportion of women who had their first child while a teen assess their child's health as excellent or very good (Moore & Peterson).

Life in a poor neighborhood also increases the child's chances of being a victim of crime and of being drawn into a life of crime, especially if the family support system is weak. Fewer than 30 percent of the juveniles and young adults detained in the youth corrections system in 1987 lived with both parents while growing up. Over one-half were raised by a single mother (USDJ 1988e). The children of single mothers also have a higher prevalence of substance abuse (AMA 1991).

The great majority of children born to adolescent mothers live in single-parent homes for long periods of time (Danziger). Those periods are longer if the birth was nonmarital or the mother is nonwhite, but even children born to married teen mothers have a greater probability of living in a mother-only household because of the higher divorce rates of teen parents. Bumpass estimates that two of five children born to women who were ever married mothers will experience the disruption of parental divorce, while three of five children born to teen mothers will experience parental divorce (in Nichols-Casebolt and Danziger).

Although living with parents who are unhappily married is not best for a child, neither is undergoing the emotional turmoil of divorce or living in a mother-only household. While nonresidential fathers, whether single or divorced, do have relationships with their children, such fathers' visits, gifts and financial contributions tend to decline rapidly and significantly as the child ages (Danziger). Many young mothers more than compensate for an absent father and many children in mother-only homes have other men such as grand-fathers or mothers' boyfriends that play supportive roles in their lives. But the strong association between growing up in a mother-only home and less successful life outcomes cannot be denied.

While perhaps most young single mothers are competent and loving parents, of all women, unmarried women under 18 are most likely to be poor mothers and their children are most at risk (USGAO 1986). The demands of childrearing are great for any parent; for one who is young and of low income they may be overgreat. The work and the life-style restrictions of motherhood may be more than offset by the pleasures it brings for someone who is mature, financially able and happy to have given birth. Someone who is young and poor and who had not intended to conceive may find the task a source of resentment and rage. A national survey evaluated by Moore and Peterson found that women who had been teen mothers were much less likely than mothers who delayed childbearing to report either happiness with their child or happiness with being a parent. Young black mothers reported markedly less happiness on both counts than young nonblack mothers. Approximately 35 percent of women who had been teen mothers reported having lost control of their emotions and feeling that they might hurt their child, compared to the 18 percent of white and 12 percent of black women who were never teen mothers who admitted such feelings (Moore & Peterson).

While data relating child abuse and teen parenthood per se is sparse, it has been observed that teenage mothers are often overrepresented in child maltreating cases. This is not unexpected since, as discussed in the preceding chapter, abuse (other than sexual abuse) is substantially greater within poor families. Holding income and race constant, the abusive family is likely to be larger, to experience more marital or quasi-marital disruptions and to be headed by a single female (NCES in Daro). These risk factors are all characteristic of families begun by teen mothers. Neglectful mothers, who tend to be of very low income, unmarried and with large numbers of unplanned, unwanted children, invariably began their families as teenagers, usually as the youngest of teen mothers (Zuravin).

The emotional, behavioral and academic problems of maltreated children described earlier are virtually identical to those experienced by the children of adolescent mothers. A 17-year follow-up of the children of black teen mothers in Baltimore found that they had a higher incidence of school problems such as grade retention, truancy and suspension, more contacts with the police and were more likely to have injured someone or to have run away than other black youth (Furstenberg et al.). Other studies have found that the children of young mothers also have a higher incidence of socioemotional problems, that is, they are more likely to feel inferior, have temper control problems and act out rebelliously or aggressively (in NRC 1987). In addition, the Baltimore study found that the children of black teen mothers are more likely to smoke, drink and take drugs and that they were likely to initiate sex at an earlier age than other black teens (Furstenberg et al.). The children of teen parents are also more likely to become teen parents, usually nonmaritally, and to become welfare dependent (Armstrong & Waszak).

Future Prospects

The birth of a child does not doom a young mother to a lifetime of poverty and despair. Nor does it doom her child to a lifetime of failure and crime. Many young mothers and their families, female headed or not, find happiness as a family unit, success in life and financial independence and security. The Baltimore follow-up of black teenage mothers found that many of the women and their children had done well. Although still disadvantaged in terms of income, education and employment status relative to their classmates who had deferred childbirth, most of the teen mothers managed to overcome the obstacles they faced and return to school or find jobs. Few went on to have large families and few became chronic welfare recipients. Not surprisingly, those whose parents had the best educations and who themselves were most academically proficient were most successful. Those who came from large or welfare-dependent families, who had poorer grades, whose parents were less educated and who had more subsequent births were less successful at finishing school and leaving welfare (Furstenberg et al.).

But while the Baltimore study gives cause for optimism, as a group, the black teen mothers and their children remained disadvantaged by virtually every measure compared to other black women and their families.

To a large extent, the difficulties the children of teen mothers face stem from their greater incidence of poverty, their mothers' lesser education and their families' instability, structure and size. How much derives from their mothers' age at maternity, which is obviously highly correlated with all of the above, is seldom clear. But while the precise source of their less-than-optimal outcomes is not easily identified, the greater life problems of the children of teen mothers are all too evident.

It is also all too evident that the personal and societal problems are going to increase in the absence of quick and effective intervention. This is true not just because births to teen mothers have been increasing but especially because births to the youngest teens have been increasing most rapidly. A growing proportion of America's children are at greater risk. And greater demands are being placed on our various social support systems.

The Public Costs of Teen Childbearing

The Center for Population Options (CPO), as reported by Armstrong and Waszak, has calculated the welfare-related costs to the public of adolescent childbearing. These were conceptualized from three perspectives.

Single-Year Costs

This is the amount the federal government spends in a particular year for AFDC, food stamps and Medicaid for families begun when the mothers were teenagers. It excludes state and local government contributions to welfare-related programs as well as expenditures for other services teen mothers and their children may require.

The CPO determined that the federal government spent $21.6 billion in 1989 on families begun by teen mothers. This includes $10.4 billion for AFDC, $3.4 billion for food stamps and $7.7 billion for Medicaid, based on the assumption that families begun by a teen birth, who comprise 53 percent of the welfare-recipient population, consume 53 percent of the funding of these programs. However, since households that do not receive AFDC may still participate in the food stamp and Medicaid programs, the 53 percent of those programs assigned to teen mothers' families is low.

Single-Birth Costs

This represents the projected cost to the federal government of a family begun by a teen birth over the following 20 years, again including only the three major benefit programs. Reflected in the calculations are the observations that (1) approximately one in three teen mothers receives welfare, (2) the average length of time a woman who begins her family as a teen remains on welfare is 2.5 years, (3) the probability a teen mother will receive public assistance declines over her lifetime and (4) the younger a woman when she first gives birth, the more children she can be expected to have.

All considered, the CPO estimates that a family begun by a teenage mother in 1989 will cost taxpayers an average of $16,975 by the time that baby reaches age 20. This figure, however, is deceptively low because it represents an average across all first births to adolescent mothers even though only one-third of families begun by a teen birth actually receive welfare. More informatively, the CPO projects that the government will spend an average of $50,925 over 20 years on each family begun in 1989 by a teen birth that enrolled in public assistance. Presumably, that figure is averaged down by the families who drop out of the welfare system.

Single-Cohort Costs

This is the projected 20-year cost to the government of all the families started by teen mothers in a given year. In other words, it is how much all the families begun by a teen mother in any one year can be expected to cost taxpayers by the time the firstborn child is 20 years old.

The CPO estimates that the families begun in 1989 by a teen birth will have cost the public treasury $6.4 billion by the year 2009.

Additional Costs

The CPO's figures are unquestionably conservative. As noted, they exclude state and local government welfare-related expenditures and overlook the fact that non-AFDC families participate in other entitlement programs, especially Medicaid, now that the eligibility requirements have been broadened to encourage the participation of mothers and children. They also omit the cost of other publicly funded services the teen mother and her family may consume, services that are less likely to be required by families begun at a later maternal age, such as parent training, job training, day care, foster care, special education and remedial education. Burt and Sonenstein found that a one-year comprehensive service package that included medical care, AFDC benefits, educational services and child care cost (in 1984) up to $7,664 for pregnant clients and up to $9,592 for clients entering the program after delivery (in USGAO 1986). These, of course, do not include the extraordinary services the family may need later. Nor do any of the cost estimates include the social costs and nonfinancial externalities generated by the inadequate or abusive parenting that all too often accompanies too-early family formation. These costs may begin with child protective services, transfer to the educational system and ultimately shift to the criminal justice system as improperly parented children grow up and act out in antisocial ways.

Nor does it include the productivity lost when young mothers and fathers fail to realize their potential because they have stopped their education short in order to rear or support a child. Neither does it include the lessened potential of the disadvantaged child or the heightened probability that that child too will become a teen parent and raise a child in great disadvantage.

A teenager's choice to give birth sets in motion a chain of events that impedes her personal progress, handicaps her child's prospects, and diverts social resources. We would, for example, have more money to spend on schools if our welfare burden were reduced; at the same time, our investment in education would reap a greater return if children attending our schools did not enter at such a disadvantage. Most people that are poor are poor because they are born into poverty. Most children born into poverty do not remain poor. But no serious reduction in poverty can occur when the ranks of the poor are continually replenished by young people who perhaps could have gone on to do well for themselves, but instead give birth and consign themselves and their offspring to years of struggle.

PUBLIC POLICY IMPERATIVES

Our public policy approach to teen pregnancy must be dual pronged. We must pursue strategies that reduce the incidence of teen pregnancy and childbirth, and we must take measures to ameliorate the negative outcomes of teen childbearing when it occurs.

Preventative Strategies

Provide More Comprehensive Sexuality Education

Most school districts provide sexuality education, but it is often too little, too late. The average amount of time devoted to sexuality education in schools that provide it is less than 42 hours. Only about five of those hours are given to discussion of birth control methods and six to sexually transmitted diseases. Only 48 percent of the girls and 26 percent of the boys who were sexually active by age 15 had received any prior sexuality education, while only 61 percent of the girls and 52 percent of the boys who were sexually active by age 18 had received any (Armstrong 1990b).

There is clearly room for improvement. One hopes that in this day of AIDS, more sexuality education will be offered to students and at a younger age. Youth must be reached before they initiate sexual activity. Although opponents of sexuality education fear that such exposure will encourage teenage sexual activity, their concerns appear unfounded. Numerous studies have revealed that adolescents provided sexuality education are no more likely to be sexually active than teens who have not received such education. The only difference is that teens who have received sexuality education are more likely to practice contraception and less likely to get pregnant (Zelnik & Kim).

Increase the Accessibility of Family Planning Services

Whether because of low income, lack of insurance, or unwillingness to seek family planning services under their families' insurance policies, adolescent women use publicly funded family planning clinics at much higher rates than any other group of women. In 1988, 36 percent of all women but 62 percent of teenaged women who had a family planning visit utilized public clinics (NCHS 1990f).

But, as discussed earlier, funding for family planning clinics has been declining in many localities. The rationale is often fiscal, as many governments have confronted growing deficits and declining revenues in the face of increased demand for government services of all kinds. However, as previously noted, such a shortsighted move is fiscally irresponsible. If, as Forrest and Singh estimate, the government saves $4.40 just on short-run medical costs for every $1.00 it spends on family planning in general, the savings must be even greater when a teen pregnancy is prevented. When an adolescent gives birth not only are the public costs of maternal and pediatric care greater, but the continuing public expenditures on behalf of the young mother and her family can be enormous.

Some family planning clinics are being closed under pressure from antiabortion activists. They claim that increased access to contraception encourages sexual activity, which results in more pregnancies and thence more abortions. They, paradoxically, argue that restricting access to contraception will result in fewer pregnancies (in Nazario). This has not proven true, and the women who are most hurt by this convoluted line of reasoning are adolescents and the poor. Both groups use publicly funded reproductive health facilities to a greater extent than other women and tend to have more unwanted pregnancies (NCHS 1990f; NCHS 1985).

Although family planning clinics are used by a disproportionate number of young women, many sexually active teenagers fail to seek them out or to seek out any birth control counseling. Thus the impetus has been building for school-based clinics. Although still few in number (only 162 were in operation as of 1990), support for school-based reproductive health care, including exams for sexually transmitted diseases, gynecological exams and pregnancy tests in addition to contraceptive services, is growing (Pascale 1990c). The state of New Jersey, for example, in which teen pregnancy is described as an "epidemic" (each year almost half the teenage girls in Camden get pregnant), has urged local school districts to open centers (IWS). School-based clinics have recently been opened in Los Angeles's Watts district, where, mimicking Camden's pregnancy rate, one-quarter of the teenaged girls in public school give birth each year (Read). But, while supporters are optimistic, school-based clinics are still too new to have posted any notable reductions in teen fertility.

Increase Access to Abortion Services

Even contracepting teens can get pregnant. Of the million or so teenage girls who get pregnant each year, many were perhaps contracepting faithfully. Since the Norplant implant, which prevents conception for over five years with 100 percent effectiveness, is not yet widely available, most women rely on conventional methods of birth control. Yet, with the exception of sterilization, which is inappropriate for all but the rare adolescent, even the best of these methods often fail. Nearly five of every 100 women using an IUD will get pregnant in any single year, as will more than two of every 100 women using the pill (PPFA). Approximately 43 percent of the women experiencing unintended pregnancies in 1987 were, in fact, practicing contraception (Gold). Since adolescent women are more likely to use less effective, nonmedical methods such as condoms or withdrawal, it is probable that contracepting teens comprise a disproportionate percentage of women who contracepted but nevertheless conceived. But regardless of the circumstances of conception, a woman experiencing an unwanted pregnancy should be allowed to terminate that pregnancy if she so chooses.

Abortions must be affordable. It is inequitable to price them out of reach of low-income women, especially since they have the highest rate of unintended pregnancies and child rearing is much more burdensome for them. Opponents of Medicaid funding protest the use of their tax dollars for abortions because they abhor the procedure on ethical grounds or they merely feel it does not warrant public expenditure. It is beyond the scope of this volume to argue the ethical issues of abortion per se, but it can be stated that whereas failure to provide public funding for abortions may result in fewer abortions, it may also result in more babies being born who are unwanted, unhealthy and forced to lead lives of severe deprivation. If the teen does raise the money to secure an abortion, it is likely to be a later-term abortion. This is both more expensive and more potentially dangerous to her; and, more to the point, it is more odious to the antiabortionist. Indeed, virtually everyone is less comfortable with the idea of later-term abortions, yet a major reason women give for having an abortion performed beyond the first trimester is the need to obtain funds to finance it (PPFA). Antiabortion activity also results in a late-term abortion when a young woman must repeatedly make appointments for the procedure but is unable to force her way past the Operation Rescue picketers outside the clinic (Marcus). She may get through eventually, but the toll on her is terrible.

Another reason frequently cited for later-term abortions is the teenager's reluctance to inform her parents of her pregnancy in those states that have parental notification laws (PPFA). As the teen delays, her pregnancy advances. Or, if a teen chooses to obtain a court-authorized bypass, the judicial process imposes a de facto waiting period that may itself result in a later-term abortion. Yet there is no indication that parental notification laws increase the probability that a teen will discuss her decision with her parents, which is the ostensible rationale behind the requirement (Blum et al.). While allegedly intended to promote family communication and protect the allegedly immature teenager from making a decision she may regret, Blum and colleagues found no increase in parental notification in states with such laws, nor did they find that girls considered such restrictions before conceiving (which of course does not require any proof of maturity beyond the obvious). Rather, teens who feel they cannot discuss the issue with their parents seek a judicial bypass, have the child (whether mature enough to rear it or not) or go to another state to obtain an abortion, which can also result in a delayed procedure. Or they undergo an illegal, less safe abortion. As more states require parental notification, the less able a pregnant teen is to exercise the option of traveling out of state and the more at risk she is.

To return to the issue of publicly funded abortions for low-income women, to deny Medicaid funding of abortions simply as a cost containment measure is fiscally shortsighted. It has been estimated that if only 20 percent of the pregnant women eligible for Medicaid who wanted an abortion were unable to obtain one and so carried to term, the public cost for maternal and pediatric care and income supports for her child's first two years of life alone would be $4 for every $1 an abortion would have cost. If all such women carried to term, the resulting health care costs would be 7 to 9 times higher and the welfare costs for their babies' first two years would be 15 to 20 times higher (Torres et al.).

If abortions were recriminalized, it has been estimated that at a minimum an additional 75,000 births to teen mothers would result (Wattleton). Births to teens in New York City could be expected to increase by 19 percent to black teens and by 14 percent to white teens (Joyce & Mocan). The public costs would clearly be huge, as would the personal costs.

Those who oppose abortion on the grounds that it too imposes personal costs, primarily emotional costs, can be assured that the psychological costs of abortion for most women are less than those of unwanted childbearing. While some women may deeply regret the decision to abort, the overwhelming feeling is generally relief (in NRC 1987). A study of conceiving low-income black teens in Maryland found that those who had terminated their pregnancies experienced no greater emotional or psychological distress and, in fact, went on to do better in school and were better off economically than their peers who had carried their pregnancies to term. The teens who aborted were also more likely to consistently use birth control following their pregnancy and to have fewer subsequent pregnancies (Zabin et al.).

Of course, not all pregnant teens would choose to abort, affordable abortions or not. And no woman of any age or economic status should be coerced into undergoing a procedure that is repugnant to her or carries such potential for emotional distress. Adoption too can be emotionally devastating to a woman, often to a far greater degree and over a much longer period of time, and is therefore a form of pregnancy resolution that is seldom chosen today. The proportion of unwed teen mothers who placed their babies for adoption had been very high in earlier decades but had fallen to 7.6 percent in 1971 and to 2.6 percent by 1976 (in Leibowitz et al.). This downward trend has been made possible by changing social mores and expanded welfare benefits. These developments have also made possible the increased incidence of teen births.

Provide Incentives to Deter Childbearing

It cannot be mere coincidence that the explosion in births to teen mothers, particularly to unwed teen mothers, paralleled the enormous growth of the welfare system that began under the Great Society antipoverty campaign of the mid-1960s. Though the concurrent changes in social mores allowed more sexual freedom and tolerated more nontraditional lifestyles and the educational and occupational progress of women in general promoted women's economic self-sufficiency, these alone cannot explain the increase in teen births.

Although some analysts claim that the trend toward female-headed households developed independently and that the welfare system either developed in response or coincidentally, most observers agree that the welfare-childbirth relationship is more direct. The degree of causality, however, is not widely agreed upon, and the question of whether the welfare system encourages births to young unmarried women or simply enables them has been contentiously debated in academic and public policy-making circles for decades. Yet research on whether potential welfare recipiency encourages noncontracepted teen sexual activity or pregnancy is lacking. Instead, studies have been conducted on the pregnancy resolution decisions of young pregnant women. When the choices offered are to carry to term or obtain an abortion, welfare eligibility does not appear to strongly influence a pregnant teenager to give birth. However, when the choices include unmarried childbirth, marriage or abortion, Leibowitz and associates found that pregnant adolescents who are on AFDC or Medicaid are far more likely than other pregnant teens to give birth and to remain unmarried. Indeed eligibility for public assistance is the only variable that significantly discriminates between the adolescents who choose to marry and those who remain single (Leibowitz et al.).

Whether welfare encourages unwed teen births or enables them, it is clear that the system of incentives is skewed in the wrong direction. Rather, we should reward teens who choose to delay or curtail their childbearing. While deferring parenthood and limiting the size of one's family does itself provide economic reward, the payoff may be too distant for a young person with a short time horizon and too low for someone who perceives her income earning ability to be small. This last point is especially relevant since, within every racial or ethnic group, the girls who bear children too early tend to be among the lowest achievers. While the goals of providing every young person with the tools she or he needs for economic success and providing opportunities for all in a fully employed economy are noble and necessary to pursue, such an idealized state is not likely to be reached soon. Though perhaps only a minor cause, too-early family formation with its productivity-limiting features inhibits our progress in achieving that state.

We must invest more in public education and job training and make higher education more affordable by increasing grants, loans and work-study earnings, but at the same time we must pay young women to avoid pregnancy.

Planned Parenthood of Denver runs a program in which it pays girls who already have had one child a modest amount for attending counseling sessions and not being pregnant. The program has apparently had more success in reducing subsequent pregnancies than other pregnancy prevention programs (Zaslowsky). But the damage, or a good deal of it, had already been done. It is imperative that we reach at-risk teens *before* they first give birth. The Norplant implant would be an excellent tool since it is safe, effective and reversible (fertility is restored within 24 hours of removal). Nearly all states now provide Medicaid funding for the implant, but what is needed is a payment to the adolescent for accepting one and a yearly bonus for retaining it up to age 20. Compensation should not be limited to Medicaid-eligible teens but should be available to all teens. The payment could be increased if the difference were applied to meeting the expenses of higher education. The program could be funded through (eventual) reductions in welfare expenditures.

The welfare system itself needs further reform. The benefit schedule should discourage unmarried pregnant or parenting teens from leaving their family of origin unless abuse is present, so that young girls do not view welfare recipiency as a means to leave home. Motherhood should not be embraced as a job that provides financial independence. Also, welfare benefits should not be increased with subsequent births. Welfare recipients should be no less fiscally responsible than working parents, none of whom get an increase in pay on the birth of a child. At the same time, we should loosen the restrictions on fathers in the home, as many states have done, and provide benefits to them if they are in school coupled with job search assistance if they are unemployed.

A more intractable problem today (and one that argues the enabling properties of welfare) is the increasing prevalence among young teens of the desire to give birth. Inner-city school nurses and family planning practitioners tell tales of 13-year-olds happy to be pregnant and 14-year-olds disappointed at not being pregnant as childbearing has essentially become a rite of passage among low-income minority youth. Teens too young to rationally consider their options are actively seeking pregnancy. The girls may want to connect with a male. Or they may want to have a baby because their girlfriends are doing it or because they think it would be fun, much like having a doll to dress up and play with. Girls from large families are especially vulnerable because they may want a baby as something to call their own or as means of getting attention (Marcus). The boys, on the other hand, often regard fatherhood as a means of proving their manhood and may pressure their girlfriends into accepting pregnancy. Parenting is thus a form of social status seeking among children who envision few other means of achieving "success." Long-term solutions to this problem, of which premature parenting is just a symptom, will be more difficult to find. But the girls, at least, might respond to the band-aid solution of a financial incentive.

In the meantime, however, teenage girls continue to get pregnant. Many would doubtless give birth even if these reforms were implemented. Therefore, we must also pursue strategies that will promote the well-being of young mothers and their families.

Ameliorative Strategies

These are designed to lessen the negative outcomes of teen births. They should reduce the cost to mother and child and, ultimately, to society as well.

Provide the Basics

Although they have been discussed earlier in this volume, the basics nevertheless bear repeating. They begin with exhortations of the "be good to your baby before it is born" type and continue with enhanced access to prenatal care (possibly in school-based clinics), affordable pediatric care and adequate nutrition, which are in fact becoming more available to pregnant and parenting teens. Just as vital to disadvantaged teens and their children are home visiting, parenting education that includes life-management training, and infant stimulation programs. Infant programs should be followed by development-oriented early childhood education and after school programs for older children. But while these basic measures are necessary, they are not sufficient. More is required if the young family is to succeed.

Enable the Teen Mother to Continue her Education

Public schools are now required by federal law to allow pregnant teens to remain in school. Some schools go further and offer programs especially for pregnant and parenting teens. All school districts should be urged to make parenting classes mandatory for all students and to provide on-site developmental day care for students' children. Although this may reduce the cost of childbearing to the adolescent and thus possibly encourage it, the benefits in terms of the mother's increased earning ability and the child's enhanced development exceed the costs. Subsidized child care should also be available to mothers enrolled in institutions of higher learning.

Assist the Adolescent Parent to Secure Employment

Job training and job search assistance should be available to all persons, but given the great need relative to resources, that may not be possible. However, it should definitely be available to young mothers and fathers.

Quality affordable child care must also be available. Surveys of young mothers have found the high cost of child care to be their greatest obstacle to self-sufficiency (USGAO 1986). The child-care income tax credit does no good for families whose income is so low they have little or no tax liability. Rather, child-care expenditures should be treated as a negative income tax similar to the earned income tax credit that accrues to low-income parents. That income tax credit should be enlarged, as should the deduction for dependents. We need to make it financially feasible for young parents to work and at the same time make it easier for all working people to have the children they want.

We must also support parental leave legislation and encourage flextime, job sharing and on-site day care at places of employment. Universal health care will make part-time work a more attractive alternative for mothers who may now work full-time primarily for the insurance. While we want to encourage self-sufficiency among young parents, we do not want to do so at the expense of the parenting to which all children are entitled.

Promote Father Involvement

We must promote greater father involvement, beginning with family life education in the schools *before* young boys become fathers. While advocating a child's right to a two-parent family, we must also inform teens of fathers' legal and financial responsibilities even when absent. Young mothers, with the help of the state, must increase the pressure on fathers to meet their obligations. Aggressive pursuit of child support payments on the part of state welfare offices has resulted in higher compliance, sometimes through wage attachments, but does not help the young mother who has not established paternity. Adolescent mothers must be encouraged to pursue adjudication even if the father is not working or is currently earning very little. His ability to provide is likely to increase. Insisting on greater paternal responsibility may motivate some young men to make more of their lives, especially if coupled with vocational training or job placement. It may also deter boys from practicing uncontracepted intercourse and becoming fathers too early.

The increasing number of teen births, especially the increase in births to very young teens and to unmarried teens, sounds an alarm that must be heeded. Failure to reverse these trends places an ever larger proportion of our children at great risk. The increasing prevalence of births to unmarried minority teens in particular has reached near crisis proportions. Almost an entire generation of minority children are at risk. When our children are at risk, our society is at risk. Failure to effectively intervene is to risk our future.

Conclusion

No one had to read this book to learn that private choices can sometimes generate great social costs. The fact that private behavior often evokes public distress is well known. This volume was intended only to more fully inform readers of the extent of those costs and to better persuade policymakers of the need to treat unhealthful behavior. Although many concerned citizens are working hard to reduce the incidence of imprudent personal choices and many policies have been formulated to reduce such choices, greater and more effective effort is urgently needed.

Economic analytical concepts contribute to our understanding of why people make ill-advised choices, the primary reason being that many people are short-term utility maximizers, sometimes risk takers, who are possessed of grievously imperfect information on the short- and long-run consequences of their behavior. Thus people may feel they are making a rational choice when in fact they are not. The risk of making an ill-considered choice is elevated by youth and by judgment that is impaired by drugs or alcohol. The consequences of making an imprudent choice are heightened when an addictive substance is involved, when the externalities are great and when the costs are intergenerational, as they frequently are. The point is made in every chapter that our poor choices often victimize or endanger our children. The costs are thence even more inequitably distributed and are resoundingly greater. To risk our children is no less than to risk our future.

Economic tools are also useful in devising effectual policies. Here the basic tools of economic incentive and disincentive, the tax and the subsidy, are joined to the concept of elasticity, which advises of the effectiveness of price incentives. The wedding of economic theory to that of education, sociology, psychology, biology and medicine strengthens our behavior modification efforts. The three legs that best support those efforts are education, research and pragmatism.

When all is considered, we find that while some of the policies we have adopted are effective, many are ineffective. Some are even counterproductive in that they may encourage the kind of behavior we want to discourage, prevent people from reducing their risk exposure, or exacerbate the social costs arising from poor behavioral choices. The intention of this volume is to help identify those strategies that will work and urge their implementation if they have not been adopted or their strengthening if they have. It is hoped that the information contained herein will provide further ammunition for those already engaged in the struggle to lessen the incidence of foolish choices and propel to action those who had not yet seen the need.

Bibliography

Abel, E. L. *Fetal Alcohol Syndrome and Fetal Alcohol Effect*. New York: Plenum Press, 1984.

Abel, E. L., and R. J. Sokol. "Incidence of Fetal Alcohol Syndrome and Economic Impact of FAS-Related Anomalies." *Drug and Alcohol Dependence* (1987): 51–70.

Abramowitz, M. "Help Urged for Pregnant Drug Users." *Washington Post*, 25 June 1989.

A. Foster Higgins & Co., Inc. *Foster Higgins Health Care Benefit Survey. Report One, Indemnity Plans: Cost, Design, and Funding*. Princeton: 1991.

Alan Guttmacher Institute. *The Cost-Benefit of Publicly Funded Family Services*. Washington: Alan Guttmacher Institute, 1990.

"Alcohol and the Fetus—Is Zero the Only Option?" *The Lancet*, 26 March 1983.

Allen, J. R., and J. W. Curran. "Prevention of AIDS and HIV Infection: Needs and Priorities for Epidemiologic Research." *American Journal of Public Health* 78, no. 4 (1988): 381–386.

Alsop, R. (of The American Association for Protecting Children, Englewood, Colo.) Oral communication, Sept. 1990.

American Association for Protecting Children, Inc. *Highlights of Official Child Neglect and Abuse Reporting: 1987*. Denver: The American Humane Association, 1990.

——. *Highlights of Official Child Neglect and Abuse Reporting: 1984*. Denver: The American Humane Association, 1986.

American Civil Liberties Union. "Pregnant Addicts and Alcoholics: Legislative Proposals and Policy Considerations for State Legislators." New York: The Women's Rights Project, Jan. 1990. Photocopy.

——. *State Legislation Pertaining to Drug Use During Pregnancy*. New York: The Women's Rights Project, Nov. 1989. Photocopy.

American Management Association. *AIDS: The Workplace Issues*. New York: AMA Membership Publications Division, 1985.

American Medical Association. "Board of Trustees Report: Drug Abuse in the United States, Strategies for Prevention." *Journal of the American Medical Association* 265, no. 16 (1991): 2102–2107.

American Psychiatric Association (APA). "Research on Mental Illness and Addictive Disorders: Progress and Prospects." *American Journal of Psychiatry* 142, Supplement A (1985): 1–41.

Anda, R. F., D. F. Williamson and P. L. Remington. "Alcohol and Fatal Injuries among U.S. Adults." *Journal of the American Medical Association* 260, no. 17 (1988): 2529-2532.

Armstrong, E. "Adolescent Males and Teen Pregnancy." In *The Facts*. Washington: Center for Population Options, May 1990a.

———. "Sexuality Education." In *The Facts*. Washington: Center for Population Options, June 1990b.

Armstrong, E., and A. Pascale. "Adolescent Sexuality, Pregnancy and Parenthood." In *The Facts*. Washington: Center for Population Options, May 1990.

Armstrong, E., and C. Waszak. *Teenage Pregnancy and Too-Early Childbearing: Public Costs, Personal Consequences*. Washington: Center for Population Options, 1990.

Arno, P. S., D. Shenson, N. F. Siegel and P. R. Lee. "Economic and Policy Implications of Early Intervention in HIV Disease." *Journal of the American Medical Association* 262, no. 11 (1989): 1493-1497.

Ball, J. C., W. R. Lange, C. P. Myers and S. R. Friedman. "Reducing the Risk of AIDS through Methadone Maintenance Treatment." *Journal of Health and Social Behavior* 29. (1988): 214-226.

Banta, W. F. *AIDS in the Workplace*. Lexington, Mass.: Lexington Books, 1988.

Barnicle, M. "Mediocrity Is the Standard." *Boston Globe*, 30 Jan. 1990.

Barthold, T. A and H. M. Hochman. "Addiction as Extreme-Seeking." *Economic Inquiry* 26 (1988): 89-106.

Becerra, J. E., C. J. R. Hogue, H. K. Atrash and N. Perez. "Infant Mortality Among Hispanics." *Journal of the American Medical Association* 265, no. 2 (1991): 217-221.

Becker, G. S., M. Grossman and K. M. Murphy. *An Empirical Analysis of Cigarette Addiction*. Cambridge, Mass.: National Bureau of Economic Research, Inc., 1990.

Becker, M. H., and J. G. Joseph. "AIDS and Behavioral Change to Reduce Risk: A Review." *American Journal of Public Health* 78, no. 4 (1988): 394-410.

Becker, M. H., and K. M. Murphy. "A Theory of Rational Addiction." *Journal of Political Economy* 96, no. 4 (1988): 675-700.

Bernier, J. *Preventing Child Abuse: A Resource for Policymakers and Advocates*. Boston: Massachusetts Committee for Children and Youth, 1990.

Besharov, D. J. "The Children of Crack: Will We Protect Them?" *Public Welfare* (Fall 1989): 6-11.

Best, J. A., S. J. Thomson, S. M. Santi, E. A. Smith and S. Brown. "Preventing Cigarette Smoking among School Children." *Annual Review of Public Health* 9. (1988): 161-201.

Blaine, T. W., and M. R. Reed. "U.S. Cigarette Demand and the Health Scare: Outlook to 1990." *Current Issues in Tobacco Economics*. Economic Papers Given at the Tobacco Workers' Conference, January 1987. (1987): 113-120.

Blair, W. G. "New York Sees a Surge in Syphilis and Will Start Testing All Babies." *New York Times*, 5 Dec. 1989.

Blendon, R. J., L. H. Aiken, H. E. Freeman and C. R. Corey. "Access to Medical Care for Black and White Americans." *Journal of the American Medical Association* 261, no. 2 (1989): 278-281.

Blum, R. W., M. D. Resnick and T. A. Stark. "The Impact of a Parental Notification Law on Adolescent Abortion Decision Making." *American Journal of Public Health* 77, no. 5 (1987): 619-620

Boodman, S. G. "Gonorrhea, Syphilis Rise Sharply Here." *Washington Post*, 6 April, 1989a.

————. "Up Against It." *Washington Post*, 5 Sept. 1989b.

Boston Department of Health and Hospitals (BDHH). *Advance Natality and Infant Mortality Data for Boston and Its Neighborhoods, 1988*. Boston: 1990.

Bowsher, C. A. "Canadian Health Insurance: Lessons for the United States." Testimony before the Committee on Government Operations, House of Representatives. GAO/T-HRD-91-35. Washington: 1991. Photocopy.

Boyer, D., and D. Fine. "Sexual Abuse as a Factor In Adolescent Pregnancy and Child Maltreatment." *Family Planning Perspectives* 24, no. 1 (1992): 4-19.

Brent, D. A., J. A. Perper and C. J. Allman. "Alcohol, Firearms, and Suicide among Youth." *Journal of the American Medical Association* 257, no. 24 (1987): 3369-3372.

Brown, L. S., and B. J. Primm. "Sexual Contacts of Intravenous Drug Users: Implications for the Next Spread of the AIDS Epidemic." *Journal of the National Medical Association* 80 (1988): 651-656.

Brown, W. J., J. F. Donohue, N. W. Axnick, J. H. Blount, N. H. Ewen and O. G. Jones. *Syphilis and Other Venereal Diseases*. Cambridge: Harvard University Press, 1970.

Bullock, K. D., R. J. Reed and I. Grant. "Reduced Mortality Risk in Alcoholics Who Achieve Long-term Abstinence." *Journal of the American Medical Association* 267, no. 5 (1992): 668-672.

Burns, T. J. "Facing Up to the Anti-Smoking Activists." *Current Issues in Tobacco Economics* (Jan. 1987): 71-89.

Canadian Cancer Society (CCS). *Sustaining a Successful Policy: The Treatment of Tobacco Taxation in the 1991 Federal Budget*. 1991.

Carrol, W. "AIDS-Related Claims Survey: Claims Paid in 1989." Washington: American Council of Life Insurance Association of America, Sept. 1989.

Catholic Health Association of the United States (CHAUS). "Systemic Healthcare Reform: Is It Time?" *Health Progress*, Jan./Feb. 1990.

Centers for Disease Control (CDC). *HIV/AIDS Surveillance Report*. Jan. 1992a.

————. "Infant Mortality—United States, 1989." *Morbidity and Mortality Weekly Report* 41, no. 5 (1992b): 81-85.

————. "Mortality Patterns—United States, 1989." *Morbidity and Mortality Weekly Report* 41, no. 7 (1992c): 121-125.

————. "The Second 100,000 Cases of Acquired Immunodeficiency Syndrome—United States, June 1981-December 1991." *Morbidity and Mortality Weekly Report* 41, no. 2 (1992d): 28-29.

————. "Sexual Behavior Among High School Students—United States, 1990." *Morbidity and Mortality Weekly Report* 40, nos. 51 & 52 (1992e): 885-888.

————. "Alternative Case-Finding Methods in a Crack-Related Syphilis Epidemic—Philadelphia." *Morbidity and Mortality Weekly Report* 40, no. 5 (1991a): 77-89.

————. "The HIV/AIDS Epidemic: The First 10 Years." *Morbidity and Mortality Weekly Report* 40, no. 22 (1991b): 357.

————. *HIV/AIDS Surveillance Report*. Sept. 1991c.

————. "Mortality Attributable to HIV Infection/AIDS—United States, 1981-1990." *Morbidity and Mortality Weekly Report* 40, no. 3 (1991d): 41-44.

————. "Premarital Sexual Experience among Adolescent Women—United States, 1970-1988." *Morbidity and Mortality Weekly Report* 39, no. 51 (1991e): 929-931.

————. "Smoking-Attributable Mortality and Years of Potential Life Lost—United States, 1988." *Morbidity and Mortality Weekly Report* 40, no. 4 (1991f): 62-71.

——— . "Trends in Fertility and Infant and Maternal Health—United States, 1980–1988." *Morbidity and Weekly Report* 40, no. 23 (1991g): 381–389.

——— . "AIDS in Women—United States." *Morbidity and Mortality Weekly Report* 39, no. 47 (1990a): 845–846.

——— . "Alcohol-Related Disease Impact—Wisconsin, 1988." *Morbidity and Mortality Weekly Report* 39, no. 11 (1990b): 178–187.

——— . "Alcohol-Related Mortality and Years of Potential Life Lost-United States, 1987." *Morbidity and Mortality Weekly Report* 39, no. 11 (1990c): 173–178.

——— . "Cigarette Advertising—United States, 1988." *Morbidity and Mortality Weekly Report* 39, no. 16 (1990d): 261–265.

——— . "Heterosexual Behaviors and Factors that Influence Condom Use among Patients Attending a Sexually Transmitted Disease Clinic—San Francisco." *Morbidity and Mortality Weekly Report* 39, no. 39 (1990e): 685–689.

——— . "HIV Prevalence Estimates and AIDS Case Projections for the United States: Report Based upon a Workshop." *Morbidity and Mortality Weekly Report* 39, no. RR-161 (1990f): 1–17.

——— . "HIV-Related Knowledge and Behaviors among High School Students—Selected U.S. Sites, 1989." *Morbidity and Mortality Weekly Report* 39, no. 23 (1990g): 383–389.

——— . Oral communication (Blunt with author), Sept. 1990h.

——— . Package of statistical tables. 1990i.

——— . "Publicly Funded HIV Counseling and Testing—United States, 1985–1989." *Morbidity and Mortality Weekly Report* 39, no. 9 (1990j): 137–140.

——— . "Risk Behaviors for HIV Transmission among IVDUs Not in Drug Treatment—United States, 1987–1989." *Morbidity and Mortality Weekly Report* 39, no. 16 (1990k): 273–276.

——— . "The Surgeon General's Report on The Health Benefits of Smoking Cessation: Executive Summary." *Morbidity and Mortality Weekly Report* 39, no. RR-12 (1990l): 1–12.

——— . "Surveillance for AIDS and HIV Infection among Black and Hispanic Children and Women of Childbearing Age, 1981–1989." *Morbidity and Mortality Weekly Report* 39, no. SS-3 (1990m): 23–30.

——— . "Counseling and Testing Intravenous Drug Users for HIV Infection—Boston." *Morbidity and Mortality Weekly Report* 38, no. 28 (1989a): 489–496.

——— . "Update: Acquired Immune Deficiency Syndrome Associated with Intravenous Drug Use—United States, 1988." *Morbidity and Mortality Weekly Report* 38, no. 10 (1989b): 165–170.

——— . "Guidelines for the Prevention and Control of Congenital Syphilis." *Morbidity and Mortality Weekly Report* 37, no. S-1 (1988a): 1–13.

——— . "Number of Sex Partners and Potential Risk of Sexual Exposure to Human Immunodeficiency Virus." *Morbidity and Mortality Weekly Report* 37, no. 37 (1988b): 565–568.

——— . "Syphilis and Congenital Syphilis—United States, 1985–1988." *Morbidity and Mortality Weekly Report* 37, no. 32 (1988c): 1–4.

——— . "Psychosocial Predictors of Smoking among Adolescents." *Morbidity and Mortality Weekly Report* 36, no. 4S (1987): 1–47.

Chaisson, R. E., P. Bacchetti, D. Osmond, B. Brodie, M. A. Sande and A. R. Moss. "Cocaine Use and HIV Infection in Intravenous Drug Users in San Francisco." *Journal of the American Medical Association* 261, no. 4 (1989): 561–565.

Chasnoff, I. J. "Drug Use in Pregnancy: Parameters of Risk." *The Pediatric Clinics of North America* 35, no. 6 (1988): 1403-1411.

——— . "Perinatal Effects of Cocaine." *Contemporary OB/GYN* (May 1987): 163-179.

Chasnoff, I. J., K. A. Burns, W. J. Burns and S. H. Schnoll. "Prenatal Drug Exposure: Effects on Neonatal and Infant Growth and Development." *Neurobehavioral Toxicology and Teratology* 8 (1986): 357-363.

Chasnoff, I. J., D. R. Griffith, S. MacGregor, K. Dirkes and K. A. Burns. "Temporal Patterns of Cocaine Use in Pregnancy: Perinatal Outcome." *Journal of the American Medical Association* 261, no. 12 (1989): 1741-1744.

Chavez, G. F., J. F. Cordero and J. E. Beccerra. "Leading Major Congenital Malformations among Minority Groups in the United States, 1981-1986." *Journal of the American Medical Association* 261, no. 2 (1989): 205-209.

Chow, R. "Program Will Pay Teens Not to Become Pregnant Again." *Los Angeles Times*, 24 Mar. 1989.

Coate, D. and M. Grossman. "Effects of Alcoholic Beverage Prices and Legal Drinking Ages on Youth Alcohol Use." *Journal of Law and Economics* 31. (1988): 145-171.

Codega, J. "CPS Treatment of the Neglectful Parent." *Protecting Children* 6, no. 3 (1989): 8-12.

Coletti, R. J. "Drugs: The Case for Legalization." *Financial World* (Oct. 1989): 32-35.

Collins, J. J., R. L. Hubbard and J. V. Rachal. "Expensive Drug Use and Illegal Income: A Test of Explanatory Hypotheses." *Criminology* 23, no. 4 (1985): 743-764.

Collins, J. W, and J. R. David. "The Differential Effect of Traditional Risk Factors on Infant Birthweight among Blacks and Whites in Chicago." *American Journal of Public Health* 80, no. 6 (June 1990): 679-681.

Congressional Budget Office. *Federal Taxation of Tobacco, Alcoholic Beverages, and Motor Fuels.* Congress of the United States. Washington: Government Printing Office (GPO) 1990.

Cook, J. "The Paradox of Antidrug Enforcement." *Forbes*, 13 Nov. 1989, 105-120.

Cook, P. J. "The Effect of Liquor Taxes on Drinking, Cirrhosis and Auto Fatalities." Working paper. Institute of Policy Sciences and Public Affairs, Duke University, 1980.

Cook, P. J., and G. Tauchen. "The Effect of Liquor Taxes on Heavy Drinking." *Bell Journal of Economics* 13, no. 2 (1982): 379-390.

Cook, P. S., R. C. Peterson and D. T. Moore. *Alcohol, Tobacco, and Other Drugs May Harm the Unborn.* Office for Substance Abuse Prevention. DHHS pub. no. (ADM) 90-1711. Rockville, Md.: 1990.

Crowley, K., and L. Standora. "O'Connor—Apple Is 'Condom City.' " *New York Post*, 3 Oct. 1990.

Danziger, S. K. "Father Involvement in Welfare Families Headed by Adolescent Mothers." Discussion Paper #856-87. Institute for Research on Poverty, University of Wisconsin—Madison, 1987.

Danziger, S. K. and A. Nichols-Casebolt. "Teen Parents and Child Support: Eligibility, Participation, and Payment." Journal of Social Service Research 11, nos. 2, 3 (1988): 1-20.

Daro, D. *Confronting Child Abuse: Research for Effective Program Design.* New York: Plenum Press, 1988.

Daro, D., and L. Mitchell. *Deaths Due to Maltreatment Soar: The Results of the Eighth Semi-Annual Fifty-State Survey.* Chicago: National Committee for the Prevention of Child Abuse, 1987.

Davis, R. M. "Women and Smoking in the United States: How Lung Cancer Became an 'Equal Opportunity' Disease." In *The Global War*. Proceedings of the Seventh World Conference on Tobacco and Health, 101–108. 1990.

Delman, F. "On Liberty, Tolerance, and Tobacco." *Current Issues in Tobacco Economics*. Economic Papers Given at the Tobacco Workers' Conference, January 1987. Ed. M. Farrell and F. Delman, 39–51.

Des Jarlais, D. C., S. R. Friedman, D. M. Novick, J. L. Sotheran, P. Thomas, S. R. Yancovitz, D. Mildvan, J. Weber, M. J. Kreek, R. Maslansky, S. Bartelme, T. Spira and M. Marmor. "HIV-1 Infection among Intravenous Drug Users in Manhattan, New York City, from 1977 through 1981." *Journal of the American Medical Association* 261, no. 7 (1989): 1006–1012.

DiFranza, J. R., and J. B. Tye. "Who Profits from Tobacco Sales to Children?" *Journal of the American Medical Association* 263, no. 20 (1990): 2784–2787.

Doweiko, H. E. *Concepts of Chemical Dependency*. Pacific Grove, Calif.: Brooks/Cole, 1990.

Drug Enforcement Administration (DEA). *Briefing Book*. United States Department of Justice. Washington: 1990a.

——— . *Drug Abuse Warning Network*. United States Department of Justice. Washington: 1990b.

——— . *Drugs of Abuse*. Washington: Government Printing Office, 1989.

Dufour, M. C., and H. Moskowitz. "The Epidemiology of Injury." *Alcohol Health and Research World* (Summer 1985): 6–10.

Enda, J. "Child Abuse Cases Up 30 Percent in City." *Philadelphia Inquirer*, 14 April 1989.

Epstein, A. M., R. S. Stern and J. S. Weissman. "Do the Poor Cost More?" *The New England Journal of Medicine* 322, no. 16 (1990): 1122–1128.

Erlich, M. "The Search for a National Health Program." *Boston Globe*, 10 June 1991.

Ernster, V. L., W. Winklestein, S. Selvin, S. M. Brown, S. T. Sacks, D. F. Austin, S. A. Mandel and T. A. Bertolli. "Race, Socioeconomic Status, and Prostate Cancer." *Cancer Treatment Reports* 61, no. 2 (1977): 187–191.

Ezzard, N. V., W. Cates, Jr., D. G. Kramer and C. Tietze. "Race-Specific Patterns of Abortion Use by American Teenagers." *American Journal of Public Health* 72, no. 8 (1982): 809–813.

Faden, R. R., A. J. Chwalow, K. Quaid, G. A. Chase, C. Lopes, C. O. Leonard and N. A. Holtzman. "Prenatal Screening and Pregnant Women's Attitudes toward the Abortion of Defective Fetuses." *American Journal of Public Health* 77, no. 3 (1987): 288–290.

Fee, F., and D. Fox., eds. *AIDS: The Burdens of History*. Berkeley: University of California Press, 1988.

Felix, A. (of Massachusetts Department of Social Services). Oral communication, Sept. 1990.

Feron, J. "Five Metro-North Workers in Crash Showed Drug Traces, U.S. Says." *New York Times*, 11 May 1988.

Fiore, M. C., T. E. Novotny, J. P. Pierce, E. J. Hatziandreu, K. M. Patel and R. M. Davis. "Trends in Cigarette Smoking in the United States: The Changing Influence of Gender and Race." *Journal of the Americal Medical Association* 261, no. 1 (1990): 49–55.

Fitzgerald, S. "Many Go without Prenatal Care, City Finds." *Philadelphia Inquirer*, 16 May 1989a.

———. "One in Six New Mothers Used Cocaine, Study Finds." *Philadelphia Inquirer*, 8 April 1989b.

Foreman, J. "Care Costs May Nearly Double by 1994." *Boston Globe*, 20 June 1991.

Forrest, J. D., and S. Singh. "Public Sector Savings Resulting from Expenditures for Contraceptives Services." *Family Planning Perspectives* 22, no. 1 (1990): 6–15.

Fox, S. H., C. Brown, A. M. Koontz and S. S. Kessel. "Perception of Risk of Smoking and Heavy Drinking during Pregnancy: 1985 NHIS Findings." *Public Health Reports* 102, no. 1 (1987): 73–79.

Freedman, A. M. "Deadly Diet." *Wall Street Journal*, 18 Dec. 1989.

French, H. "Rise in Babies Hurt by Drugs is Predicted: 5 Percent in New York City Could Need Care by 1995." *New York Times*, 18 Oct. 1989.

Friedman, L. S., E. Lichtenstein and A. Biglan. "Smoking Onset among Teens: An Empirical Analysis of Initial Situations." *Addictive Behaviors* 10 (1985): 1–13.

Fullilove, R. E., M. T. Fullilove, B. P. Bowser and S. A. Gross. "Risk of Sexually Transmitted Disease among Black Adolescent Crack Users in Oakland and San Francisco, California." *Journal of the American Medical Association* 263, no. 6 (1990): 851–855.

Furstenberg, Jr., F. F., J. Brooks-Gunn and S. P. Morgan. "Adolescent Mothers and Their Children in Later Life." *Family Planning Perspectives* 19, no. 4. (1987): 142–151.

Garbarino, J., C. Schellenback and J. M. Sebes. *Troubled Youth, Troubled Families*. New York: Aldine, 1986.

Garcia, C. A. "Drug-Exposed Infants and Their Families: Issues and Policy Options." Policy Analysis Exercise. John F. Kennedy School of Government, Harvard University, 1990.

Garrison, J. "The AIDS Research Backlash." *San Francisco Chronicle*, 17 Dec. 1989.

Gayle, H. D., R. P. Keeling, M. Garcia-Tunon, B. W. Kilbourne, J. P. Narkunas, F. R. Ingram, M. F. Rogers and J. W. Curran. "Prevalence of the Human Immunodeficiency Virus among University Students." *New England Journal of Medicine* 323, no. 22 (1990): 1538–1541.

Gelles, R. "The Family and Its Role in the Abuse of Children." *Psychiatric Annals* 17, no. 4. (1987): 229–232.

Gibbs, N. "Shameful Bequests to the Next Generation." *Time*, 8 Oct. 1990.

Gilliam, D. "The Children of Crack." *Washington Post*, 31 July 1989.

Gladwell, H. "Failures Seen in Education on 'Safe Sex.' " *Washington Post*, 24 June 1990.

Glazer, S. "Who Smokes, Who Starts, and Why." Editorial Research Reports. *Congressional Quarterly* (Mar. 1989): 149–163.

Glebatis, D. M., L. F. Novick and A. Stacey. "Hospitalization of HIV-Seropositive Newborns with AIDS-Related Disease within the First Year of Life." *American Journal of Public Health* 81S (May 1991): 46–49.

Global AIDS Policy Coalition. *AIDS in the World 1992*. ed. by J. M. Mann, D. J. M. Tarantola and T. W. Netter. Cambridge: Harvard University Press, in press.

Golan, K. (of Centers for Disease Control Press Office.) Oral communication, Aug. 1991.

Gold, R. B. *Abortion and Women's Health: A Turning Point for America?* Washington: Alan Guttmacher Institute, 1990.

Goldstein, P. J. "Drugs and Violent Crime." In N. A. Weiner and M. E. Wolfgang, eds., *Pathways to Criminal Violence*. Newbury Park, Calif.: Sage,1989.

Goldstein, P. J., P. A. Bellucci, B. J. Spunt and T. Miller. "Volume of Cocaine Use and Violence: A Comparison between Men and Women." *Journal of Drug Issues* 21, no. 2 (1991): 345–367.

Gordis, E. "Alcohol: A Special Risk for Youth." *The Challenge* 4, no. 2 (1989): 1–10.

Gordon, B. "Crack's Incredible Cost to San Francisco." *San Francisco Chronicle*, 21 Feb. 1989.

Greene, M. S. "Abuse, Neglect Rising in D.C." *Washington Post*, 10 Sept. 1989a.

——— . " 'Boarder Babies' Linger in Hospitals." *Washington Post*, 11 Sept. 1989b.

——— . "Sitting on a Time Bomb Waiting for Kids to Die." *Washington Post*, 12 Sept. 1989c.

Grise, V. N. "Economic Importance of the U. S. Tobacco Industry." *Tobacco: Situation and Outlook Report*, United States Department of Agriculture (April 1991): 30–34.

——— . "Trends in Tobacco Consumption in the U.S. and Future Prospects." *Current Issues in Tobacco Economics*. Economic Papers Given at the Tobacco Workers Conference, January 1987 (1987): 121–138.

Grise, V. N., and K. F. Griffin. *The U.S. Tobacco Industry*. United States Department of Agriculture. Agricultural Economic Report no. 589. Washington: 1988.

Gwinn, M., M. Pappaioanou, J. R. George, W. H. Hannon, S. C. Wasser, M. A. Redus, R. Hoff, G. F. Grady, A. Willoughby, A. C. Novello, L. R. Peterson, T. J. Dondero and J. W. Curran. "Prevalence of HIV Infection in Childbearing Women in the United States." *Journal of the American Medical Association* 265 no. 13 (1991): 1704–1708.

Haberman, P. W. "Alcohol and Alcoholism in Traffic and Other Accidental Deaths." *American Journal of Drug and Alcohol Abuse* 13, no. 4 (1987): 475–484.

Hadley, J., E. P. Steinberg and J. Feder. "Comparison of Uninsured and Privately Insured Hospital Patients." *Journal of the American Medical Association* 265, no. 3 (1991): 374–379.

Haffner, D., and S. Casey. "Approaches to Adolescent Pregnancy Prevention." *Seminars in Adolescent Medicine* 2, no. 3 (1986): 259–267.

Haglund, B., and S. Cnattingius. "Cigarette Smoking as a Risk Factor for Sudden Infant Death Syndrome: A Population-Based Study." *American Journal of Public Health* 80, no. 1 (1990): 29–32.

Hahn, R. A., I. M. Onorato, T. S. Jones and J. Dougherty. "Prevalence of HIV Infection among Intravenous Drug Users in the United States." *Journal of the American Medical Association* 261, no. 18 (1989): 2677–2684.

Halpert, D. "White Americans Living Longer; Black Lifespan Declines." *Philadelphia Inquirer*, 3 Mar. 1989.

Hartley, R. "A Program Blueprint for Neglectful Families." *Protecting Children* 6, no. 3 (1989): 3–7.

Hebel, J. R., N. L. Fox and M. Sexton. "Dose-Response of Birth Weight to Various Measures of Maternal Smoking during Pregnancy." *Journal of Clinical Epidemiology* 41, no. 5 (1988): 483–489.

Hellinger, F. J. "Updated Forecasts of the Costs of Medical Care for Persons with AIDS." *Public Health Reports* 105, no. 1 (1990): 1–12.

Henry, T. "School Administrators Confronted with New Problem." *Brockton Enterprise*, 24 Sept. 1990.

Hingson, R. W., L. Strunin, B. M. Berlin and T. Heeren. "Beliefs about AIDS, Use of Alcohol and Drugs, and Unprotected Sex among Massachusetts Adolescents." *American Journal of Public Health* 80, no. 3 (1990): 295–299.

Hodgson, B. "Alaska's Big Spill: Can the Wilderness Heal?" *National Geographic* 177, no. 1 (1990): 2–43.

Hofmann, M. B., M. Krakow and J. Kwass. *Drug Use Trends in Greater Boston and Massachusetts*. Boston: Health and Addictions Research, Inc., 1990.

Howland, J., and R. Hingson. "Alcohol as a Risk Factor for Injuries or Death Due to Fires and Burns: Review of the Literature." *Public Health Reports* 102, no. 5 (1987): 475–483.

Hubbard, R. L., M. E. Marsden, J. V. Rachal, H. J. Harwood, E. R. Cavanaugh and H. M. Ginzberg. *Drug Abuse Treatment: A National Study of Effectiveness*. Chapel Hill: University of North Carolina Press, 1989.

Hundleby, J. D., and G. W. Mercer. "Family and Friends as Social Environments and Their Relationship to Young Adolescents' Use of Alcohol, Tobacco and Marijuana." *Journal of Marriage and the Family* (Feb. 1987): 151–164.

Hunt, D. E., D. S. Lipton and B. Spunt. "Patterns of Criminal Activity among Methadone Clients and Current Narcotics Users Not in Treatment." *Journal of Drug Issues* (Fall 1984): 687–702.

Inciardi, J. A., and A. E. Pottieger. "Kids, Crack, and Crime." *Journal of Drug Issues* 21, no. 2 (1991): 257-270.

Inquirer Wire Services (IWS). "State Urges Birth Control Counseling in Schools." *Philadelphia Inquirer*, 15 Jan. 1989.

Institute of Medicine, National Academy of Sciences. *Mobilizing against AIDS: The Unfinished Story of a Virus*. Cambridge: Harvard University Press, 1986.

Isikoff, M. "Resurgence of Heroin Smuggling Feared." *Washington Post*, 14 July 1991.

Jackson, S. E., D. Chenoweth, E. D. Glover, D. Holbert and D. White. "Study Indicates Smoking Cessation Improves Workplace Absenteeism Rate." *Occupational Health and Safety* (Dec. 1989): 13–18.

Johnson, B. D., P. J. Goldstein, E. Preble, J. Schneidler, D. Lipton, B. Spunt and T. Miller. *Taking Care of Business: The Economics of Crime by Heroin Abusers*. Lexington, Mass.: Lexington Books, 1985.

Jones, R. "Youths' Suit Ends Stores' Cigarette Habit." *Boston Globe*, 19 June 1991.

Joyce, T. J. "The Social and Economic Correlates of Pregnancy Resolution among Adolescents in New York City, by Race and Ethnicity: A Multivariate Analysis." *American Journal of Public Health* 78, no. 6 (1988): 626–630.

Joyce, T. J., and N. H. Mocan. "The Impact of Legalized Abortion on Adolescent Childbearing in New York City." *American Journal of Public Health* 80, no. 3 (1990): 273–278.

Judson, F. N., and T. M. Vernon. "The Impact of AIDS on State and Local Health Departments: Issues and a Few Answers." *American Journal of Public Health* 78, no. 4 (1988): 387–393.

Kaighan, H. V. "Substance Abuse Abuses the Bottom Line." *Pension World* (July 1989) 16–19.

Kegeles, S. M., N. E. Alder and C. E. Irwin. "Sexually Active Adolescents and Condoms: Changes over One Year in Knowledge, Attitudes and Use." *American Journal of Public Health* 78, no. 4 (1988): 460–461.

Kennedy, E. M. "An Affordable Health Care Plan for All." *Boston Globe*, 6 June 1991.

Kent, J. "A Follow-Up Study of Abused Children." *Journal of Pediatric Psychology* 1, no. 2 (Spring 1976): 23–31.

Kerr, P. "Crack and Resurgence of Syphilis Spreading AIDS among the Poor." *New York Times*, 20 Sept. 1989.

———. "Addiction's Hidden Toll: Poor Families in Turmoil." *New York Times*, 23 June 1988.

Kerrigan, M. J. "Smokeless Tobacco and the Anti-Tobacco Movement." *Current Issues in Tobacco Economics*. Economic Paper Given at the Tobacco Workers Conference, January 1987 (1987): 59–63.

Kidder, Peabody. "Tobacco Outlook." *Equity Research*, 29 Oct. 1990.

Kirn, T. F. "Laws Ban Minors' Tobacco Purchases, but Enforcement Is Another Matter." *Journal of the American Medical Association* 257, no. 24 (1987): 3323–3324.

Kleiman, M. A. R. *Marijuana: Costs of Abuse, Costs of Control*. New York: Greenwood Press, 1989.

Knox, R. A. "AIDS Kills Women at Faster Rate." *Boston Globe*, 16 Dec. 1990.

——— . "HMO Researchers Warn of Burden of AIDS Care." *Boston Globe*, 7 June 1989.

Koretz, G. "Canada Makes Smoking Hazardous to the Wallet." *Business Week*, 20 May 1991.

Krauthammer, C. "Worse Than 'Brave New World': Newborns Permanently Damaged by Cocaine." *Philadelphia Inquirer*, 9 June 1989.

Kumpfer, K. L. "Special Populations: Etiology and Prevention of Vulnerability to Chemical Dependency in Children of Substance Abusers." *Youth at High Risk for Substance Abuse*. DHHS pub. no. (ADM) 90-1537, 1–72. Washington: GPO, 1990.

Landrum, S., C. Beck-Sague and S. Kraus. "Racial Trends in Syphilis among Men with Same-Sex Partners in Atlanta, Georgia." *American Journal of Public Health* 78, no. 1 (1988): 66–67.

Lang, P. "Poll Reveals Californians' Ambivalence on AIDS." *San Francisco Chronicle*, 12 May 1989.

Law, B. F. (or Cardinal B. F.) letter to parishioners reprinted in *Boston Globe* 21 May 1989.

Leavit, R. (of March of Dimes Birth Defects Foundation, White Plains, N. Y.) Oral communication, Sept. 1990.

Leibowitz, A., M. Eisen and W. K. Chow. "An Economic Model of Teenage Pregnancy Decision Making." *Demography* 23, no. 1 (1986): 67–77.

Leonard, K. E., E. J. Bromet, D. K. Parkinson, N. L. Day and C. M. Ryan. "Patterns of Alcohol Use and Physically Aggressive Behavior in Men." *Journal of Studies on Alcohol* 46, no. 4 (1985): 279–282.

Lessner, L. "Projection of AIDS Incidence in Women in New York State." *American Journal of Public Health* 81S. (1991): 30–34.

Leventhal, H., K. Glynn and R. Fleming. "Is the Smoking Decision an 'Informed Choice'?" *Journal of the American Medical Association* 257, no. 24 (1987): 3373–3376.

Levit, K. R., H. C. Lazenby, C. A. Cowan and S. W. Letsch. "National Health Expenditures." *Health Care Financing Review* 13, no. 1 (1991): 29–54.

Lewit, E. M., and D. Coate. "The Potential for Using Excise Taxes to Reduce Smoking." *Journal of Health Economics* no. 1. (1982): 121–145.

Lippiatt, B. C. "Measuring Medical Cost and Life Expectancy Impacts of Changes in Cigarette Sales." *Preventive Medicine* 19 (1990): 515–532.

Lodge, J. H. *Drug and Alcohol Abuse in the Workplace*. New York: Marcel Dekker, 1987.

Lubitz, J., and R. Prihoda. "The Use and Cost of Medicare Services in the Last Two Years of Life." *Health Care Financing Review* 5, no. 3, (Spring 1984): 117–131.

Lynch, M. A., and J. Roberts. *Consequences of Child Abuse*. London: Academic Press, 1982.

MacDonald, D. I. "An Approach to the Problem of Teenage Pregnancy." *Public Health Reports* 102, no. 4 (1987): 377–385.

MacGregor, S. N., L. G. Keith, S. J. Chasnoff, M. A. Rosner, G. M. Chisum, P. Shaw and J. P. Minogue. "Cocaine Use during Pregnancy: Adverse Perinatal Outcome." *American Journal of Obstetrics and Gynecology* 157, no. 3 (1987): 686–690.

Maddux, J. F., and D. P. Desmond. "Relapse and Recovery in Substance Abuse Careers." In *Relapse and Recovery in Drug Abuse*, ed. F. T. Tims and C. G. Leukefeld. 49–71. DHHS pub. no. (ADM) 86-1473 Washington: GPO, 1986.

Magura, S., J. L. Shapiro, Q. Siddiqi, and D. S. Lipton. "Variables Influencing Condom Use among Intravenous Drug Users." *American Journal of Public Health* 80, no. 1 (1990): 82–84.

Mahar, M. "Going Up in Smoke? The Tobacco Industry's Image Grows Increasingly Tarnished." *Barron's*, 9 July 1990, 8–27.

"Majorities Now Support Ban on Public Smoking, Cigarette Advertising . . ." *The Gallup Report*. Rep. 286. (Sept. 1988): 37–40.

Manning, W. G., E. B. Keeler, J. P. Newhouse, E. M. Sloss and J. Wasserman. "The Taxes of Sin: Do Smokers and Drinkers Pay Their Way?" *Journal of the American Medical Association* 261, no. 11 (1989): 1604–1609.

March of Dimes Birth Defects Foundation (MOD). *Public Health Education Information Sheets*. White Plains, N.Y.: 1989.

Marcus, E. (Director of Gynecare, Boston). Oral communication, Nov. 1991.

Massachusetts Department of Public Health (MDPH). *Adolescents at Risk 1991: Sexually Transmitted Diseases*. Boston: 1991.

——— . *Advance Data: Births 1988*. Boston: 1989.

Massachusetts Department of Public Welfare (MDPW). *Medicaid's Costliest Cases*. Boston: 1991.

Massachusetts Department of Social Services (MDSS). *Child Maltreatment Statistics January 1–December 31, 1990*. Boston: 1991.

——— . *Child Abuse Fact Sheets*. Boston: 1990a.

——— . *Children-at-Risk—Effects of Substance Abuse on Family Violence: A Statistical Summary*. Boston: 1990b.

——— . *Substance Abuse and Family Violence: Part II*. Boston: 1990c.

——— . *Substance Abuse and Family Violence: Part I*. Boston: 1989.

Massachusetts Task Force on Infant Mortality (MTF). *Unfinished Business: Poverty, Race and Infant Survival in Massachusetts*. Boston: 1990.

Mattson, M. E., E. S. Pollack and J. W. Cullen. "What Are the Odds that Smoking Will Kill You?" *American Journal of Public Health* 77, no. 4 (1987): 425–431.

McCord, C., and H. P. Freeman. "Excess Mortality in Harlem." *New England Journal of Medicine* 322, no. 3 (1990): 173–177.

McCusker, J., A. M. Stoddard, K. H. Mayer, J. Zapka, C. Morrison and S. P. Saltzman. "Effects of HIV Antibody Test Knowledge on Subsequent Sexual Behaviors in a Cohort of Homosexually Active Men." *American Journal of Public Health* 78, no. 4, (1988): 462–465.

McIntosh, I. D. "Smoking and Pregnancy: Attributable Risks and Public Health Implications." *Canadian Journal of Public Health* 75 (1984): 141–148.

McKusick, L., W. Horstman and T. J. Coates. "AIDS and Sexual Behavior Reported by Gay Men in San Francisco." *American Journal of Public Health* 75, no. 5 (1985): 493–496.

McNulty, M. "Combating Pregnancy Discrimination in Access to Substance Abuse Treatment for Low-Income Women." *National Health Law Program Clearinghouse Review* (May 1989): 21–25.

Mercer-Meidinger-Hansen, Inc. *Substance Abuse in the Workforce*. New York: 1988.

Mezzacappa, D. "Survey Finds Most Philadelphia Tenth Graders Have Had Sex." *Philadelphia Inquirer*, 24 Jan. 1989.

Miller, B. "Drugs, Guns Push Homicide Rates to Record Levels in Nation's Cities." *Philadelphia Inquirer*, 8 Dec. 1990.

Miller, T. R. "High Cost of Highway Crashes." *The Urban Institute Policy and Research Report* 21, no. 2 (1991): 16–17.

Moore, K. A. *Facts at a Glance*. Washington: Child Trends, 1989: 3 pgs.

Moore, K. A., and J. L. Peterson. *The Consequences of Teenage Pregnancy*. 5th ed. Washington: Child Trends, Inc., 1989.

Moore, K. A., and R. F. Wertheimer. "Teenage Childbearing and Welfare: Preventive and Ameliorative Strategies." *Family Plannings Perspectives* 16, no. 6 (1984): 285–289.

Moss, K. L. "Legal Issues: Drug Testing of Postpartum Women and Newborns as the Basis for Civil and Criminal Proceedings." *National Health Law Program Clearinghouse Review* (March 1990): 1406–1414.

Mott, J. "Opium Use and Crime in the United Kingdom." *Contemporary Drug Problems* (1980): 437–451.

Murray, F. J. "Administration Hails 'Startling' Cocaine Falloff." *Washington Times*, 20 Dec. 1990.

Nardone, J. M., and L. Steriti. *A Profile of Women Admitted to Substance-Abuse Treatment in Fiscal Year 1989*. Boston: Health and Addictions Research, 1990.

National Association for Perinatal Addiction Research and Education (NAPARE). *Substances Most Commonly Abused During Pregnancy and Their Risk to Mother and Baby*. Englenook, Colo.: 1989.

National Center for Health Statistics (NCHS). *Health United States, 1990*. DHHS pub. no. (PHS) 91-1232. Hyattsville, Md.: 1991.

——— . "Advance Report of Final Mortality Statistics, 1988." *Monthly Vital Statistics Report* 39, no. 7, supplement (1990a).

——— . "Advance Report of Final Natality Statistics, 1988. *"Monthly Vital Statistics Report* 39, no. 4, supplement (1990b).

——— . "Americans Assess Their Health: United States, 1987." *Vital and Health Statistics*. Ser. 10, no. 174. Hyattsville, Md.: 1990c.

——— . "Health of Black and White Americans, 1985-1987." *Vital and Health Statistics*. Ser. 10, no. 171. Hyattsville, Md. 1990d.

——— . *Health, United States, 1989*. DHHS pub.no. (PHS) 90-1232. Hyattsville, Md.: 1990e.

——— . "Use of Family Planning Services in the United States: 1982 and 1988. *Advance Data*. No. 1984. DHHS pub. no. (PHS) 90-1250. Hyattsville, Md.: 1990f.

——— . "AIDS Knowledge and Attitudes of Black Americans." *Advance Data*. No. 165. DHHS pub. no. (PHS) 89-1250. Hyattsville, Md.: 1989a.

——— . "AIDS Knowledge and Attitudes of Hispanic Americans." *Advance Data*. No. 166. DHHS pub. no. (PHS) 89-1250. Hyattsville, Md.: 1989b.

——— . "Characteristics of Persons Dying from AIDS." *Advance Data*. No. 173. DHHS pub. no. (PHS) 89-1250. Hyattsville, Md.: 1989c.

——— . "Smoking and Other Tobacco Use: United States, 1987." *Vital and Health Statistics*. Ser. 10, no. 169. Hyattsville, Md.: 1989d.

——— . "Relationships between Smoking and Other Unhealthy Habits: United States 1985." *Advance Data*. no. 154. 1988.

——— . *Prenatal Smoking and Childhood Morbidity*. Hyattsville, Md.: 1987.

——— . *Wanted and Unwanted Childbearing: United States, 1973–1982. Advance Data*. No. 108. DHHS pub. no. (PHS) 85-1250. Hyattsville, Md.: 1985.

National Committee for the Prevention of Child Abuse (NCPCA). *Fact Sheet on Child Abuse Deaths*. Chicago: 1987.

National Conference of Catholic Bishops. "Called to Compassion and Responsibility: A Response to the HIV/AIDS Crisis." *Origins* 19, no. 26 (1989): 421–434.

National Fire Protection Association (NFPA). *National Fire Incident Reports: 1984–1988*. Quincy, Mass.: National Fire Protection Association, 1991.

National Highway Traffic Safety Administration (NHTSA). *A Decade of Progress*. DOT HS 807 693. Washington: Government Printing Office, 1991.

——— . *Drunk Driving Facts*. RPO717. Washington: 1989.

——— . *The Economic Cost to Society of Motor Vehicle Accidents*. Washington: 1987. Mimeo.

National Institute on Drug Abuse (NIDA). *National Household Survey on Drug Abuse: Population Estimates 1990*. DHHS pub. no. (ADM) 91-1732. Rockville, Md.: 1991.

——— . *National Household Survey on Drug Abuse: Main Findings 1988*. DHHS pub. no. (ADM) 90-1682. Rockville, Md.: 1990.

——— . *NIDA Capsules. High School Senior Drug Use: 1975–1989*. Rockville, Md.: 1989. Mimeo.

National Narcotics Intelligence Consumers Committee (NNICC). *The NNICC Report: 1989*. GPO, 1990.

National Research Council (NRC). *AIDS: Sexual Behavior and Intravenous Drug Use*. Washington: National Academy Press, 1989.

——— . *Risking the Future*. Washington: National Academy Press, 1987.

Navarro, V. "Race or Class Versus Race and Class: Mortality Differentials in the United States." *The Lancet* 336 (1990): 1238–1240.

Nazario, S. L. "Abortion Foes Pose Threat to the Funding of Family Planning." *Wall Street Journal*, 8 Mar. 1990.

Nichols-Casebolt, A. and S. K. Danziger. "The Effect of Childbearing Age on Child Support Awards and Economic Well-being among Divorcing Mothers." *Journal of Divorce* 12, no. 4. (1989): 34–38.

Noble Lowndes Consultants and Actuaries. *1991 Survey of Health Insurance Companies*. New York: Noble Lowndes 1991.

Novick, L. F., D. Berns, R. Stricof, R. Stevens, K. Pass and J. Wethers. "HIV Seroprevalence in Newborns in New York State." *Journal of the American Medical Association* 261, no. 12 (1989): 1745–1750.

Novotny, P. L., K. E. Warner, J. S. Kendrick and P. L. Remington, "Smoking by Blacks and Whites: Socioeconomic and Demographic Differences." *American Journal of Public Health* (Sept. 1988): 1187–1189.

Nurco, D. N., J. C. Ball, J. W. Shaffer and T. E. Hanlon. "The Criminality of Narcotics Addicts." *Journal of Nervous and Mental Disease* 173, no. 2 (1985): 94–102.

Nurco, D. N., T. E. Hanlon, T. W. Kinlock and K. R. Duszynski. "Differential Criminal Patterns of Narcotic Addicts over an Addiction Career." *Criminology* 26, no. 3 (1988): 407–423.

O'Connell, M., and C. Rogers. "Out-of-Wedlock Births, Premarital Pregnancies and Their Effect on Family Formation and Dissolution." *Family Planning Perspectives* 6, no. 4 (1984): 157–162.

Office of Management and Budget (OMB). *Budget of the United States Government: Fiscal Year 1991.* Washington: GPO, 1990.

Office of National Drug Control Policy. *National Drug Control Strategy.* Washington: GPO, 1991a.

——— . *National Drug Control Strategy: Budget Summary.* Washington: GPO, 1991b.

——— . *Leading Drug Indicators.* Washington: GPO, 1990.

Office of Policy and Program Evaluation (OPPE). *Indices: A Statistical Index to District of Columbia Services.* Washington: 1990.

Office of Technology Assessment (OTA). *Smoking-Related Deaths and Financial Costs.* Washington: 1985. Photocopy.

O'Neill, J. A., D. A. Wolf, L. J. Bassi and M. T. Hannan, "An Analysis of Time on Welfare." Abridged in *The Urban Institute Policy and Research Report* 15, no. 1 (1985): 4–6.

Otten, M. W., S. T. Teutsch, D. F. Williamson, and J. S. Marks. "The Effect of Known Risk Factors on the Excess Mortality of Black Adults in the United States." *Journal of the American Medical Association* 263, no. 6 (1990): 845–850.

Pascale, A. "Adolescent Contraceptive Use." In *The Facts.* Washington: Center for Population Options, June 1990a.

——— . "Adolescent Sexuality, Pregnancy and Parenthood." In *The Facts.* Washington: Center for Population Options, May 1990b.

——— . "School-Based Clinics." In *The Facts.* Washington: Center for Population Options, June 1990c.

Pear, R. "The Hard Thing About Cutting Infant Mortality Is Educating Mothers." *New York Times,* 12 Aug. 1990.

Pennsylvania Perinatal Association. *Facts on Infant Mortality in Pennsylvania.* Bryn Mawr: 1990.

The Pepper Commission. *A Call for Action.* Washington: GPO, 1990.

Pittman, K. J. "Reading and Writing as Risk Reduction: The School's Role in Preventing Teenage Pregnancies." In D. J. Jones and S. F. Battle, eds., *Teenage Pregnancy: Developing Strategies for Change in the Twenty-first Century.* New Brunswick, N.J.: Transaction, 1990.

Planned Parenthood Federation of America (PPFA). Questions and Answers about Abortion. New York: Planned Parenthood Federation of America, 1986. Photocopy.

Plaut, J., and T. Kelley. *Childwatch: Children and Drugs.* New York: New York Interface Development Project, Inc., 1989.

Plotnick, R. D. "Welfare and Out-of-Wedlock Childbearing: Evidence from the 1980's." Discussion Paper #876-89. Institute for Research on Poverty, University of Wisconsin—Madison, 1989.

Polit, D. F. "Effects of a Comprehensive Program for Teenage Parents: Five Years after Project Redirection." *Family Planning Perspectives* 21, no. 4 (1989): 164–169.

Price Waterhouse. *The Economic Impact of the Tobacco Industry on the United States Economy.* Tobacco Institute. Washington: Price Waterhouse, 1990.

Pytte, A. "Tobacco's Clout Stays Strong Through Dollars, Jobs, Ads." *Congressional Quarterly* (19 May 1990): 1542–1548.

Quinlan-Rowley, A., and A. Schlesinger. *Services for Teen Parents and Their Children, Evaluation Results, September, 1988.* Department of Social Services, Commonwealth of Massachusetts. Boston: 1988.

Ralph, N., and C. Spigner. "Contraceptive Practices among Female Heroin Addicts." *American Journal of Public Health* 76, no. 8 (1988): 1016–1017.

Read, E. W. "Birth Cycle: For Poor Teenagers, Pregnancies Become New Rite of Passage." *Wall Street Journal*, 17 Mar. 1988.

Reid, D. "Diseases from Sex Rise among Teenagers." *Boston Globe*, 11 April 1990.

Reid, D., and N. Smith. "What Is The Single Most Important Intervention for the Prevention of Smoking-Related Disease?" In *The Global War*. Proceedings from the Seventh World Conference on Tobacco and Health, 309–313. 1990.

"Reports of Congenital Syphilis Rise." *New York Times*, 12 Dec. 1989.

Revkin, A. C. "Crack in the Cradle." *Discover*, Sept. 1989, 62–69.

Richardson, J. L., K. Dwyer, K. McGuigan, W. B. Hansen, C. Dent, B. Brannon and B. Flay. "Substance Use Among Eighth-Graders who Take Care of Themselves after School." *Pediatrics* 84, no. 3 (1989): 556–566.

Rimm, E. B., E. L. Giovannucci, W. C. Willett, G. A. Colditz, A. Ascherio, B. Rosner, M. J. Stampfer. "Prospective Study of Alcohol Consumption and Risk of Coronary Disease in Men." *The Lancet* 338 (Aug. 1991): 464–468.

Robert Wood Johnson Foundation. "In the Midst of Dramatic Changes in U.S. Health Care, Americans Generally Report Satisfaction with the Care Received, Says a New National Access Survey." *Special Report Number Two*. Princeton: The Robert Wood Johnson Foundation Communications Office, 1987.

Rogers, M. G., P. A. Thomas, E. T. Starcher, M. C. Noa, T. J. Bush and H. W. Jaffe. "Acquired Immune Deficiency Syndrome in Children: Report of the Centers for Disease Control National Surveillance, 1982–1985." *Pediatrics* 79, no. 6 (1987): 1008–1014.

Rolfs, R. T., M. Goldberg and R. G. Sharrar. "Risk Factors for Syphilis: Cocaine Use and Prostitution." *American Journal of Public Health* 80, no. 7 (1990): 853–857.

Ross, H. E., F. B. Glaser, and T. Germanson. "The Prevalence of Psychiatric Disorders in Patients with Alcohol and Other Drug Problems." *Archives of General Psychiatry* 45 (1988): 1023–1031.

Saffer, H., and M. Grossman. "Beer Taxes, the Legal Drinking Age, and Youth Motor Vehicle Fatalities." *Journal of Legal Studies* 16, no. 2 (1987): 351–374.

Salomon Brothers. "Stock Research: Tobacco." New York: Jan. 1990. Report.

Sandler, D. P., G. W. Comstock, K. J. Helsing and D. L. Shore. "Deaths from All Causes in Non-Smokers who Lived with Smokers." *American Journal of Public Health* 79, no. 2 (1989): 163–167.

Schelling, T. C. "Economics and Cigarettes." *Preventive Medicine* 15 (1986): 549–560.

Schilling, R. F., N. El-Bassel, L. Gilbert and S. P. Schinke. "Correlates of Drug Use, Sexual Behavior, and Attitudes Toward Safer Sex among African-American and Hispanic Women in Methadone Maintenance." *Journal of Drug Issues* 21, no. 4 (1991): 685–712.

Schilling, R. F., S. P. Schinke, S. E. Nichols, L. H. Zayas, S. O. Miller, M. A. Orlandi and G. J. Botvin. "Developing Strategies for AIDS Prevention Research with Black and Hispanic Drug Users." *Public Health Reports* 104, no. 1 (1990): 2–11.

Schmidt, F. "Cigarette Advertising Is Fraud on the Consumer." In *The Global War*. Proceedings of the Seventh World Conference on Tobacco and Health, 428–429. 1990.

Schmidt, W. E. "Fiery Crash Kills 27 in Kentucky as Truck and Youths' Bus Collide." *New York Times*, 16 May 1988.

Schuckit, M. A. "Biological Vulnerability to Alcoholism." *Journal of Consulting and Clinical Psychology* 55, no. 3 (1987): 301–309.

———. *Drug and Alcohol Use: A Clinical Guide to Diagnosis and Treatment.* 2nd ed. New York: Plenum Press, 1984.

———. "The History of Psychotic Symptoms in Alcoholics." *Journal of Clinical Psychiatry* 43, no. 2 (1982): 53–57.

Schwartz, E., V. Y. Kofie, M. Rivo and R. V. Tuckson. "Black/White Comparisons of Deaths Preventable by Medical Intervention: United States and the District of Columbia, 1980–1986." *International Journal of Epidemiology* 19, no. 3. (1990): 591–598.

Scitovsky, A. A., and D. P. Rice. "Estimates of the Direct and Indirect Costs of Acquired Immunodeficiency Syndrome in the United States, 1985, 1986, and 1991." *Public Health Reports* 102, no. 1 (1987): 5–17.

"Secondhand Smoke Kills 53,000 a Year, Says EPA-Sponsored Study." *Boston Globe*, 30 May 1991.

Selwyn, P. A., R. J. Carter, E. E. Schoenbaum, V. J. Robertson, R. S. Klein and M. F. Rogers. "Knowledge of HIV Antibody Status and Decisions to Continue or Terminate Pregnancy among Intravenous Drug Users." *Journal of the American Medical Association* 261, no. 24 (1989): 3567–3571.

Serdula, M., D. F. Williamson, J. S. Kendrick, R. F. Anda and T. Byers. "Trends in Alcohol Consumption by Pregnant Women." *Journal of the American Medical Association* 265, no. 7 (1991): 876–879.

Silverman, S. "Interaction of Drug-Abusing Mother, Fetus, Types of Drugs Examined in Numerous Studies." *Journal of the American Medical Association* 216, no. 12 (1989): 1689–1693.

Simpson, D. D., and K. L. Marsh. "Relapse and Recovery among Opoid Addicts Twelve Years after Treatment." In *Relapse and Recovery in Drug Abuse*, ed. F. T. Tims and C. G. Leukefeld. 86–103. DHHS pub. no. (ADM) 86-1473. Washington: GPO, 1986.

Skirrow, J., and E. Sawka. "Alcohol and Drug Abuse Prevention Strategies: An Overview." *Contemporary Drug Problems* 14 (Summer 1987): 147–241.

Slade, D. "Cigarette Machine Ban May Be Worth It." *Boston Globe*, 2 May 1991.

Sloan, I. J. *AIDS Law: Implications for the Individual and Society.* New York: Oceana Publications, 1988.

———. *Child Abuse: Governing Law and Legislation.* New York: Oceana Publications, 1983.

Smith, P. F., P. L. Remington and the Behavioral Risk Factor Surveillance Group. "The Epidemiology of Drinking and Driving: Results from the Behavioral Risk Factor Surveillance System, 1986." *Health Education Quarterly* 16, no. 3. (1989): 345–358.

"Smoking 101." *Fortune*, 27 Feb. 1989, 134.

Sonenstein, F. L., J. H. Pleck and L. C. Ku. "Sexual Activity, Condom Use and AIDS Awareness among Adolescent Males." *Family Planning Perspectives* 21, no. 4 (1989): 152–158.

Sonnefeld, S. T., D. R. Waldo, J. A. Lemieux and D. R. McKusick. "Projections of National Health Expenditures through the Year 2000." *Health Care Financing Review* 13, no. 1 (1991): 1–27.

Sparadeo, F. R., and D. Gill. "Effects of Prior Alcohol Use on Head Injury Recovery." *Journal of Head Trauma Rehabilitation* 4, no. 1 (1989): 75–82.

Spolar, C. "AIDS Cases Rise among the Homeless." *Washington Post*, 1 May 1990.

St. Louis, M. E., G. A. Conway, C. R. Hayman, C. Miller, L. R. Petersen and T. J. Dondero. "Human Immunodeficiency Virus Infection in Disadvantaged Adolescents: Findings from the U.S. Job Corps. *Journal of the American Medical Association* 266, no. 17 (1991): 2381-2391.

State Center for Health Statistics (SCHS). *The Impact of Maternal Smoking on Infant Birth Weight: New Hampshire Residents, 1987-1989.* Pub. no. 90-018. Concord: 1991a.

———. *Patterns of Maternal Smoking during Pregnancy: New Hampshire Residents, 1987-1989.* Pub. no. 91-001. Concord: 1991b.

State of California Department of Social Services (SCDSS). *Child Maltreatment Tables 1985-1989.* Sacramento: 1990.

———. *Preplacement Preventative Services: Survey of Selected Characteristics for Cases Closed during January 1989.* Sacramento: 1989.

Steinglass, P. "The Impact of Alcoholism on the Family." *Journal of Studies on Alcohol* 42, no. 3 (1981): 288-303.

Steinhausen, H. C., D. Gobel and V. Nestler. "Psychopathology in the Offspring of Alcoholic Parents." *Journal of the American Academy of Child Psychiatry* 23, no. 4 (1984): 465-471.

Stephens, R. C., T. E. Feucht and S. W. Roman. "Effects of an Intervention Program on AIDS-Related Drug and Needle Behavior among Intravenous Drug Users." *American Journal of Public Health* 81, no. 5 (1991): 568-571.

Stigler, G. J, and G. S. Becker. "De Gustibus Non Est Disputandum." *American Economic Review* 67, no. 2 (1977): 76-90.

Stokes III, J. "Why Not Rate Health and Life Insurance Premiums By Risks?" *The New England Journal of Medicine* 308, no. 7 (1983): 393-395.

Streissguth, A. P., J. M. Aase, S. K. Clarren, S. P. Randels, R. A. LaDue and D. F. Smith. "Fetal Alcohol Syndrome in Adolescents and Adults." *Journal of the American Medical Association* 265, no. 15 (1991): 1961-1967.

Stricof, R. L., J. T. Kennedy, T. C. Nattell, I. B. Weisfuse and L. F. Novick. "HIV Seroprevalence in a Facility for Runaway and Homeless Adolescents." *American Journal of Public Health* 81S (1991): 50-53.

Thompson, D. "Should Every Baby Be Saved?" *Time*, 11 June 1990.

Tobacco Merchants Association (TMA), Princeton. Oral communication (Darryl Jayson with author), June 1991.

Torres, A., P. Donovan, N. Dittes and J. D. Forrest. "Public Benefits and Costs of Government Funding for Abortion." *Family Planning Perspectives* 18, no. 3 (1986): 111-118.

Treviño, F. M., M. E. Moyer, R. B. Valdez and C. A. Stroup-Benham. "Health Insurance Coverage and Utilization of Health Services by Mexican Americans, Mainland Puerto Ricans, and Cuban Americans." *Journal of the Americal Medical Association* 265, no. 2 (1991): 233-237.

Tye, J. B., K. E. Warner and S. A. Glantz. "Tobacco Advertising and Consumption: Evidence of a Causal Relationship." *Journal of Public Health Policy* (Winter 1987): 492-508.

Uhlig, M. A. "A System that Couldn't Save a Child from Lethal Abuse." *New York Times*, 6 Nov. 1987.

United States Bureau of the Census (USBC). *Statistical Abstract of the United States, 1990.* 110th ed. Washington: Government Printing Office, 1990.

United States Conference of Mayors (USCM). *The Impact of AIDS on America's Cities.* Washington: 1991.

United States Department of Agriculture (USDA). *Tobacco: Situation and Outlook Report.* Economic Research Service. TS-214. Washington: April 1991.

United States Department of Health and Human Services (USDHHS). *Drug Abuse and Drug Abuse Research.* DHHS pub. no. (ADM) 91–1704. Rockville, Md.: 1991a.

———. Office of Smoking and Health. Oral communication (McDougal with author), Jan. 1991b.

———. *The Economic Costs of Alcohol and Drug Abuse and Mental Illness: 1985.* Rockville, Md.: 1990a.

———. *The Health Benefits of Smoking Cessation: A Report of the Surgeon General.* DHHS pub. no. (CDC) 90-8416. Rockville, Md.: 1990b.

———. *Seventh Special Report to the U.S. Congress on Alcohol and Health.* Rockville, Md.: 1990c.

———. *Reducing the Health Consequences of Smoking: 25 Years of Progress. A Report of the Surgeon General.* DHHS pub. no. (CDC) 89-8411. Rockville, Md. 1989a.

———. *Smoking Tobacco and Health: A Fact Book.* DHHS pub. no. (CDC) 87-8397 (revised 1989). Rockville, Md.: 1989b.

———. *Study Findings: Study of National Incidence and Prevalence of Child Abuse and Neglect: 1988.* Rockville, Md.: 1988.

———. *Report of the Secretary's Task Force on Black and Minority Health.* Vols. 1–8. Washington: Government Printing Office, 1985–1986.

United States Department of Justice (USDJ). *Drugs and Crime Facts, 1990.* Bureau of Justice Statistics. Rockville, Md.: 1991a.

———. *Drug Use Forecasting: Second Quarter: April to June 1990.* National Institute of Justice Research in Action. Washington: April 1991b.

———. *1988 Drug Use Forecasting Annual Report.* National Institute of Justice Research in Action. Washington: Mar. 1990a.

———. *Sourcebook of Criminal Justice Statistics—1989.* Bureau of Justice Statistics. Washington: 1990b.

———. *Drug Law Violators, 1980–1986.* Bureau of Justice Statistics Special Report. Washington: 1988a.

———. *Drug Use and Crime.* Bureau of Justice Statistics Special Report. Washington: 1988b.

———. *Drunk Driving.* Bureau of Justice Statistics Special Report. Washington: 1988c.

———. *Profile of State Prison Inmates, 1986.* Bureau of Justice Statistics Special Report. Washington: 1988d.

———. *Survey of Youth in Custody, 1987.* Bureau of Justice Statistics Special Report. Washington: 1988e.

United States Department of Labor (USDL). *CPI Detailed Report for November 1991.* Bureau of Labor Statistics report ISSN 0095-926X. Washington: 1992.

———. *Alcohol and Drug Abuse Provisions in Major Collective Bargaining Agreements in Selected Industries.* Bureau of Labor Statistics Bulletin 2369. Washington: 1990.

United States General Accounting Office (USGAO). *Canadian Health Insurance: Lessons for the United States.* GAO/HRD-91-90. Washington: 1991a.

———. *The War on Drugs: Arrests Burdening Local Criminal Justice Systems.* GAO/GGD-91-40. Washington: 1991b.

———. *AIDS Education: Gaps in Coverage Still Exist.* GAO/T-HRD-90-26. Washington: 1990a.

———. *Defense Health Care: Effects of AIDS in the Military.* GAO/HRD-90-39. Washington: 1990b.

——. Dichotomy between U.S. Tobacco Export Policy and Antismoking Initiatives. GAO/NSIAD-90-190. Washington: 1990c.

——. *Drug Abuse: Research on Treatment May Not Address Current Needs.* GAO/HRD-90-114. Washington: 1990d.

——. *Drug-Exposed Infants: A Generation at Risk.* GAO/HRD-90-138. Washington: 1990e.

——. Health Insurance: Availability and Adequacy for Small Businesses. GAO/T-HRD-90-33. Washington: 1990f.

——. *Home Visiting: A Promising Early Intervention Strategy for At-Risk Families.* GAO/HRD-90-83. Washington: 1990g.

——. *Methadone Maintenance: Some Treatment Programs Are Not Effective: Greater Federal Oversight Needs.* GAO/HRD-90-104. 1990h.

——. *AIDS Education: Issues Affecting Counseling and Testing Programs.* GAO/HRD-89-39. Washington: 1989a.

——. *AIDS Forecasting: Undercount of Cases and Lack of Key Data Weaken Existing Estimates.* GAO/PEMD-89-13. Washington: 1989b.

——. *Health Insurance, an Overview of the Working Uninsured.* GAO/HRD-89-45. Washington: 1989c.

——. Pediatric AIDS: Health and Social Service Needs of Infants and Children. GAO/HRD-89-96. Washington: 1989d.

——. *Teenage Smoking: Higher Excise Tax Should Significantly Reduce The Number of Smokers.* GAO/HRD-89-119. Washington 1989e.

——. *AIDS Education: Reaching Populations at Higher Risk.* GAO/PEMD-88-35. Washington: 1988.

——. *Drinking-Age Laws: An Evaluation Synthesis of Their Impact on Highway Safety.* GAO/PEMD-87-10. Washington: 1987.

——. *Teenage Pregnancy: 500,000 Births a Year but Few Tested Programs.* GAO/PEMD-86-16BR. Washington: 1986.

United States House of Representatives Select Committee on Children, Youth and Families (USHR). *U.S. Children and Their Families: Current Conditions and Recent Trends, 1989.* 101st Cong., 1st sess. H. Report 101-356. Washington: GPO, 1989.

Vaughn, D. H. "Smoking in the Workplace: A Management Perspective." *Employee Relations Law Journal* 14, no. 3. (1988): 359–386.

Vlahov, D., T. F. Brewer, K. G. Castro, J. P. Narkunas, M. E. Salive, J. Ulrich and A. Munoz. "Prevalence of Antibody to HIV-1 among Entrants to U.S. Correctional Facilities." *Journal of the American Medical Association* 265, no. 9 (1991): 1129–1132.

Walsh, D. C., and N. P. Cordon. "Legal Approaches to Smoking Deterrence." *American Review of Public Health* no. 7 (1986): 127–149.

Warner, K. E., L. M. Goldenhar and C. G. McLaughlin. "Cigarette Advertising and Magazine Coverage of the Hazards of Smoking: A Statistical Analysis." *New England Journal of Medicine* 326, no. 5 (1992): 305–309.

Warner, K. E. "Tobacco Taxation and Economic Effects of Declining Tobacco Consumption." In *The Global War.* Proceedings of the Seventh World Conference on Tobacco and Health, 81–87. 1990.

——. "Effects of the Antismoking Campaign: An Update." *American Journal of Public Health* 79, no. 2 (1989): 144–151.

——. "Smoking and Health Implications of a Change in the Federal Excise Tax." *Journal of the American Medical Association* 255, no. 8, (1986): 1028–1032.

Warner, K. E., and H. A. Murt. "Economic Incentives for Health." *American Review of Public Health* 5 (1984): 33–107.

Wattleton, F. "Teenage Pregnancies and the Recriminalization of Abortions." *American Journal of Public Health* 80, no. 3 (1990): 269–270.

The White House. "The President's Comprehensive Health Reform Program." Office of the Press Secretary. 6 Feb. 1992.

Williams, A. F., and R. S. Karpf. "Teenage Drivers and Fatal Crash Responsibility." *Law and Policy* 6 (1984): 101–113.

Williams, C. N., M. Krakow, M. B. Hofmann, D. A. Traniello, R. N. Breen and D. McCarty. Alcohol Use Trends among Massachusetts Adolescents: 1984–1987. Boston: Health and Addictions Research, Inc., 1989.

Williams, W. L. Testimony on Homicide before the United States Senate Judiciary Committee. 101st Congress, 2nd Session. July 1990.

Winkenwerder, W., A. R. Kessler and R. M. Stolec. "Federal Spending for Illness Caused by the Human Immunodeficiency Virus." *New England Journal of Medicine* 320, no. 24 (1989): 1598–1603.

Witteman, A. "First Mess Up, Then Mop Up." *Time*, 2 April 1990, 22.

Woititz, J. G. *Adult Children of Alcoholics*. Washington: Health Communications, Inc., 1990.

Wolock, I., and B. Horowitz. "Child Maltreatment and Material Deprivation among AFDC-Recipient Families." *Social Service Review* (June 1979): 175–194.

Wong, D. S. "Killer of Boy Given 18–20 Year Term." *Boston Globe*, 18 July 1989.

Wright, S. J. "SOS: Alcohol, Drugs, and Boating." *Alcohol Health and Research World*, (Summer 1985): 28–33.

Zabin, L. S., M. B. Hirsch and M. R. Emerson. "When Urban Adolescents Choose Abortion: Effects on Education, Psychological Status and Subsequent Pregnancy." *Family Planning Perspectives* 21, no. 6 (1989): 248–255.

Zaslowsky, D. "Denver Program Curbs Teenagers' Pregnancy." *New York Times*, 16 Jan. 1989.

Zelnik, M., and Y. J. Kim. "Sex Education and Its Association with Teenage Sexual Activity, Pregnancy and Contraceptive Use." *Family Planning Perspectives* 14, no. 3 (1982): 117–126.

Zuckerman, B., D. A. Frank, R. Hingson, H. Amaro, S. M. Levenson, H. Kayne, S. Parker, R. Vinci, K. Aboagye, L. E. Fried, H. Cabral, R. Timperi and H. Bauchner. "Effects of Maternal Marijuana and Cocaine Use on Fetal Growth." *New England Journal of Medicine* 320 (1989): 762–768.

Zuravin, S. "Child Neglect Research Findings—Some Implications for the Delivery of Child Protective Services." *Protecting Children* 6, no. 3, (1989): 13–18.

Index

About the Author

NANCY HAMMERLE is Assistant Professor of Economics at Stonehill College in Massachusetts.

DATE DUE